Divorcing the Corporation

One woman's fight to save her family from multinational maneuvers

Rosalyn M. Reeder

Hapi Haus
St. Joseph, Michigan

The contents of this book derive from the author's personal experience plus court transcripts, letters, and other materials of record. To the best of her knowledge and according to her perceptions, her account is true. As in any history, all names used are actual names.

Inquiries should be addressed to:
Hapi Haus Publishing
P. O. Box 916
St. Joseph, Michigan 49085-0916

Editing & Layout: Chris Roerden, Edit It

Printed in the United States of America
First edition February 1999

ISBN 0-9666586-0-4 HC

LC Card Catalog Number 98-94069

Publisher's Cataloging-in-Publication
(Provided by Quality Books, Inc.)

Reeder, Rosalyn M.
  Divorcing the corporation : one woman's fight to save her family from multinational maneuvers / Rosalyn M. Reeder. -- 1st ed.
    p. cm.
    Includes bibliographical references and index.
    ISBN: 0-9666586-0-4

  1. Executives' spouses--Biography. 2. Reeder, Rosalyn M.--Marriage. 3. Reeder, Rosalyn M.--Trials, litigation, etc. 4. Corporate culture. 5. Work and family. 6. Whirlpool Corporation. I. Title.

HQ759.6.R44 1999   306.8'72 [B]
                        QBI98-1475

To Attorney Karen E. Werme, without whose counsel and support I would not have survived emotionally and the story could not have been told.

Let those who would have peace, seek justice.

To the reader

Writing this manuscript began in 1989 as I jotted down every detail I could recall to use in suing the Whirlpool Corporation for breach of its oral contract with me. This breach led to the dissolution of my thirty-eight-year marriage to one of its vice presidents. In 1992, having lost both my husband and the lawsuit, I shaped the jottings into a narrative aimed at explaining to my four children what had happened to their family.

Next came my realization that I am not alone in this experience, that corporations breaking up families has become an American sociological phenomenon. With the help of an editor whose own marriage and family were similarly disrupted, I developed the manuscript to its current state for publication and distribution.

—*Rosalyn M. Reeder*

Contents

Overview

Passion and pain—like so many responses set in motion with
out apparent intellectual engagement—formed the impe-
tus for my filing suit. I was fighting for my sanity.

When the first of a series of migraine headaches gripped my
head like a vise, sickening and debilitating my whole body, I
knew only that I had to find relief. I did not know at the time
that relief from the headaches and return to a sane way of life
would require divorcing my husband of thirty-eight years and
suing the corporation for which he had worked almost as long.

I had every reason to believe the unremitting, nausea-pro-
ducing ache in my head was the result not of diet or other poor
health habits, but of the incredible stress under which I had been
living in São Paulo, Brazil, for more than two years.

Days of overwhelming pain dragged by as I struggled to
focus on what conditions in my life I had the power to change.
Nothing diminished either the throb or the nausea. Then something inside me broke through and softly screamed, "I've got to
get out of here!" Instantly my body relaxed and all discomfort
disappeared, though I did nothing more at the time than permit
the thought to exist.

A migraine gripped me again next morning. I sensed the

cause immediately. The next question—"When?"—pulsed against my skull.

As the answer gradually came to me, the vise relaxed its grip once more. Our son Curt would soon be arriving from Germany, where he was stationed, to celebrate Carnaval in Rio with us. I couldn't leave before his visit, but I could do so as soon as he returned to his Army post.

This thought bought me one more day of respite from pain before the voice forced me to consider the most difficult question of all. "How?"

Slowly, a plan formed. Perhaps a medical crisis would give me the excuse I needed to break free. Exaggerating a minor condition, I said I needed to go back home for surgery. The condition had become so uncomfortable, I said, that I couldn't wait out the next few months until my husband's assignment was over.

His employer had insinuated its monolithic presence into my private life almost three years earlier, making decisions for me and eroding my structure of values. Thus, I had grown more and more to mistrust the corporation, and to trust less and less my husband, Emanuel Von Koenig, who had evolved into a corporate henchman.

I could barely trust myself. I had grown incredibly tired and depressed, with deteriorating social skills. At one time I could effortlessly call up English, German, or Portuguese—whatever tongue was called for when I faced people who spoke one or more of these languages. No longer was I able to shift into the right language, much less say anything coherent in it.

It was raining in Detroit when friends met me at the airport. Their house was my first stop before I continued my journey home to St. Joseph and my house, about two hundred miles west. One of my four sons was living in the house with his family until Manny and I would need it again. Before temporarily relocating us to Brazil in 1986, the company had tried to get us to sell that family home. If the corporation had succeeded in that plan as well, I would not even have had a home to return to.

I was in no hurry to leave my friends' home, a comforting cave-like refuge. Even the dark, dreary February weather that enveloped me in moistness whenever we went out was soothingly womb-like. My friend Millie took a few days off from work to be with me. Day after day, she let me share the source of my depression, until we both realized I was afraid to go home. St. Joseph–Benton Harbor was where the corporate offices were located.

Wisely, Millie recognized I might never leave if she did not help me find what I thought I needed—a lawyer. She arranged an appointment for me with an attorney she knew, Irene Piccone, an advocate for women. Elderly and infirm, Irene wore over her shoulders and back some kind of life-support system—oxygen, I think. I saw in this frail woman a vital part of my own life-support system. Although she had reduced her practice to part-time, she could not refuse a sister in need.

During our meeting in her small, cluttered office, I told her how, in 1985, Whirlpool Corporation had begun to manipulate and deceive my husband and me into delaying his retirement, due in two years, because they needed his help in setting up a trust company in South America, *Whirlpool do Brasil.*

I talked to her about Manny's emotional abandonment of me; about the growing psychological and verbal abuse, at first periodic, eventually, every day; and about his not being my advocate when no one else could be. I was not in denial, but I had acted forgiving and understanding because I knew that Manny, working in and through the *Whirlpool do Brasil* office, was under even greater pressure than I. For each of us, the strain was caused by our having been coerced into living and working arrangements not of our choice.

The elderly attorney listened intently, taking notes from time to time. When she interrupted occasionally, the message I heard was always the same: "I think your husband is responsible for this."

I knew Irene was right, but I'd needed to hear her say it. I knew my husband was in complicity with his captors. The corporation held his retirement rights and professional reputation hostage, demanding in exchange that he perform work for them no one else could do. But being the key man was not an honor. What had been done to me in the process appeared to be, in the corporation's opinion, incidental and unimportant. Manny seemed to think that in the long run I would see everything had been for the best, that we would be financially better off and able to retire with respect within the Whirlpool community.

The downside was that the key man's spouse had been hijacked into the role of second lady. When I gave up the struggle and accepted the inevitability of going to Brazil, I was acting upon insufficient as well as incorrect information given to me by the corporation and by its representative, my husband. The terms presented to me and to which I implicitly agreed were breached. Looking back, I now firmly believe neither Whirlpool nor my husband had any intention of honoring what they promised. Theirs was a hidden agenda.

Enlightened and fortified by Irene Piccone's observations, I gathered strength for the next stage of my journey and boarded the bus to St. Joseph. Being once again embraced by my family felt good. Not wanting the confusion of my life to overtake my children, I decided not to move into the house with Jeff and his family. Instead, I rented a one-bedroom apartment at Briarwood in Benton Harbor, saying I needed quiet to write. A few days later, I bought a car with the help of another son, Doug.

Suspecting my health insurance would soon disappear along with the other underpinnings of life-as-I-had-known-it, I made plans for my minor surgery the following month at a clinic in Grand Rapids.

On February 27, I retained an attorney to represent me in divorce proceedings. I knew if I remained married to Manny, he would not "let me" sue Whirlpool. What the corporation had done was unjust and indefensible, but Manny seemed not to realize the corporation had done anything to him. Of course I still loved Manny, but what he and the corporation were doing was causing my mental and physical health to deteriorate. In my struggle to survive, I had to forget about love for the time being.

All my sons and daughters-in-law were supportive and helpful: Doug and Jo, Jeff and Nancy, Ed and Lori, and—from his post in Germany—Curt. They didn't know what was going on, but they knew something was up.

Manny also must have known the day he took me to the São Paulo airport. Because I was leaving under the guise of desperately requiring surgery, we did not discuss the real reason, but I believe he knew. Most of our communication with each other for the three years since going to Brazil had been either silent or quarrelsome, but a current of understanding still ran deep.

We had gone to Brazil for Whirlpool once before, in 1969. With four young sons, Manny and I had accepted that first assignment enthusiastically. But seventeen years later I exerted every effort possible to avoid becoming, again, an expatriate whose lifeline was held in the dictatorial hands of a heartless corporation.

With chicane maneuvers, the corporation made it impossible for us to refuse the second time. The result, reckoned into social statistics, turned out to be merely one more broken family—a small price for a corporation to pay for what it accomplished in the world market, a large price for the Von Koenig family.

Starting out—1951. (See page 26)

Part One

The Family and Its Values

When it became necessary to divorce Manny, I could find no fault in him for his actions. As Irene Piccone had noted, many of the causes seemed directly attributable to him. But deeper analysis explains his behavior as responses to dictatorial demands made of him by the corporation. Because of Manny's childhood conditioning under similarly dictatorial situations in Germany, where he was born in 1927, he was susceptible and vulnerable.

Manny and I were married in 1951. After we'd settled in the United States, his mother, Elise Jadoul Von Koenig, visited from Munich the summer of 1967. She enjoyed her walks, and one evening she asked me to walk with her around the block. The air that evening still held the freshness that follows a good storm.

This stroll had a purpose beyond exercise. Elise wanted to relieve her conscience by telling me some things about her life that she felt were affecting mine. One was about her unsatisfactory marriage. I suspect this is something neither her daughter nor her son ever heard in such detail.

Elise had been a beautiful young Belgian from Liege. She'd

married a German officer she came to know while he was part of the enemy forces occupying her country after World War I. Shortly after, he suffered mental incompetence and was institutionalized. She was granted a divorce but could not go back to her family, which had disowned her because of her defection. Her only recourse had been to marry again, this time out of expediency, not love. Her second husband was Ludwig Von Koenig, the father of Manny and his sister, Wolfhilde, called Lulu for Little Wolf.

As Elise and I walked through the scattered twigs and branches that recalled the thunder and lightning of the previous night, she told me about the passions that had stormed inside her many years earlier. When her second husband lost interest in her while they were still in their late thirties, she considered taking a lover. However, even though it was difficult for her to go on in the physically loveless relationship, she decided she, too, would be chaste. She made that decision out of consideration, she said, for her children. She preferred, for their sake, that there never be cause for divorce, recrimination, or scandal.

Elise also confirmed something Manny had told me about the reason his parents had not sent him to college. During the last days at the front in Berlin, Manny had been captured by the Russians and imprisoned in a camp in Czechoslovakia. His parents believed he had been killed. By the time he managed to escape and make his way back to Munich, his sister was already enrolled at the university, and the family could not afford tuition for two.

Happy though Elise was over her son's return, she was nevertheless adamant that Lulu continue. Elise had decided her daughter should become a doctor, and Ludwig concurred. Elise's own post–World War I experiences convinced her the world was not safe for a woman who could not support herself. Men, she said, always managed. She was sorry, but circumstances being what they were, Manny would have to fend for himself. He could, of course, live at home, but he would have to finance his own education.

This story was one of the first Manny told me about his life, and he never fully forgave his mother. His resentment was based in part on the personality differences between Manny and his sister that surfaced in early childhood. Lulu was, first of all, older. In addition, she was a "goodie-two-shoes" who frequently tattled on her cute but mischievous little brother. To Manny, their mother's funding Lulu's education over his seemed not only another instance of her playing favorites, but also an umbrella declaration of favoritism.

Manny noticed, of course, that his father was silently acquiescent in the matter.

As Elise and I continued our walk, she said: "I apologize to you if you find my son not as good as he should be. I take the blame for this. But you must understand I always did the very best I knew how to do. There were the wars, you know. We had so little control."

I knew her reference to doing the best she could had a broad meaning, encompassing her efforts in trying to instill Belgian values in her German children, especially during the Hitler years of forced mis-education.

I also understood instantly what she meant by finding her son "not as good" as he should be. The year we were married, 1951, I went with Manny to Germany for fourteen months to live with his family—Elise, Ludwig, and Lulu. In the process I learned a great deal that helped me understand his truly abnormal childhood. War is child abuse.

We lived in a once beautiful fifth floor walk-up apartment. The kitchen balcony overlooked the Isar River and the palace of former King Maximilian on the opposite bank. But the enamel had been bombed off the bathtub, and the kitchen badly needed paint, which was unavailable. Because of the post-war housing shortage, the provisional government had ordered the Von Koenigs to rent out their largest room to a working class couple, both of whom drank heavily. Manny's family also had to share their kitchen and bath with the renters.

No matter where I went in Munich, I was presented with views of what war leaves in its wake—crumbled castle walls, fragments of bombed baroque angels, all my own dreams of Old European fairy tales fallen in the dust. Having become a German citizen by marriage, I lived among my fellow citizens, experiencing how they grasped for security by holding onto the rigid protocols of their fallen civilization, and how timorously, with baffled confusion, they attempted to construct the New Age they did not understand.

Periodically Manny reminisced about a cake he almost had on his sixteenth birthday. It was March 1943. Only through great ingenuity and planning, his mother produced what had become a rare luxury. The family was seated at the table, about to indulge, when an Allied bombing attack began. They all scurried to the basement shelter. They returned to find the apartment in shambles and the cake shot through with splinters of glass. The lesson he told me he learned from this was to not delay gratification. Who knows when you may get another birthday cake?

After the war when Manny returned to finish his senior high school year and enroll at the University of Munich, he earned his tuition by the only path that seemed open. He black-marketed cigarettes.

This did not diminish my perception of Manny as a good person. Considering the devastation of his home and homeland, the destruction of his civilization, and his forced entry into the chaos of emergent democracy, his sensitivity and morality were better, I believe, than anyone could have expected.

Although Manny may never have been able to totally forgive his mother, in later years he did forgive his sister for the advantages she received. I think he found this possible because of Lulu's generosity toward us both. She also assumed complete care of their aging widowed mother, as though she considered it solely her obligation because of the educational advantages she had been given.

My mother could well have made the same declaration to Manny as Manny's mother made to me: "I apologize to you if you find my daughter not as good as she should be." My mother, too, had done the very best she could under the circumstances that engulfed her.

Esther Bullis's family had been reasonably prosperous for at least three generations. In historical records, the family is recognized as contributing to the early agricultural development of eastern South Dakota. The farm at the edge of Brookings, thirty miles west of the Minnesota border, belonged to my grandfather, Frederick Morton Bullis (widowed in 1928), until he lost it during the Depression. He became a renter of the very buildings and acreage that had once been his, yet he provided shelter and a dairy-based livelihood for two daughters; a son-in-law; my mother; and two grandchildren, my brother and me.

Born in Brookings in 1930, I was three and my brother, Ronald, two, when Esther took us to nearby Oldham to live with her in-laws, the Reeders. When the neighbors learned our shameful secret—that Donald, the oldest son of Ethel and John, was serving time in the Minnesota State Penitentiary for armed robbery in a town across the border—the Reeders moved us all to a farm near Aiken, Minnesota, far enough away so the secret would not be known. The shame was mine, too; Donald was my father.

I did not know what the word "father" meant until I was six or seven, or maybe eight. Even then, the understanding I had of the concept "father" was of someone I loved very much but who could be discussed only in hushed tones. I recall going with my brother, my mother, and my father's parents to visit him in the prison when I was a preschooler.

My mother did not find living with her in-laws entirely pleasant. Even though it meant becoming a welfare recipient, she moved us to Stillwater, Minnesota, so we could be near the prison for visits. Not until 1939 did my mother give up pretending Donald Reeder would be able to rejoin us and complete our family. His in-prison behavior was as rebellious as that which led him there. Periodic infractions extended his sentence. Although she never let anyone say bad things about him, my mother divorced him for her children's sake.

Her subsequent marriage to Fred Nygren moved us all out to his farm in the Minnesota Swedish community that extends from Scandia to Forest Lake. Scandia had achieved a certain short-lived fame for having been visited, simultaneously, by Ingrid Bergman and *Life* magazine. Until my brother and I each completed eighth grade, we walked a mile and a half through all kinds of weather to and from the one-room schoolhouse. Big Lake School had been situated to serve the community of farms that encircled it.

Throughout those years, Ronald and I devotedly corresponded with our father, receiving from him doting letters and personally designed birthday cards. About once every two years we were able to visit him.

According to my older relatives, such a tragic and disgraceful thing as going to prison had never happened in either the Bullis or Reeder families. Theories about its cause, which need not be recounted here, still are debated at family reunions. Its relevance to this narrative is that this shadow cast over my life a darkness I was totally innocent of having created, in the same way that Manny, as a member of the Hitler Youth, was innocent of the Nazi darkness. Each of us bore scars from our life experiences and from being discriminated against for our guilt by association—he for having been a prepubescent Nazi and I for being the daughter of a felon.

Half a century later we were caught again—as we each had been in our youth—in the eddy of someone else's immoral conduct. Our thirty-eight-year marriage was rent asunder.

The year after my father went to prison, when I turned three and went to live on the Reeders' farm in Oldham, Emanuel Von Koenig, already six, was living a very different life. A few blocks from his parents' well-appointed fifth floor apartment on Thierschstrasse, in the ancient city of Munich, lived Adolph Hitler.

Hitler rose to power that year, 1933. His little neighbors, Manny and Lulu, became members of the Hitler Jugend. It mattered not that they, like thousands of other children in Germany at the time, were confirmed in Catholicism.

At Dachau on the outskirts of Munich, homosexuals, communists, and Jews were beginning to be interred. Elise spoke less and less French as the Nazi movement grew, to the point where she feigned not knowing the language at all. Manny, with his youth group, was invited to tea with Adolph Hitler at the *Haus der Kunst*, and his parents dared not object to his going. Manny recounts the event, from his childhood perspective, as innocuous. It was like American Boy Scouts hobnobbing with a governor.

Manny's father was often away in the summer working as a surveyor. Elise, a homemaker, spent her time at home cultivating flowering plants and going daily to the city market to buy fresh produce.

Manny was eleven when Neville Chamberlain came to his

city to sign the infamous agreement which, in a domino effect, capitulated Europe to Hitler's whims. He was twelve when Poland fell and thirteen when Denmark and Norway joined the ranks of the defeated, followed by the Netherlands, Belgium, and France.

At the time of these world changes, I was focused mostly on the basics of arithmetic. My world was made up of sunrises and sunsets across gently rolling hills. I went with my brother to bring home the cows at milking time. He and I played with domesticated raccoons, had a pet pig named Peggy, romped with a dog named Sport, and caressed so many cats they didn't even have names. Our new dad showed us where the Baltimore orioles nested.

Mom, who had taught school for a time before marriage, skillfully planned and grew a garden from which she canned enough fruit and vegetables to feed us all until the next harvest. She gloried in the orchard she planted with her own coarse hands and in the lawn she brought forth where none had grown. In 1940, my and Ronald's little sister, Nanci, was born.

When Elise and my mother eventually met nearly thirty-five years later, they liked each other. Their nurturing personalities had more in common than their link through shared grandchildren.

As I was growing up, there was no indoor plumbing on the Scandia or Forest Lake farms in my area or at the school I attended—unlike the apartment where Manny grew up. Although neither Munich nor Forest Lake had central heating, Manny's home had electricity; mine did not. Big Lake had a library of only two dozen books. Manny had daily access to the renowned Deutsches Museum, within blocks of his family's apartment. From his kitchen balcony, where his family breakfasted or took afternoon coffee, he could see the Isar River and the palatial Maximilianeum—a view he eventually shared with me.

Mussolini joined with Hitler in 1940, spreading the front into Africa and the Balkans. Stalemated with England, Hitler moved against Russia. Manny was almost sixteen. I was in the eighth grade of a one-room country school in the middle of Minnesota. When the tide of the Afro–Eurasian war turned and the German troops retreated from Stalingrad in January 1943, among them was a soldier from Leipzig named John Eser—who twenty-six years later would become Manny's boss at Whirlpool.

By 1942 America had joined the Allies and Japan joined the Axis. Manny's father was inducted and off at the front. The bombing of Munich began. High school classes met in anti-aircraft trenches so that Manny and his classmates could fire against the bombers in between parsing Latin phrases. Joining the Navy at age sixteen, he had the good fortune to be on shore when his ship was sunk. Reassigned to ground forces, he was in Berlin fighting hand-to-hand against the Russians when the war ended in April 1945.

At age eighteen, not even graduated from high school, he was transported to a prisoner-of-war camp in Czechoslovakia, from which he escaped with the help of a German doctor in the camp's hospital. Emaciated, and thought by his family to be dead, he literally walked most of the way home to Munich— which was at the time occupied by American forces.

Following their capture of the city, these heavily armed soldiers entered every dwelling in search of possible resisters. In the dark of night, they knocked on the door behind which Lulu and her mother waited in terror, not knowing what would come next. In contrast, I knew only that my mother's brother, Robert, was serving in the Navy and was at Pearl Harbor December 7, 1941. My stepbrother, Roger, also served in the Navy in the Pacific. The greatest conflagration of all time, World War II, barely touched me. Its ending the year I turned fifteen did not occupy my consciousness as much as the reality of being a sophomore at Forest Lake High School and having moved on to geometry.

In 1945 I spent the first of three summer vacations working as a maid, uniform and all, for a Minneapolis family, the Shearers, at their island in the St. Croix River. I swam, canoed, and served meals to house guests. From conversations I overheard and from social interactions, I acquired a wisdom about class divisions that surpassed my desire to participate in them. I learned what "my place" was and how to keep in it. While Manny had been taught "master race," I learned master "economic class."

Nineteen forty-seven was a heady year of change and initiation for me. First, the high school principal, Floyd Cohoes, encouraged the student council to sponsor my candidacy for Miss Forest Lake. I became my little Swedish town's first winner of that title and its first Fire Queen representative to the St. Paul Winter Carnival.

That same year my father, who had been paroled to his parents one year earlier, died violently in a sawmill accident in Missouri. Ronald and I, who had corresponded with him and visited him on rare occasions, took the bus to Mountain Grove for the funeral. The experience was nothing we could talk about to anyone but each other, because, for the sake of social appearances, our father had ceased existing in 1939. Our mother pretended the death of her first husband didn't matter to her, although we knew she grieved terribly.

The third event that marked my seventeenth year was my graduation from high school as valedictorian, receiving Elk's Club and Tozer Foundation scholarships and the American Legion School Award for courage, character, service, companionship, and scholarship.

The scholastic rewards were neither a surprise nor a source of elation. I had always been a diligent student interested in learning for learning's sake as well as being driven, I think, by a

Lutheran-inspired need to atone for my father's sins against society. I felt a need to bring joy to my mother in the rather hard life I felt she lived. As I had sown, so did I reap.

I was so burdened by my perception of the community's watching to see if the children turned out to be like their father, that I was introverted and dull, scarcely aware that I might be physically attractive. My principal had the notion that entering me in a beauty pageant might round out my personality. Did he know I would win? The thought never occurred to me. I entered because he pushed.

Winning the beauty title, and observing that this—for which I had done nothing—impressed my community far more than did the valedictory, confused me. Thrown into this mixture was the death of the phantom father, whose genetic and sub-cultural contributions were substantial. Confused though I was, but surrounded by Swedish stoicism, I, too, was stoic.

We had no counselors in those days to help troubled teens resolve conflicting issues induced by major trauma. Struggling within me even today are the 1947 conflicts between dreams dashed and dreams engendered.

That fall, when I started attending the University of Minnesota, I stayed at the Shearer home in Minneapolis, providing part-time service in exchange for room and board. I had scholarships, yes, but they were for modest amounts that presupposed being supplemented with part-time work.

When the *St. Paul Dispatch* ran a full-page feature on Forest Lake's "Scholarly Queen," the Shearers were quite upset, feeling such publicity was inappropriate for a maid—specifically *their* maid. The Woodhill Country Club, to which the Shearers and their friends belonged, apparently had no etiquette guidelines for such a situation. I sympathized with the Shearers' dilemma, but hardly knew what to do about it. The title of "maid" did not define who I was, and "queen" was incompatible with the role I filled in their household. I left their employ in the spring at the end of our contracted time.

At the time the "Scholarly Queen" article and photographs were published, I met a young man at the Lutheran Student Association. Because we met during my "fifteen minutes of fame," Dick may have felt there was more to me than there really was. We quickly became inseparable and eventually were engaged, with every intention of marrying. In the spring of 1950, acting out of confusion and insecurity, I called it off.

Marriage to Dick would have meant filling a role he and his prominent family already had defined for me. I sensed my personal karma required more freedom of range. I could not be a mere accouterment on the arm of a man destined to be successful with me or without me.

In Munich after the war, Manny finished high school. He became president of the student body and had a summer job with a yacht club at the Starnberger See, where he acted as skipper for U.S. Army personnel seeking recreation.

He met and loved Erika, who was planning to go to Chile to live with an uncle. They planned that Manny would follow, and they would then marry. Elise intercepted their mail, however, causing each of the lovers to believe the other had not written because of a change of heart. Whatever can be said of Elise's actions, they are understandable in the context of her own youthful defection to another country and the great unhappiness she experienced as a result. She acted in a way she thought best for her son.

Manny remained in Germany and went on to complete one year at the University of Munich before being sponsored by the U.S. Department of State to study in America for a year. The purpose of sending a group of promising young Germans to America was to have them learn democracy and return home as models for its practice in Germany. Offered his choice of location in the United States, Manny replied, "Somewhere in the middle." Thus he found himself at the University of Minnesota. He had certainly not been chosen for his English skills, which were minimal at the time. I had been studying German for several years as my second language, which was recommended, if not required, for graduation.

I was sharing a room on campus with Dorothy Johnson, a good friend from Scandia who had graduated with my brother. Having joined the Cosmopolitan Club, Dot and I had met Maung Khin, a young man from Burma, who was living at the Delta Tau Delta fraternity house. One afternoon in late September 1950, as Dot and I were walking past the frat house, Maung Khin saw Dot and called out of an upstairs window for us to come in. In the living room we were introduced to Manny, fresh off the boat except for a brief stop in New York where all the German students were introduced to Eleanor Roosevelt. That event had marked the shift of an era for the young man who, with a preteen group, had sipped tea with Hitler in Munich.

My studies were keeping me too busy to let me share the love-at-first-sight intensity Manny later claimed to have experienced. Moreover, after two and a half years in an intimate relationship, I wasn't ready for another. It happened anyway.

No particular anti-German sentiment existed anywhere among my friends. If anything, to others in the university milieu and to me, Manny was all the more interesting because he was a real live specimen of what we so recently had been taught to hate. He belied our prejudices with his wonder at having been reborn into a world so abundant and promising.

Among the qualities Manny and I shared was a tremendous backlog of suffering—he, under the lie of the Nazi master-race mania; I, under the lie that socioeconomic upward mobility made some of us better than others.

I had grown up deluded, fed Shirley Temple movies in which

the central problem was generally solved by a rich daddy. Upward mobility was the theme in the radio soap operas to which
I was exposed as a child: "Pepper Young's Family," "Stella Dal-
las," "Mary Noble, Backstage Wife." As an adult, when I listen
to the ongoing debates about whether media affects young
people, I am amused—aware of the influence the media had on
shaping my youthful romanticized aspirations.

In my father's letters and during my visits to the prison, I
had been enchanted by my father's tales of eventual riches and
his dreams of our going away to Mexico, maybe Brazil. When
he was paroled in 1945, he awoke from his fantasy world to
experience the same Depression-era poverty that had catapulted
him into prison in 1932. After he died, I no longer believed in
riches or in daddies.

I couldn't be Shirley Temple to my daddy, who was no more
up to the part than I. Nor could I be Mary Noble to Dick. I required a partner whose need for me would be the same as my
need for him; one with whom I would start out equal, as together we built our own unique set of values within the post-
war new-world view.

My character was in the same chaotic upheaval because of
family and community origins as Manny's was because of the
rise and fall of the Third Reich. He said to me, "You have no
idea what it feels like to have been taught one way all your life
and then, suddenly, to be told by the U.S. Occupation Forces
and most of the rest of the world that everything you believe is
wrong."

I did know what it felt like. In my case, I had not needed to
be told it was wrong to believe rich and successful is somehow
inherently better than poor and unnoticed. Hadn't I walked away
from a Mary Noble marriage and felt the better for it? Nor had I
needed to be told it was wrong to whisper, "Do you know their
father is in prison?" causing the children to believe it was some-

how their fault. Hadn't I "made myself" valedictorian?

My father's failure was no more my fault than Hitler's career was Manny's doing. Coming together as we did at that critical time in both our lives, when each of us had also known the loss of a first love, we determined we would pool our diverse cultural experiences and co-create a new value system for the better world in which we would live.

Manny's father's family held the title of *Edler und Ritter;* which, literally translated, means "nobleman and cavalier," a knight on horseback. The Von Koenigs had paid little heed to this minor heritage until required, by the rise of Hitler, to produce genealogy records proving they were not Jewish.

"Once upon a time" Manny's ancestors had owned a castle in Paumshausen, but hadn't I been the actual living queen-for-a-year of the principality of Forest Lake, which may, who knows, have been as large as Paumshausen? He brought to me, out of the Old World, a title—which was romantic. I, a daughter of the New World, gave him my country.

We were both poor, bitterly so, literally living from hand to mouth. Manny lived at the fraternity house but stoked the furnace for the privilege, somewhat as I had lived in upscale Kenwood Park wearing a maid's uniform.

In their naïveté, Manny's frat brothers sought, at their parties, to pair him with young women from their affiliated sorority. To no avail. His modest amount of pocket money and his great depth of soul stood in the way of any such alliances. To the Greek letter crowd, neither Manny nor I was any great prize, but we were to each other.

We applied for a marriage license using Manny's full legal German name. Years later when he became an American citizen, he chose to delete three of the four first names required of nobility. He transformed himself from Emanuel Anton Felix Ludwig Koenig von Paumshausen to Emanuel (no middle name)

Von Koenig. Von Koenig was the name used by his family in Munich.

Our application for a marriage license appeared in a list published in the *Minneapolis Star*. Boxed in an upper corner on the front page of the same edition, the *Star* highlighted our impending union under the caption, "This bride's going to need Koenig-sized calling card."

The *Forest Lake Times* followed up on the feature, noting I had placed an order with them for "Koenig-sized wedding invitations."

In the same issue, the Forest Lake Study Club invited the public to attend a program at which this curiosity-arousing visitor would speak.

Manny did not advise his parents of our forthcoming marriage. He would have married Erika and gone to live in Chile had his mother not interfered. Why, he reasoned, would she not attempt to stop him from marrying someone else to whose country he most probably would immigrate? His family was to be presented with a *fait accompli*.

My brother arranged leave from the Navy to be our best man, saying, "I wouldn't miss it, even though I still think of a German as someone who sneaks around in a trench coat, spying."

Our marriage on March 26, 1951, marked the beginning of a family unit that endured for the next thirty-eight years. It was eroded by the very force that Manny and I, as youths, thought we had overcome—a "master class" thinking imposed on us from without.

When we married, being together seemed as natural for us— who had recently met—as it was for our Burmese friends whose parents had pledged them to each other in childhood. Maung Khin and Gladys (her English name) were married in 1952 while we were living in Munich. When we returned to the United States in December of that year, we stayed with them one night in New York, where Maung Khin was working at the United Nations.

Two members of our wedding party, Dorothy Johnson and Mohammed Gheith, also married during that time and went to live in Egypt. International marriages were, perhaps, part of the post-war enlightenment that college students, as well as armed forces personnel, were experiencing. At any rate, internationalism has been a major force characterizing my entire adult life.

In contrast, internationalism played very little part in the lives of the Whirlpool staff who, in 1986, set about engineering my life. The puppeteers pulling my strings had no more understanding of the rich interweaving of cross-enculturation I had experienced than the frat brothers had of Manny's background when they hosted his first year in America in 1950–1951. While one cannot fault either of these organizations for their naïveté, it must be noted that years later, when I said "no" to going to Brazil for Whirlpool, I did it because I knew far better than the corporation that I was not up to the particular cross-cultural experience they proposed for me.

As newlyweds, we struggled like any other couple. During the hot summer of 1951 following our early spring wedding, I continued my student job at the University of Minnesota Library. I was in my junior year as a psychology major. Manny found work as a welder at Bros Brothers in Minneapolis. The hard, dirty work paid well.

We needed the money because I had determined to return to Germany with him in September when his student visa expired. I feared if I didn't return with him—if I waited in the United States for his immigrant clearance and his return—I would never be able to understand him as fully as I could if I accompanied him.

He would guide me through the aftermath of World War II and enable me to experience it at its nucleus. Having experienced Munich, I was able to understand, thirty-eight years later, how his childhood fears under Hitler were reactivated by the corporate powers' eerie similarities to Nazism. Failing to cooperate with either Nazism or Whirlpool meant annihilation.

Manny's earliest, most tender years taught him that to obey meant to survive. Bertold Brecht's plays explained that mentality, in which the moral imperative is, "First, you survive."

Manny survived Nazism and later was able to kick it with the help of world opinion, which convinced him it had been all wrong. However, mine was the only voice telling him that the doctrine of corporate infallibility was wrong. My single voice was not strong enough for him to hear. I lost him to Whirlpool, which he survived only by becoming absorbed into it.

I had to get out of the marriage dominated by the increasingly amplified corporate voice, but I do not blame Manny. I understand why he did what he did.

One thing Manny said to me the summer we married held the key to my understanding of our dissolution. He made a promise to me of some sort—the specifics have long escaped my memory—and he followed it by saying, "On my word of honor." Among my friends such a proclamation was taken lightly, somewhat jokingly. When I heard it spoken by my new husband, I raised some question about the seriousness of his promise. Manny replied he was making this statement quite seriously, in the courtly European tradition. My having taken it as a joke offended him, and he delivered quite a lecture on the meaning honor held for him. The concept was so much the essential element of his existence that it survived intact, even through the Nazi era. The bond between us did not dissolve until it appeared to me that Manny had lost this sense of honor through his assimilation into the Whirlpool culture.

Honor, to him, meant all the things we mean by contractual law. It meant adhering "to the letter" of any agreement, verbal or written. It meant following instructions and doing the job to the very best of one's ability, without need of prodding. I observed two experiences he had with Minnesotans who understood this concept and how integral it was to the German character. In 1951 when we purchased a few furniture pieces on short-term credit, the owner of the small store exclaimed, "Oh, I know I won't have to worry about payment from *you*. Germans *always* pay their bills."

A few years later, when we had returned to Minnesota's Twin Cities after living in Germany, we were introduced to Werner von Braun at a gathering of the Volksfest Association, an organization of Germanophiles. Dr. von Braun pumped Manny's hand and told him he would be welcome to come to work at the Redstone Arsenal, if he were interested. The mere fact of his having been raised and trained in Germany was recommendation enough for another German.

Honor, in Germany, was a social value strongly internalized within the individual. In reality honor served the regime better than it did the individual, moving people to inform the regime about others who were not conforming to the regime's code. Honor, so dichotomized, embodies an element of fear. To whom is one loyal first: family, or state or corporation?

The U.S. State Department paid Manny's return passage following his year at the university. For my ocean passage we barely had enough money. Bus fare from Forest Lake, Minnesota, to New York Harbor, where the SS *Washington* awaited the return of students it had brought from Germany the year before, was out of the question.

We hitchhiked cross-country with the apprehensive support of my mother and stepfather who, even though they thought our action strange, could see the sense of it. They drove us to the intersection of Route 61 and Old Highway 8, about five miles from their farm, dropping us off at the side of the road with our two meager suitcases. They parked nearby to snap a photo of us. They waited until we caught our first ride and waved good-bye. We knew we would be back, but we had no idea when.

Before we left, Manny completed, with my help, all the necessary immigration forms. Manny's was a privileged immigration, because he was married to an American. My special friend and matron of honor, Shirley Brisson, and her husband, Dennis, did not hesitate to sign as his sponsors.

I had never been beyond the boundaries of the United States before and had no concept of what I was heading into. We only knew we would both be back. For his year of study in America, Manny's only obligation to the State Department was to put into practice what he had learned in his metamorphosis from Nazi to democrat. He could do that wherever he was. We planned for our stay in Germany to be a learning experience for me, for as long as I could handle it.

My introduction to Germany occurred as it does for many travelers, at customs control in Bremerhaven. Unlike most travelers, however, I was in the company of hundreds of students returning from various universities across the United States. None of them identified any longer as members of the "master race," and they derided the border guards for their goose-stepping attire and manner. In a way, the students were modeling a lesson democracy had taught them. I trust they became more compassionate later, without losing their basic sense of democratic values.

We boarded a train in the dark. Hours later, bombed-out Frankfurt became my first full daylight view of the country of which I was an instant citizen. As stark black and white as the newsreels I'd seen, the city seemed to *be* those very films, magically made life-sized. I stood inside the scene and wept.

Munich was the same, but I was a little more prepared for the desolation by the time we arrived there later the same day.

Elise, whom I quickly learned to call *Mutti* (an affectionate variation of *Mutter*, meaning Mother), demonstrated her acceptance of me and of the liaison with her son that brought me into her home, by having Manny translate her thoughts and write this to my parents:

> *Now your nice daughter arrived at our home. We welcomed her to our hearts as our daughter. You can be sure we do for Rosalyn everything we can according to our conditions. We know that here the life is entirely different from that in the States, that it is hard, but with our love we are sure she will spend a happy time and have a nice remembrance of our family. Thank you for the greetings, which we heartily return.*

Elise did not know, and probably would not have believed it had she been told, of the very humble conditions out of which I had come to be with them. In 1946, my folks had moved from the spacious two-story house we had lived in since Mom, Ron and I had become part of the family in 1939, to what had been the old Nygren homestead. There the farm land was better and the barn was adequate, but the tiny two-bedroom house, built without closets, provided truly substandard shelter. It was not insulated, and it was heated only by wood-burning stoves in the kitchen and living room. Personal needs were served by an outhouse. Today I marvel that we survived those winters. To the credit of our pioneer-spirited parents, another marvelous big house eventually arose in place of the other, as they persevered in their gardening and dairy farming. At no time, I think, did they view themselves as poor. Their wealth lay in their perspectives.

Even as the Von Koenigs showed acceptance, they resented

me for intruding and yet valued me as model and link to the new American-controlled bureaucracy. When *Mutti* and I walked in Munich, shopping and doing errands together, she told me about the magnificent buildings that used to stand where there was only rubble. She always carefully explained the devastation was the result of British bombs. In her rhetoric to me, she held Americans guilty of nothing.

As she had with other cosmic shifts in her life, Elise set about adjusting herself to the inevitable. She knew she was going to lose her son eventually—if not to Erika in Chile, then to me in America.

At Christmas, when I wanted to hear the Bach concert at the nearby St. Lukas Kirche, I went alone because *Mutti* was not interested and could see no reason why her son, who "didn't understand such things," should go simply to escort his wife. She preferred to have him with the family, sitting around the table, as we did most evenings.

Manny's family displayed quite a bit of this attitude during the fourteen months we lived with them. Still, I never felt the pull for his affection was unbalanced. The old ways prevailed within the apartment walls, but outside, everywhere, all traditions were shifting toward American-style democracy.

The bottom line was that Manny would eventually emigrate to the United States. Everyone knew I was the one who held the magic wand. We would stay in Munich for as long as I needed to study it. The more pleasant the family made my stay, the longer they would have their son with them. None of us were conscious of these dynamics at the time we played them out; nonetheless, that's the way it was.

Manny found a job with the U.S. Military Post Exchange working as a liaison between American supervisors and German employees. The American International Underwriters Corporation, which wrote insurance coverage for armed forces personnel, hired me to give the girl-next-door touch to its office on the Neubiberg Air Force Base.

Together with Manny's old friends and our new friends from each of our jobs, plus seven students we had met aboard the *SS Washington,* we led a richly educational social life that ranged from attending grand receptions at the American Consulate to acknowledging the gradual dying from war-related malnutrition of several native neighbors (Hannelore, Helmut: may you rest in peace)—and the suicide of one of the students (Martin).

Thanks to Manny's job with the PX and his training course in Nuremberg, we spent a weekend there together and stood behind the lectern at the great stadium, the *Parteitag-gelände,* where Hitler orated the masses into frenzied passion.

Although neither of us had been there before, the different backgrounds we brought to the experience surely caused different reactions in each of us, even if only in intensity. The stadium was empty of all human life, save us. It stood cold and harsh in the November wind, and seemed as much an antiquity as the Coliseum in Rome. This Nuremberg stadium stood as an anachronistic remnant of a Rome within our lifetime. I sensed it as such. Eerily empty, it was a stage from which all the actors had gone, never to return.

Manny's sensations had to have been more immediate. On a stage that was part of the same franchise, a few hours away in Munich, he had been one of the actors. How his role had changed! His pensiveness that day in 1952 was matched in 1988 when I stood with him in Munich on a street corner near the Church of St. Anne. In reverie, his gaze circled the rooftops in all directions. Finally he said, "The last time I was here, everything all around me was on fire."

In contrast, on an outing with my company, AIUC, we were in never-never land, watching castles on the Rhine parade past our excursion boat.

Mutti was an artist of sorts. She arranged for me to take voice lessons from her friend, Marta Starziewski, and accompanied me on the piano when I practiced. We went to the theater together. She was also a skilled shopper and cook, and she taught me much about household arts.

During our first months in Munich, Lulu was in Hannover doing medical residency. She came home for Christmas 1951, and we all lived amicably together for the next year.

Manny and I paid our fair share of family living expenses. We took one extensive camping trip into Italy, Switzerland, and France with a German couple. For this, Manny purchased a movie camera. We were not frugal, and we did not plan ahead.

When we eventually left Germany, we did it less because of family friction than because of the situation as a whole. The German environment, seeming at first to offer an atmosphere of freedom, really didn't. So many senseless "rules" controlled what one must always do (*"Sowas tut mann immer"*) or what one must never do (*"Sowas tut mann nie"*). My inappropriate responses became shrill and impatient "WHYs?" and "WHY NOTs?" My breathing had begun to feel constricted. I did the best I could to blend in, but I reached the limits of my adaptability.

Although Manny welcomed the start of a new life in the States, he had not been unduly eager for that moment, knowing eventually it would come. I recognize now that reaching my limits of adaptability in Germany—and knowing it—foreshadowed the Brazil experience. My mind and body are one. When dissonance becomes too great, my body will not allow conditions my mind will not accept. My body rebels, with either constricted breathing or migraine headaches.

We caught a midnight train to meet our ship in Genoa. We were able to leave only because the Brissons had signed the necessary affidavit of responsibility. To Manny's credit, he is still grateful to them.

The easy stage of our partnership was over. We had then to define ourselves and put our untested beliefs into practice. That's what we thought. Actually, what we had to do was find jobs. Not easy. We had no money, and we already owed my stepfather the amount of our passage home. The Korean War was in progress, and Manny's alien status limited access to the tool-and-die job he sought.

The Seeger Refrigerator Company in St. Paul had one department that did not require security clearance, and there Manny found work, providing the entrée to his entire career. The Whirlpool Corporation purchased the Seeger Refrigerator Company and Manny along with it.

Every example of American democracy's triumph over other forms of government was news. The headline in a spring 1953 issue of the *St. Paul Pioneer Press* read: "Job here taught ex-Nazi democracy best."

Reporter Carl Hennemann wrote:

> *American democratic principles, taught after World War II in a Munich, Germany, high school, changed an ardent young Nazi into a student of democracy. . . . Von Koenig decided to finish his high school (education), interrupted by the war. Americans had taken over and were running the school like an American high school. Von Koenig was elected president of the school's self-government council and a representative to Munich's high school council.*
>
> *This was his first contact with democratic government and he became curious.*
>
> *"Soon all students were reading all the American and English books they could get," he said. "And we read, and read, and read trying to find out what we really were."*

Reporting on our return to St. Paul, the article quoted Manny's observation, "It is much easier for a German to transfer to America than for an American to transfer to Germany."

FOURTEEN   1☆

Job Here Taught Ex-

By CARL HENNEMANN

American democratic principles, taught after World War II in a Munich, Germany, high school, changed an ardent young Nazi into a student of democracy who has become an American worker at the Seeger Refrigerator Co. plant in St. Paul.

Emanuel von Koenig, a uniformed Nazi grade school student at 10—back in 1937—progressed in his teens to the German air force, the German labor service, and the German navy.

"We got everything we wanted," he said. "We were Hitler's **children. We got all the** athletic goods and overnight camping trips we wanted, we could study art, architecture, sculpture. We were told all kindness came to us from Hitler. We knew nothing but Hitler and his kindness. We served him fervently to the end."

After the war, Von Koenig declined from 210 pounds to 102 in a Russian prison camp. He came back to Munich and the reproaches which older Germans, who had known democracy under the republic, heaped on the younger ones who had supported Hitler.

Von Koenig decided to finish his high school, interrupted by the war. Americans had taken over and were running the school like an American high school. Von Koenig was elected president of the school's self-government council and a representative to Munich's high school council.

This was his first contact with democratic government and he became curious.

"Soon all students were reading all the American and English books they could get," he said. "And we read, and read, and read trying to find out what we really were."

Graduating in 1948, Von Koenig took a job in youth education. He was a student at the University of Munich when he became an exchange student and came to the University of Minnesota. Before he left the state university in 1951 and went back to Munich, he married Rosalyn Reeder of Forest Lake. In Munich, both husband and wife found good jobs. But Von Koenig felt he was already an American. Fourteen months later the Von Koenigs were back in America.

"It is much easier for a German to transfer to America, than for an American to transfer to Germany," is the way Von Koenig explained it.

The young German soon caught on to Americanism. He went to a Twin Cities employment agency and applied for a factory job as a metal worker, a skill he had learned in Munich. In January he went to work at Seeger's as a production clerk. In five weeks he was an assembly line foreman.

"And there," he said succinctly, "is where I really learned about American democracy. For in a German factory, the foreman is a dictator. He hires a number, fires a number, reprimands a number. There is no human element. You know you've got a boss and what he says goes.

"I wasn't only a young squirt, and a foreigner at that, but also somebody who had to make a lot of psychological adjustments in winning the workers I was supposed to boss. It took two or three months to make the adjustment. Now I can go

---

ST. PAUL DISPATCH

Nazi Democracy Best

Emanuel von Koenig, 271 Summit, and his wife, Rosalyn, cut out name cards for a card party sponsored by the Newcomers club. It is all part of Emanuel's transformation from a former Nazi soldier and sailor to an American citizen and worker.—Staff Photo.

● ● ●

to any guy in the factory and we know just how to act toward each other."

Von Koenig is now assistant die job supervisor.

He and his wife live at 271 Summit. Mrs. Von Koenig is an insurance agent, and Von Koenig says she is an advocate of democracy in the family.

Back in Munich, Von Koenig's father, a railroad surveyor, and his mother, a native of Belgium,

who survived the war, have a daughter, Wolfhilde, 27, who has become a doctor. Their savings and hopes all went into making her an independent professional woman. The elder Von Koenig never joined the Nazi party, and evaded such action by joining in welfare work.

Young Von Koenig is awaiting the year 1955. His transfer to democracy will become complete in that year. He will become an American citizen.

The article, which was poignantly prophetic, went on to describe how he had started at Seeger's as a production clerk and in five weeks became an assembly-line foreman. Manny was quoted as saying: "And there is where I really learned about American democracy. For in a German factory, the foreman is a dictator. . . . There is no human element. You know you've got a boss and what he says goes."

Ultimately, however, this dictatorial manner of World War II Germany is exactly what Manny experienced again from the CEO of the Whirlpool Corporation, who apparently believed the end justified the means. The 1953 article refers to me with Manny's observation that I was "an advocate of democracy in the family." Whatever else changed, that did not.

Glad to be back in Minnesota, we settled into a pleasant social life with old friends and new. I worked for a time in insurance sales, as I had in Munich, and later as a placement counselor in a personnel agency. At the same time I was soprano soloist with the boys' choir at St. Paul's Episcopal Church in Minneapolis, followed by a year at a Presbyterian church in St. Paul.

When I became pregnant in late 1956, both of us had for some time been enrolled in University of Minnesota extension courses, studying evenings toward completing the degrees we had "vacationed from" in 1951. Manny had advanced at Whirlpool, and I was quite happily employed in the finance department of the Weyerhaeuser Lumber Company.

Ironically, I was then offered the one job likely to have developed into a satisfying career. A Ph.D. in the research branch of 3M's personnel department taught the statistics course I was completing. He offered me a job, pregnant or not, mother or not, with part-time hours at my convenience. I can't believe I said no. I, who had thought I didn't even want to be a mother, *chose* to engage in the role full time.

Not until 1957 when Doug, our first child, was born, did

Manny's and my life together take on real meaning and present its greatest challenges. I still took extension courses aiming toward a degree. Toward what end, I might have asked myself: A good job? I had already received a best-of-all-probable offers and turned it down.

Lulu came to visit us the fall of 1957 to see her infant nephew. The following summer we took our year-old son to Munich to meet his *Grosseltern* (grandparents), who by then lived with Lulu, a practicing anesthesiologist, in the Bogenhausen district.

Our second child, Jeff, was born in 1959. Manny took a leave of absence to complete his degree and graduated from the University of Minnesota in 1960. I graduated, finally, in 1961.

Manny was tapped for a transfer to Hamilton, Ohio, and he moved to the new location ahead of the rest of us. I was a college graduate with no outside-the-home employment, giving full care to a toddler and an infant, about to resettle in a strange house and community in which my outside world would be defined for the first time in terms of my husband's employment. This was the reverse of my situation in Munich, where the outside world had been mine.

Before the children and I moved to join him, Manny voiced our new situation over the phone to me: "I feel I am moving ahead, and you are standing still." I felt the same way about it but had insufficient time and will to fully analyze the sensation. We loved each other very much. Edward was born in 1962.

Once in a rare while, in this still-early stage of our lives within the Whirlpool framework in Hamilton, Manny brought visiting colleagues home for dinner. One such was Sam Bateman, who was to play a key role in later events. I was merely fringe that evening. Sam and Manny talked; I served dinner.

Manny respected Sam's work and said he was an okay person. As for me, Sam and I did not have enough communication between us to enable me to say whether he was a nice person or not. What did make a lasting impression on me was a purely household *faux pas:* I forgot to thoroughly stir the potato salad before putting it on the table. As a result, Sam got a dry portion. Asked about it some years later, he did not remember the incident, the evening, or me.

When the Hamilton plant was phased out, we were transferred back to St. Paul and settled on Portland Avenue, the most child-friendly neighborhood we ever experienced. I set up a *Deutsche Schule* in our dining room to teach German to our boys and to tuition-paying neighbor children. I continued post-grad extension courses at the University of Minnesota, primarily studying German literature.

Manny went to Munich for a solo visit with his parents and sister in 1963. In 1964 Lulu crossed the Atlantic to be with us a second time. That was the year the best-ever picture of our family was taken (reproduced on page 104).

Accepted into the ensemble of the St. Paul Civic Opera, I sang in most of its productions for several years until becoming pregnant with Curt.

Through opera connections, we met Alfred and Lorraine Mohr, founders of the Volksfest Association. German-born Alfred fully understood the royal implications of "Von" and treated Manny with special respect. I remember one of the Mohrs' glitteringly giddy parties honoring Prince Konstantin, honest-to-goodness heir to the Bavarian throne should the Royalist Party ever be successful. Manny, a knight who did indeed know such courtly skills as how to kiss a lady's hand properly, was asked to help the prince "receive." Konstantin did not take himself at all seriously and worked out signals with Manny about when they would click heels and when they wouldn't.

I arrived at the party late, after performing in "I Pagliacci."

Still in the clown mode, I wore an orange dress with one orange stocking and shoe, the other leg and foot in chartreuse, and fit right into the gaiety in progress.

In 1966, when our eldest was nine, we shipped him off via nonstop Lufthansa to spend six weeks in Munich. Consequently, Doug is the only one of our boys who has memories of his grandfather, still alive then. The summer after Doug's visit, *Mutti* made her only trip to the United States.

I was a Cub Scout den mother when Doug and Jeff were ten and eight; Manny helped not only his own sons with their derby cars, but other children as well. He was a wonderful father. He changed diapers, wiped noses, did laundry, shopped for groceries, cooked, and cleaned. Routinely on Friday evenings, we had an easy-to-prepare supper of pancakes and apple sauce, followed by Manny's taking all four of his sons—even Curt, barely out of diapers—for a Family Night swim at the health club. It allowed me one evening of much-needed peace.

Manny was a competent carpenter and craftsman, as well. He designed and built a kitchen and supply trailer that enabled the six of us to camp at Yellowstone Park the summer of 1968. During the few years before we packed up for our first international transfer, he had a Sunfish sailboat for his own getaways, but he frequently took the older boys aboard. On occasion, with a sitter in charge at home, he and I sailed White Bear Lake.

Life was rounded out for all of us by having grandparents, aunts, uncles, and cousins nearby. July 4 was always a Forest Lake occasion. Thanksgiving, Christmas, and birthdays shifted from house to house.

How could a mother of four get herself out of the house from time to time? Such outings were necessary for my mental health, because Manny was frequently out of town on business. I became active at the St. Paul College Club (American Association of University Women), starting as a topic chair, going on to chair

a twenty-four-member Creative Arts Committee, and then serving on the state board from 1967 to 1969.

In 1967, AAUW offered College Faculty Program scholarships to members interested in preparing to teach at that level. I
applied, was successful, and enrolled in the University of Minnesota Graduate School for an M.A. in linguistics. Still a psychologist at heart, I had determined language was a major part
of socialization, and linguistics could answer for me many of
the questions I had about psychology not addressed directly by
that discipline.

I vividly recall my initial discussion of my grad work with
Manny, who was daily becoming more "corporate." I felt I had
to start by saying, "There's something important I need to talk
to you about. I've been waiting to catch you in a good mood,
but I can't wait any longer."

Though my words were a bit dour, they succeeded in getting his attention. After I had explained what I proposed to do
with my scholarship, which covered every expense, even to
baby-sitters and housecleaning, he said, "Well, I suppose it's
something we could consider."

I responded, "You don't seem to understand. I'm not asking
for your permission. I'm showing you the courtesy of informing you." I rejoiced that the world outside our doors did not
belong only to him and other ladder climbers, after all. An avenue had reopened for me. This is an example of how my advocacy for "democracy in the family" required, on occasion,
vigorous exercise.

I enrolled in the fall of 1968. By midwinter, Manny was made
a spectacular offer, the kind he had dreamed about all his life.
His role model in life had not been his father, a government
surveyor; it had been his mother's engineer brother, who had
traveled all of Europe and much of Russia in practice of his profession.

Brastemp, Whirlpool's affiliate in Brazil, requested technical assistance in the area of foam insulation. Key-punched cards representing all likely candidates were run through the selector. Manny was first choice, even though his work at the time was with vacuum cleaners. Salivating at the prospect, he coaxed me to move to Brazil with, "I can't spend the rest of my life cutting a fraction of a cent off the cost of vacuum cleaner cords."

He had no trouble persuading me. I was then thirty-eight, but I had the spark of the twenty-one-year-old who had hitch-hiked into post-war Europe with a husband she had known for only ten months. The AAUW scholarship had no strings attached. Each student was to be fully supported for one year. If we didn't achieve our degrees within that time, the rest was up to us. With the next term, I audited Portuguese. What a linguistic opportunity!

Manny left for Brazil on March 16, 1969, his forty-second birthday. Before taking a cab to the Minneapolis airport, he gazed deep into what he called my "one-hundred-thousand eyes" with his, equally intense, and said, "I don't want to go. I'm scared." Then I did for him what I so often did, with or without words, sometimes simply by empathy. Affirming for him that all his previous careful and deliberate choices had brought him to that point, I said, "You *have* to go. It is your destiny."

Our attorney relieved me of dealing with the sale of our house and other extraordinary legal and financial matters so I could finish my student year and get our children through theirs. Doug was in sixth grade, Jeff in fourth, and Ed in first. Curt attended Crocus Hill preschool in the mornings, and a neighbor cared for him on weekday afternoons.

Manny returned for a short visit in June to participate in the garage sale, final packing, and farewells. I made most of the decisions about what would go into storage. Based on information he had sent me, I had also purchased the kitchenware, electric blankets, linens, and clothing we would need in Brazil over the next two years. Manny came home exhausted, but no more so than I was.

John Eser, who as a young soldier in the German army was part of the retreat from Stalingrad, was director of the International Division at Whirlpool's home office in Benton Harbor, Michigan. He introduced himself to me on the phone and invited me to the home office so I could become familiar with corporate personnel and expatriate policies before going to Brazil. I appreciated this gesture and still do, as I fondly remember everything about John's manner and motives during the years that followed. Given my responsibilities—running a household with four children while being a full-time graduate student—I had to decline, even though I knew it was something I *should* do. That the visit was offered not once, but several times and insistently, gave me confidence, at the time, in the corporation's integrity.

This experience with John Eser in 1969, under the Whirlpool presidency of Elisha Gray, stands in marked contrast to the orientation offered me in 1986, when Whirlpool, under the presidency of Jack Sparks, again sought Manny's services in Brazil. For this second relocation, Whirlpool deliberately concealed rules from me, regulations to which I was later held.

Beginning with the Hamilton, Ohio, assignment, Manny had been at the manager level with Whirlpool. In Brazil he became superintendent of the Brastemp factories, working closely with its president, Miguel Etchenique, whom we called Mike. His wife, Helen, worked with Manny to locate a house for us to rent. Staff members from Mike's office assisted him in partially furnishing it with locally purchased items.

Manny and I knew living in Brazil would provide outstanding educational experiences for our children as well as for us. We chose not to enroll them in the American School, but to immerse them as much as possible in the local culture. At Manny's request, the Etcheniques sought to gain admission for the boys at the school their own children attended. That did not work out, but Manny persisted and found the Instituto MacKenzie which was, at least, willing to try us out. One of our first experiences was an interview with the principal, Irene Gusmão. Yes, she decided, our family commitment was such that our children had a good chance of succeeding in learning Portuguese and being trained as good Brazilian citizens over the next few years.

I was proud of my husband for his integrationist attitude, and I suppose he must have been equally proud of me. We were living out our dream of building, together, a unique set of values, replacing much of what we had been taught as children.

By the end of six months, our children spoke better Portuguese than we did, including playground slang. Manny's vocabulary included factory and business jargon, while mine tended toward household management and linguistic form.

Aside from several neighboring American families who befriended us, we oriented our social life toward Brazilians. I didn't even join the Newcomer's Club. After the house and school situations were under control, I went to the União Cultural Brasil–Estados Unidos to enroll in a Portuguese language class.

I was surprised to find that enrollment included a one-on-one interview with the assistant director of courses, but I later realized this was not routine. Based on information I had given on my application form, I was being "set up" to deliver a series of lectures on psycholinguistics.

True, I was fresh from the University of Minnesota, having taken state-of-the-art courses in the Linguistics Department on Noam Chomsky's *Transformational Grammar* and courses in the Psychology Department from Kenneth MacCorquodale, who had been the editor of B.F. Skinner's book, *Verbal Behavior.* When

I later took my first oral exam in Portuguese, all three of my examiners were teachers who had been students in classes I taught. Because I had expected so much of them, I was compelled to perform in Portuguese much better than had been my original intent.

This launched me into academia, a world apart from Manny's manufacturing environment. Academia allowed me to maintain a sense of self and broadened the social base for both of us. For example, at the União I met a teacher of English, Trude Hauptmann, a Berlin Jew who had escaped the Nazis. She remains a close and special friend of mine to this day.

John Eser came from the home office to visit from time to time and never failed to ask me with the utmost sincerity how things were and what he could do for me. He always responded sympathetically. Once he rush-ordered a WaterPik for us when we needed to replace one our young son had destroyed at a neighbor's house while trying to "find out how it worked."

Between John's and Manny's positions was another held by Frank Livingston, who came through from time to time to check on things at Brastemp, and he also accepted invitations to our house.

I first met Julio Caicedo, another corporate employee, in São Paulo. He and his wife, Gloria, were also to become close friends of ours—that is, as close as is possible in a corporate structure, where the first rule always has to be "watch your back."

Mike and Helen Etchenique were models of solicitous hosting. Regularly, at least once a month, they entertained us either at their home or for dinner out—sometimes alone, sometimes in company. Initially, both they and John Eser treated me with such respect that when I was unable to attend a party to include Brastemp functionaries, John said, "Well, then, we won't have the party." My concern about attending was the lack of baby-sitter service available in the city. Brazilian families either had other relatives living with them or had a permanent live-in *baba* for their children.

Manny and I reasoned we would never be able to go anywhere if we could not resolve this problem. Hiring just any Brazilian on an as-needed basis didn't work, because on the one hand, those who were educated enough for the responsibility would be insulted at the suggestion, and on the other hand, those who would baby-sit would be so cowed by the status of our children they would allow the children to overrun them.

We weighed the facts: Doug was twelve; our house had bars on every window and double locks on every door; it was made of fire-retardant materials, marble, stone, and cement; and it was patrolled by a uniformed guard carrying a gun. We decided the children were probably not in danger from anything other than themselves. The party could go on.

We did not know until several years later, about the time we were getting ready to leave Brazil and return to the United States, the real reason our house had been available for rent: the son of the owner had been shot to death by a prowler on the second-floor balcony. Understandably, the family had not wanted to live there anymore.

The first renters moved out following the terrorist assassination of an American major who lived down the street. After his death, flyers appeared on the car windshields of Americans living in the area notifying them they would be next.

###

During the two years the boys and I were with Manny in São Paulo, he was not asked, even once, to attend meetings back in Benton Harbor, although Mike and others went several times. Manny wondered why he wasn't included. I think, now, he was not invited because our guardian angel, John Eser, knew he should stay in Brazil with us.

The only time Manny left us alone for any length of time while we were in Brazil was when he went to Salvador on business in December 1969. Thinking of us even then, he arranged things so all of us could share in the adventure. While the boys were finishing their school terms, Manny went on ahead, driving our car on the long journey so we could all return in it together. We hired the guard's cousin to live in our house while we were gone, so it would be protected days as well as nights. School out, the boys and I flew to Salvador where we spent a memorable Christmas in the tropics. The holiday was so different from any of our other December celebrations the boys did not realize it was Christmas.

We tried to take in all the local culture we could in São Paulo. Sunday was our family day. Each week we planned exciting child-oriented outings that familiarized us with the area while keeping us tightly bonded.

After a few bad starts with maids, whom I did not hesitate to send packing at the first sign of trouble, we were fortunate to be adopted by Maria Antonio, a woman so beautiful we called her Crosby because she looked like a black version of Kathy, Bing Crosby's second wife.

Maria Antonio could come to us only two days a week, but she brought us her husband's eighteen-year-old sister, Eunice, to be our "live-in." Crosby trained her sister-in-law to give "proper" service while continuing to come twice weekly herself. She sometimes brought her little son Roberto to play with Curt. She asked if she could do her family's laundry in our machines, and I could see no reason why not.

Crosby was patient with me. She eavesdropped on my conversations with solicitors who came to the door. When they were gone, she would ask me in the simplest Portuguese possible— the only kind I really understood in those first months—whether I had comprehended what they were offering or what they wanted. My answer was invariably no, and she would explain to me in every which way possible until I finally understood. I miss her gentle heart.

When people ask me today whether I like Brazilians, I think of Crosby as I answer in glowingly positive terms.

Our neighbor, bureau chief for Associated Press, told us about a Brazilian journalist friend of his who had disappeared, Gulag-fashion, and no one could find out why, much less do anything about it. There was no habeas corpus protection under the Brazilian dictatorship. This information succeeded in raising by a few degrees the sense of danger we constantly felt.

Nelson Rockefeller came to the city to speak, and the elevators of the building in which he was to appear were bombed. The movie theater on Avenida Paulista, which we sometimes frequented, also was bombed. A prominent politician was gunned down at an intersection our children's school bus had passed through only an hour before.

Having accepted an invitation to a dinner party given by Brazilian friends introduced to us by our landlady, we were asked ahead of time not to talk about political matters. The daughter of one of the couples to be present was a terrorist who had left the country to avoid being arrested.

Against this background, we were further disturbed to learn that Mike Etchenique had become dissatisfied with Manny's performance. Manny and I pillow-talked about it a great deal. The life we were living as a family was not separable from Brastemp. We depended on the Brastemp office for everything: currency exchange, meat delivery, travel arrangements, document updates, references, even safe conduct, if needed.

Manny's assessment of the developing problem was that Mike had forgotten why he had originally brought Manny down from the States. The purpose had been for Manny to teach Brastemp how Whirlpool in the U.S. handled manufacturing, not for Manny to learn to function in the Brazilian manner.

In the Brazilian culture at large, we had experienced any number of differences, which we understood and therefore respected, even though we had no intention of incorporating them into our way of life. For example, people in Brazil commonly disregarded lines, whether in the MacKenzie school bookstore or at the open produce market. The most commandeering person was waited on next, no matter how long others had been waiting.

Employees in the Brastemp factory practiced similar culturally rooted behaviors. Department heads reached beyond the boundaries of their areas to effect changes in departments headed by others. There was little signing of memos and directives, as though to deliberately evade responsibility and possible repercussion. Obscured channels of authority complicated the task of tracking a problem to its source and had adverse effects on meeting production goals and schedules. These practices conflicted with the way things were done in the U.S.

More and more, it seemed to Manny, Mike was resisting suggestions on what to change and how. Manny had to go through daily meditations to remind himself that no matter how Mike acted, his own mission there was to teach Brazilians how he—representing Whirlpool—did things. He had not come to learn how Brazilians worked, which seemed, increasingly, to be what Mike was trying to teach him.

I supported Manny totally in his holding firm to his job description and in continuing to do the best he could, whatever the changing circumstances.

As Mike became ever more disenchanted with Manny, even considering him, probably, as a thorn in his side, he withdrew from us, bit by bit, the umbrella Brastemp had provided to us. That umbrella had allowed us to live in the security of knowing, for instance, that none of us would disappear into the Gulag, be gunned down on the praça, or be murdered in our own home.

Mike apparently was complaining about Manny to John Eser and others at the Michigan home office. Manny's, and our family's, ultimate life support system 7,000 miles to the north was being undermined.

Invitations from the Etcheniques and other Brastemp executives came less regularly. When they did come, they were usually rude, last-minute thoughts, and if we couldn't make it, "too bad." Quite a change from the solicitousness of the early months.

During our "honeymoon" with Brastemp, our requests for conversion of dollars from Manny's pay into cruzeiros had been carried out the same day. Toward the end of our stay, the transaction, without explanation or forewarning, could take up to four days. There were times when I had to borrow local currency from one of our American neighbors before I could go to the market for food.

Manny had the chameleon's gift for changing into the color of whatever culture he was in. He chose to be Brazilian-macho on the matter of my driving. He purchased a car and got himself licensed, but told me driving in São Paulo was difficult and dangerous, and if there were an accident, it was so complicated that it would be better if only one of us were exposed to it. I was given no choice.

I could do nothing about it, because obtaining a driver's license could have been facilitated only through Manny and Brastemp. Taxis were abundant and inexpensive, so I never experienced great inconvenience. However, the first recognizable seed of inequity in our marriage/partnership had been planted. I keenly felt the injustice, and I was embarrassed at having followed bait that led me into a trap of powerlessness.

In that same period, another attempt at culture-inspired coercion stands out in my memory. Our family was invited to a Brastemp employee picnic. We were ready to leave when Manny let me know what I was wearing wasn't conservative enough for his image or his posture. "Posture" was the big corporate word in the States that year. He suggested I change my clothes. I didn't. He phoned a Brazilian colleague who would be attending the picnic to ask what *he* thought women would be wearing. Manny turned to me and said, "Azi thinks it would be better if. . . . "

I dealt with that humiliation by simply not responding and by going as I was. I have no recollection of feeling out of place at the picnic because of what I was wearing.

I think Manny had put his own twist on whatever Azi said. A slender, gentle descendent of Lebanese parents, Azi, as well as his family, befriended us at every turn. I felt I knew him well enough to criticize one thing about Brazil that causes all Americans to squirm in discomfort—the poor, miserable, homeless beggars of all ages and genders everywhere. I asked Azi, "Why don't you *do* something about that?"

Tears filled his eyes as he replied, "We don't know what to do."

Today I am ashamed of the arrogance I had at the time as I see similar conditions developing in my own country. We Americans, like the Brazilians, don't know what to do about it, either.

###

What saved me from oppressive machismo and from being engulfed by the corporation was involvement in the lives of my children and in my own separate life in academia. After the União succeeded in drawing in all possible students who had an interest in my courses, thereby "using me up," they did me the immense favor of assisting my enrollment at PUC, the Pontifícia Universidade Católica, for a semester of graduate linguistics courses to be taught by a visiting American.

The professor for these two graduate courses turned out to

be a native Argentinean who taught one of the classes in Spanish. Spanish overlaps Portuguese about 90 percent, so the Brazilians had little difficulty learning it. For me, who had barely a grip on Portuguese, the challenge was huge. To me fell the advantage that the texts were in English, and the professor, although she wrote out the exams in Spanish, was willing to accept my answers in English.

Had I been able to spend one term more at PUC, I would have earned the M.A. I set out to get under the AAUW College Faculty Program. However, this was not to be. Manny's welcome was worn out, even if his work was not finished. We were going home.

At that time, home leaves were granted every second year. We had previously negotiated with Whirlpool, through John Eser, to forego the round trip leave Manny had earned many months earlier in favor of the corporation's paying for a stopover in Germany when we left in July 1971. Well-traveled Brazilians call this "the triangle route."

I don't know the details of Manny's farewell to the factory on his last day at Brastemp. I know no executives or their wives said any kind of farewell to me. The only people to see us off at the airport were two friends I had made through the União Cultural and one of our neighboring American families.

Once we arrived in Rio, we were on our own. I was terrified, knowing that if any little thing went wrong, we had no protectors on whom we could call. The visa control official checked our names against a list. I don't know what kind of list it was. What if we had been on it? We were searched, every one of us. Even the youngest child, who was only six, was taken to a separate compartment for a search. We passed on into the No Man's Land from which, theoretically, there was no going back.

Our Alitalia flight to Rome was delayed, putting a little more agony into the exit. I did not relax, even after eventual take-off.

Flight time was ten hours. Only as we moved into the sixth hour of the flight did I relax, knowing we had passed the point of no return. In case of emergency, the plane would proceed rather than turn back.

Manny had been through much worse under Hitler and in the hands of the Russians. He was alert and on guard, but I think he believed our U.S. citizenship protected us, even if Mike and Brastemp did not.

We spent a wonderful few weeks in Munich. Manny's family lived on Kufsteiner Platz, and they housed us across the bridge, past Radio Free Europe, at a delightful pension called Gasthaus Monopteros at the edge of the Englische Garten. Manny's friend from the students' round-trip crossing on the *SS Washington*, Wolfgang Schleich, who was then working with RFE in Berlin, had married, and he brought his family through the Russian-occupied sector to visit with us.

Finally, we went home to St. Paul, even if we no longer had a house there. The boys and I lived at the Holiday Inn while Manny went on to St. Joseph–Benton Harbor in Michigan to integrate into John Eser's department and investigate housing.

Then we moved to the St. Joseph Holiday Inn, where we lived for a month without receiving a true welcome from anyone in the corporation or the community. One afternoon, after I had completed the struggle of obtaining a Michigan driver's license and a car, Gloria Caicedo, whose husband I knew from his business trips to São Paulo, invited the boys and me for an afternoon at her house.

Julio Caicedo and Manny held equal rank within the International Division at the home office. Because no one else voluntarily socialized with us, and her hospitality was not particularly cordial, I knew she had been "ordered" to entertain us. Later, after Gloria and I endured a few other indignities together, we became friends.

When the Whirlpool Management Club held a dinner at the House of David facility, we went, but we did not feel welcome. I found it both awkward and foreboding to be only grudgingly greeted by some six different executives whom I had entertained while they were on business trips to Brazil. Each had enjoyed dinner in our home and been taken by us on excursions to nearby Santos.

I was experiencing first-hand what had been described to me by the Whirlpool wives in Hamilton, Ohio. These women, having lived in the home office territory, had told me, "Your social status on any given day will be directly proportional to your husband's standing at the office." Manny was in disrepute.

We bought a house on Niles Road, into which we would move over Labor Day weekend. Still living at the Holiday Inn, I tried to enroll the children in the schools appropriate to the location of the new house. The principal told me the children could not be enrolled until we actually lived in the house. I had not given my name when making my initial request, so I simply waited a day and started over. I gave the address on Niles Road as our current address; the lie for my children's welfare was entirely justified.

What was that about? As nearly as I have ever been able to determine, it was rooted in the fears of that time that the St. Joseph schools—predominantly white—might be court-ordered to integrate with the Benton Harbor schools—predominantly black. St. Joseph evaded such an order, integration occurring instead with the Eau Claire and Coloma schools. During that wait-it-out interim, my new hometown was being ridiculously cautious about whom it admitted into its schools.

Medical referrals through Whirlpool were also quite dismal. They brought us to the least qualified general practitioner, who, within a few years, had to give up his practice. The recommended ophthalmologist refused to see our son until the first available appointment in mid-October, even though Jeff had broken his glasses and needed good vision as he entered a new school system.

After we moved into our house, a pot of mums arrived from John Eser and his wife, Edith, whom I had not yet met. We did not meet until December, when Manny was out of town on business and the Esers threw a holiday party I attended alone.

The furnishings we had in storage in St. Paul arrived in September. Because of a New York dock strike, our belongings from Brazil did not join us until February. When I invited relatives from Minnesota to come for Thanksgiving, I asked them to bring their own silverware.

Once the children's school and health care were taken care of and drapes were hung in the house, I set about determining how to complete the M.A. I had begun four years earlier. Independent studies through the University of Minnesota were only a remote possibility. A University of Chicago program I checked into welcomed only doctoral students. Finally I went with all my varied credentials in hand to enroll at Andrews University. This time I was interested in the quickest route, no longer caring into what field it took me. My advisor recommended educational psychology/child development, which I completed over the course of exactly one year, graduating in 1973.

At the end of Manny's first business year in St. Joseph, John Eser and others considerably underrated his year's performance. According to procedure, the evaluation was to be discussed with the employee, who was then to sign it to certify its content had been discussed and agreed upon. Manny read it but refused to sign.

This was not an easy stance for him to take, but it was justified and necessary. At home I gave him total support. For both of us, and for the value system we had worked out together, honor was the keystone; justice was its corollary.

Manny took the unprecedented action of going over the head of John and of John's in-between superiors. He wrote a letter of explanation to CEO John Platts. Mr. Platts did not respond directly, but the negative pressure on Manny diminished, so it is safe to assume something happened "up there."

John Eser continued to work closely with Brazil, as did Julio Caicedo. Although Manny had been conspicuously removed from the Brazil scene, he worked with nearly all of Whirlpool's other international affiliates: Colombia, Venezuela, Italy, Australia, Canada, Iran, Mexico, and Nigeria.

I met most of these countries' representatives when they came to Benton Harbor, because entertaining visitors was an integral part of Manny's job—and mine, as the corporate extension of my husband. I served dinners at our home and went out with them on the Whirlpool round of Tosi's, Grand Mere, Captain's Table, Schuler's, Coral Gables in Saugatuck, and the Black Swan in Kalamazoo. Not solely because I *had* to; I am a cosmopolitan internationalist, and I enjoyed all the visitors for their interesting differences.

Frequently I was part of the International Division's cadre when it hosted international associates at the Berrien Hills Country Club and the Point O'Woods Golf and Country Club. Sometimes we boarded a plane to the corporate lodge, Dunrovin', near Baldwin, Michigan, where I was part of the "host team." I was never a guest. I was working, and I knew it.

Manny's problems of entry into the home office had been worked out. He again seemed to be ascending the corporate ladder. He remarked to me one day, "I'm beginning to understand how this corporate system really works. It's not much different from the Nazi party." This statement was more prophetic than either of us was aware of at the time. We both took heed, but we should have taken more.

For many years I had no contact with the Brazilians with

whom, for two years as a guest in their country, I had frequently interacted: Mike and Helen Etchenique and Rudolpho and Ruth Bertola. These were the people whose desertion had struck fear into my heart, and who lacked the courtesy to bid me farewell when I left their country. When business relations break down at the corporate level, so does socializing.

A new Brazilian company, Consul, was added to the fold of Brastemp and Whirlpool. Its young president-elect, Ivens Freitag, came to live in St. Joseph–Benton Harbor for a year of Whirlpool indoctrination. Yvonne, his wife, and their young children, came too. I had no contact with them until I found myself at their farewell party, the result of a shift in Manny's assignments which came, again, to include Brazil.

At that first meeting, Yvonne bluntly asked, "Who are you? Why haven't I met you before? Why are you here?"

I answered, "Because of some long political story I don't understand myself."

Yvonne and I, in the ensuing years, came to a level of understanding different from the posturing at which Helen and Ruth were adept. Yvonne and I occasionally could speak to each other directly and honestly.

There were good things about living in St. Joseph. The house, for instance—in which I still live. On his first reconnaissance of the area, Manny spotted a piece of property dominated by oak trees in the township on the river. He knew the five-bedroom, two-story house with a gambrel roof was "the one" I would want. He also said—fatigued by the very thought of raking all those leaves in the fall—I couldn't have it, because of the maintenance it would require. Eventually we bought it anyway, as it was so much more suitable than any other. It was big, old, and friendly, and each of our four boys could have his own room.

Manny was there a time or two for the fall yard and gutter cleanup, but usually not. When he was, he issued militant orders regarding how—and how fast—we should all proceed to get the odious chore out of the way. When he was off on a business jaunt, the rest of us rather enjoyed the "harvest."

One year when Doug, Jeff, and Ed were all grown and gone, Curt and I labored alone, some days until after dark. I look back on that fall with genuine nostalgia, as I now do the work with more modern equipment alone—and yet not alone—because of the wealth of autumn memories.

The space is shared with cardinals. My most wonderful winter memory is of a snowed-in period when Manny set up his tripod and camera at the bird feeder he had attached to the sunroom window. He became a cardinal portrait specialist.

In the spring, cardinals nested outside his office window at the Whirlpool Corporation, and he brought me daily stories of their progress. Unfortunately, they were frightened away and abandoned the nest. He brought me an egg he salvaged. I have it still.

When we lived in St. Paul, Manny had served on the PTA board one year. Almost immediately after coming to Michigan, he was asked to do the same for St. Joseph's E.P. Clarke School. I was proud of Manny's underdog advocacy in siding with the teachers, who complained about the principal's unreasonable demands on them and his harsh treatment of students. Ultimately, the principal decided to seek other employment.

Manny's community volunteerism was a short-lived luxury that had to give way to business travel demands. Instead, he supported my candidacy for school board trustee in 1975 and again in 1978, even though I was quoted in the *Herald-Press* making inflammatory statements such as, "The Advisory Council [to the St. Joseph school board] is the most useless organization to which I have ever belonged."

I lost the election; the Advisory Council, an emperor without clothes, was disbanded. Unfortunately, a council through which community members could make a genuine impact was not instituted to replace it. Thereafter, advice was sought from "blue ribbon" committees, whose members were carefully selected.

When I first became critical of the Council, one of my colleagues, who worked at Whirlpool, suggested that before I proceeded I might want to check with my husband to see how much he liked his job. When I repeated this to Manny, he was incensed. He said he would never like any job well enough to be intimidated or have any member of his family intimidated. That was then; less than ten years later, he became my intimidator on behalf of his employer.

Our oldest son, Doug, showed signs of independent thinking as he went through the St. Joseph school system, objecting strongly—albeit in good humor—to policies and administrator behaviors he found nonsensical. At first we found this trait puzzling, because he had proven himself a model of adaptability in Brazil. Toward the end of his term at the Instituto MacKenzie in São Paulo, some ideological differences arose and he asked us what he should do. Because we were guests in the country and at the school, we advised him to act diplomatically. Let it go, we said. We'd be leaving soon.

If he were in his own culture, we told him, we would expect him to speak up—to make a difference. This seemed to be what he was doing once back in his own country. In retrospect, I see that Manny and I were doing the same through our activism in school matters. By so doing, we set an example Doug followed.

Manny's and my relationship was better than good for many years. I didn't mind his being gone approximately half the time on either domestic or foreign trips. As his income rose steadily, that and our house took good care of us.

We had variety in living patterns at our house under two equally pleasant sets of conditions—when Manny was there and when he wasn't. When he was home, he set a good example for his sons by cleaning bathrooms, doing laundry, and cooking. He especially liked to cook and was fond of trying new recipes. When he was gone, the boys took on more responsibility but also enjoyed more freedom to be themselves. The same was true for me.

When we went out, I was his lady. I remember one occasion when we were entertaining visitors at Tosi's with another Whirlpool couple. Manny had returned from a three-week trip, and we were still in our reunion "honeymoon." He was so wrapped up in me that he, most inappropriately, turned to me first for my menu selection, rather than to the guests. The other hosting couple was annoyed at the *faux pas*, but I remember it fondly, because I need it to warm my heart. I'm glad it happened, because it is a remembrance of how things were before the corporation drove its wedge between us.

Once during a long weekend of entertaining corporate visitors at Dunrovin', a co-hostess and I separated briefly from the group to make personal purchases. As we came out of a shop, Manny drove up for us. My companion remarked at the intuitive synchronicity. "Wow! How many years does it take to work out that kind of togetherness?"

Life became especially pleasant for me, even as a half-time "corporate widow," when as a result of publicity surrounding the 1975 school board election, Southwestern Michigan Community College in Dowagiac invited me to interview for an especially challenging summer position. I was hired to teach introduction to the Social Sciences to a group of twelve young men, none of whom wanted to be taking the required course.

It went well. Then in the fall, I taught psychology. The following year, I taught both there and at Lake Michigan College.
That was as close as I ever came to fulfilling the destiny intended
for me by the American Association of University Women. They
had forecast a shortage of community college teachers; actually,
there came to be a glut.

In 1976, Doug graduated from high school and joined the
Army. In April of the following spring, he married his "most
wonderful girl in the world," Joelene Nichols, who went with
him to Hawaii for his tour of duty.

Trude Hauptmann, my colleague from the União Cultural
Brasil Estados Unidos, had become Director of Courses at the
Associacão Alumni and invited me to São Paulo in 1977 to work
for her. Through the Sociology Department of Western Michigan University, where I was a doctoral student and an instructor, I issued a press release, which appeared on June 2 in the
Herald-Palladium. The article announced that I was to be guest
lecturer at a series of language-learning seminars July 18–30 in
Brazil. It further stated:

> *She will be the featured speaker at the seminar for Brazilian
> teachers of English in São Paulo, delivering the keynote ad-
> dress on "The Nature-Nurture Dichotomy: An Update on the
> Chomsky-Skinner Controversy." She will also lecture and di-
> rect workshops on the cultural dimensions of second-language
> acquisition because of her experience in the area of psycho-
> sociolinguistics. This summer's invitation is the outgrowth of
> a series of lectures she gave in São Paulo at the União Cultural
> Brasil–Estados Unidos.*

The twelve days I spent in Brazil were heady ones for me. I
stayed at Trude's house. She had a call from her counterpart in
Santos who was conducting similar seminars a few days in advance of those in São Paulo. Their guest speaker had canceled;
could they borrow me for one day? I was escorted by limousine

down the escarpment to a hotel where I was called for the next morning. Taken to an auditorium, I delivered as rousing an address as one can on the subject of linguistics. Then I was whisked away to a board member's private mansion for lunch with her family, back to the school to conduct a class, and, finally, deposited back in São Paulo at Trude's door.

In and around the lectures and courses I gave the following week, I was aware that the Esers resided in Joinville, in the southern state of Santa Caterina. John had begun serving there in 1976 as president of Consul while continuing to train young Ivens Freitag to become his successor. Back in Benton Harbor, John's office as director of the technology wing of the International Division had been taken over by Bill Grimes.

A second Whirlpool couple, whose rank was more comparable to Manny's, was also living and working in São Paulo. Inviting his wife to attend my final lecture and to have lunch was as close as I dared get to the Whirlpool Corporation.

Vice President Bob Willemin and his wife, Velva, on a combination of business and tourism, were in both cities and were in São Paulo at the same time I was. Because of what I had learned about hierarchy during my teen years working part-time as a maid, I knew rank likes to initiate the social moves. Overtures from below are rarely appreciated. I did not contact them or any of the Brazilians I knew would be entertaining them. Only if I had been there with my husband, and only if there had been some direct reason for including him in a social event, would there have been an appropriate slot for me.

Upon my return from this, my one and only professional business trip to Brazil, Manny and I dined out with another Whirlpool couple. Although the return from Brazil of any of the Whirlpool men was always the occasion for storytelling and updates on current conditions there, all three of my dinner companions seemed embarrassed when I expressed opinions related to what I had experienced in Brazil. I sensed that even the other woman was embarrassed that I should presume to have my observations taken as seriously as the men's would be in a similar circumstance.

The academic scene is, in many ways, like the corporate. The reaction among my colleagues at Western Michigan University was similar to Whirlpool's indifference.

The department chair, David Chapman, and all the other men on the staff—there was only one woman professor in the department—avoided conversation on the subject of my Brazilian adventure until one social-event evening to which spouses were invited. The department's men gathered around my husband to hang on his every word about Brazil—as though only he had been there or as though, yes, we had both been there, but only the male viewpoint mattered. Each of my accomplishments represented a long-overdue acknowledgment of the range of my capabilities, yet each was dampened by some reminder—by both the corporation and academia—that I was in some way deficient. I can only suppose it was because I am a woman.

I did not live my academic or spiritual life in St. Joseph. Having run for school board twice, losing the second time by a larger margin than the first time, I felt I had shown my willingness to serve the public. The public had shown me they did not want me on my terms, which promised more voice and creative participation for ordinary people.

Thereafter, I supported philosophy and actions when I could. When I couldn't, I either kept silent or, if a matter directly affected me, I raised objections. I fed, clothed, counseled, and transported my children, attended their school functions, and welcomed their peers into our friendly house. When Manny was in town, so did he.

In 1979, the summer Curt was fourteen, Manny and he drove to Canada and hopped a bush plane to a Jungian camp on Lake Temagami. They spent time in sweat lodges under Indian guidance, in sessions led by Jungian analysts, and in wandering the primal forest for days at a time to learn basic survival skills. The experience was good for each of them, individually, and for their father-son relationship.

When each of our four boys were fourth and fifth graders, they spent one or more summer sessions at Concordia College's German Language Village in Minnesota. The summer Curt was eighteen, we sent him on Concordia's six-week finishing school experience—the "Germany Abroad" trip under supervision of the Language Villages. In Munich, he was able, briefly, to see his father's family.

###

We hoped these enriching experiences for Curt would compensate for some of the trauma of his first years in St. Joseph, while his father and I were still learning the intricate steps of how the corporation dances with the home life of its employees. When in second grade, Curt had been excited about being in a school program his father would be home to attend. But Manny, brutally overworked and fatigued from too much travel, snapped at me in Curt's presence, saying one parent was going to have to be enough.

Our marriage and our family were under constant push-pull strain between family values and corporate loyalty. When Manny wasn't gone, he was either recovering from the most recent trip or getting ready to go on the next one. In 1980 he missed, by one day, being home for Ed's high school graduation. We fought about that, because I believed he could have, and certainly should have, been home. His choosing, instead, to see some business meeting through to the end had the element of proving his dedication to Whirlpool by demonstrating its business was more important to him than his family.

To reconstruct what was going on in our lives next, I quote from a letter I wrote to my Aunt Carol in Boise, dated August 7, 1981.

> *I used to teach psychology at Lake Michigan College, then at Southwestern Michigan College—both near here. Then, in '76, I started commuting the fifty miles to Kalamazoo to teach sociology at Western Michigan University while also working on a Ph.D. in social psychology. I have now dropped out of the program and will no longer teach. I wasn't sure about this until yesterday, when I actually finalized the withdrawals, on both counts.*
>
> *I was a good teacher, a good student, and a dedicated scholar. On three occasions I presented papers at behaviorist conventions, finally combining all I thought I knew into a metatheory that synthesized B.F. Skinner, Carl Jung, Emile Durkheim, and Max Planck. For this, I sought publication on the grounds that I was building a bridge between psychology and sociology. Professor Richard Malotte said best what most of my mentors and quasi-mentors must have thought: "You'll build it all right. You'll stand on it, and we won't let you off at either end."*

Giving up on academia as a pathway for my thoughts, I started to write my version of "the great American novel." I settled down to four to five hours a day of fantasy production, underpinned by my metatheory.

While I was working on my book in July 1981, Dick Devine retired and Manny was promoted to his position (the slot Frank Livingston held while we were in Brazil 1969–1971). His title was still "manager," but he was to manage something bigger. I wrote to my parents in November:

> *It involves even more entertaining of foreign visitors than he was already doing, and it is necessary that "his wife" be more*

involved. I don't mind, both because I like people and because these are especially interesting people. October was a very busy month. Manny is leaving tomorrow for Munich (personal business), then Nigeria. I have been told his boss's wife will be calling me to ask if I will "help out," even while he's gone, by taking the wife of some visiting Brazilian businessman to lunch.

Marilyn Grimes did call me and, although I had very much the feeling I was working for her rather than with her, I did not then feel that such involvement with Whirlpool was an imposition. I found it interesting and still had ample daily time for my four to five hours of writing.

I recall objecting only once. Ivens Freitag's parents, major stockholders in the Brazilian company, Consul, were coming to St. Joseph. Mrs. Freitag had expressed an interest in visiting Minneapolis, and Manny approached me with the office-generated suggestion that I escort her on the corporate jet to Minneapolis for a day of sightseeing.

I was familiar with Minneapolis, but I had never been on the corporate jet. Nor had I ever met Mrs. Freitag. I didn't believe I could successfully pull off such an adventure and have everybody—Mrs. Freitag, the pilot and crew, and Whirlpool personnel we would meet along the way—happy at the end of the day. If Whirlpool really thought I could, why would they believe such an accomplished person was available to them at the crook of a little finger? I said "no."

Even though I was aware of having a fairly well-defined, though unwritten and never openly acknowledged, job description within the corporation, this hostessing suggestion far exceeded any others up to that point. It turned out to be small potatoes, though, compared to what the corporation expected of me in 1986, and which they extracted from me, even though, again, I said "no."

#

The Esers returned from Brazil mid-1981. John came back as a corporate vice president, not merely a division vice president, and was responsible for both departments of the International Division, sales and technology.

In December, the Esers held an at-home Christmas party for the division. Typical of Whirlpool at-homes, the party was politically correct and stratified—only personnel above a certain level were invited. Manny and I were included. Herb Ansbach, then president of Whirlpool, and his wife, Betty, were long-time friends of the Esers. They were at the party, as were Jerry Southland, head of international sales, and his wife.

I don't recall much beyond sitting at a round table with Herb and Jerry and deliberately saying at least one controversial thing, probably a feminist remark, to let them know I was not a "yes wife." This didn't disturb Herb, because Betty wasn't either.

John Eser, having by then spent five years in Brazil, had come to thoroughly understand how Brazilian and U.S. systems can clash and how the fallout can be misinterpreted by the uninitiated. He eased Manny back into the Brazilian circle, first having an impact on me when I was invited to the farewell party for Ivens and Yvonne Freitag, sometime during 1982, when Herb Ansbach was still corporation president. I remember his and Betty's being there.

Sometime during 1982 or early 1983, John and Manny traveled to São Paulo together on business, staying at the Hotel Jaguar. One evening, Tony Etchenique, Mike's brother and a director of Brastemp, whose practices Manny had criticized during 1969–71, invited John Eser to his home for dinner—but not Manny. When Manny related this to me following the trip, I said I thought John should have declined, knowing this to be a deliberate insult to Manny and, hence, to Whirlpool. Manny shrugged it off, but he was clearly disturbed by it, or he wouldn't have mentioned it.

In December of 1982, Jack Sparks became CEO of Whirlpool. Being close to the inner circle at that time, I heard Herb Ansbach talk about how his days were numbered. Earlier in his and Jack's work history, a clash of wills culminated in Herb's doing something he knew Jack could never forgive. Jack disposed of Herb and made himself president as well as CEO.

I met Jack Sparks for the first time two seasons before he became CEO. We were in the cafeteria of the St. Joseph High School at the Orchestra Awards Dinner—we with our son Edward, the Sparks with their daughter Kate. Jack's wife, Fredda, introduced us. Fredda had been a long-time school board trustee. In that position, she had dealt with my protests and suggestions a number of times. I liked and respected her and had a sense that the feeling was at least partially mutual.

Manny and I were in quite a favored position that evening, because Ed, if not big-man-on-campus, was surely big-man-in-music. He was concert master and recipient of the most-valued member award. Fredda's introduction verged on gushing—to the point where Jack gave her a signal of "enough, already."

We seated ourselves at a table across the room from theirs. Several times Manny called my attention to the fact that Jack often cast his gaze in our direction—as though he might be sizing me up. He already knew Manny.

Once Jack Sparks became CEO and disposed of Herb Ansbach, would Herb's close friend, John Eser, be far behind? In no time at all, the whole Whirlpool team lineup was changing. Social events such as Management Club functions and the summer picnic became almost totally political and military, requiring study time before attendance to know where the mines might be laid.

"Accidents" and "coincidences" don't happen in St. Joseph.

If some unusual little event seems to be significant, it probably is. The second time I ran for a school board position, our son Jeff's picture appeared in the school paper. I did not consider this a coincidence. He was news because I was. "Who knows," someone on the staff had thought, "maybe she'll win and be someone we have to reckon with."

Upon entering the grounds to the Whirlpool summer picnic in 1983, when Manny was back in grace, I was greeted by a costumed coyote hired to clown around and add an air of festivity. The brief waltz we shared was recorded in a picture published in the next *Full Line News*. Media people, in-house or out, are not told whom to cover. Successful journalists have their own highly developed sense of who's in and who's out. In later times, when I was "out," I couldn't get either media coverage or a lawyer for love or money.

By this time, my level of political awareness was high. I observed Jack and Fredda Sparks in their new role as First Family. Wherever they strolled, the walkways cleared before them. Whirlpool people on all sides returned their smiles, often adding some pleasant commentary. On a small scale, this response from employees was similar to how we Americans respond to the President of our country and the First Lady.

I think Whirlpool executives foster the image of the corporation as "family" to soften the reality of its dictatorial nature. The spouse of a Whirlpool employee may think of her or himself as a member of the Whirlpool family by derivation. The grammar of this works well as long as the spouse benefits from the liaison, and as long as whatever services required of the spouse are pleasant and willingly given.

Fredda clearly had a line of authority and commanded a respect that went beyond her individual personality. However, like the First Lady of our land, the corporate First Lady is equally without a job description. Hence, all the ambiguities inherent in the role of First Lady also exist for the wife of the chief executive officer of a major corporation. The same holds true for wives of powerful men throughout the political structure and the armed forces.

The basic rule of the grammatical structure underlying these ambiguous concepts and behaviors is, or has been, that men own the women to whom they are married. These women are empty vessels into which men pour their own importance and then carry them around as accouterments.

As a psycholinguist, I tried, on that Whirlpool picnic day in 1983, to discover what could be the behavioral grammar underlying and tying together the surface structure phrases which, upon examination, contradicted each other.

I did not figure that out all in one day. Full awareness came only late in 1988 in Brazil, where, as a mere adjunct to my husband, I had become troublesome because I refused to have no values of my own. The "aha" experience came when Manny cleared the air of all murky ambiguities by curtly informing me that the "family" he and the home office were worrying about was the staff at the office; it did not include me. This was evident even though he had been signing my name along with his on Christmas cards I never saw, and sending them out from the office to an unseen-by-me list of Whirlpool business associates "and their wives," all of whom were maintaining the illusion— which I now saw as pure fiction—that we were all "family."

By the time I danced with the coyote at that 1983 Whirlpool picnic, John Eser had literally "cleaned out his desk." Jack Sparks anointed two probable candidates for the office of president, a spot he did not intend to occupy indefinitely. They were George Wardeberg, championed by former CEO Elisha Gray, and David Whitwam, his own favorite. Manny's explanation to me was these two "knights" would have to fight it out, more or less to the death, until a winner was declared.

I attended a Whirlpool Management Club dinner in the Upton Room at Lake Michigan College, in the building now called the Mendel Center, during the first exhilarating flush of this new death-match arrangement. Manny reintroduced me to Sam Bateman who, I was told, was the fourth-highest ranking man in the corporation, following Jack Sparks, George Wardeberg, and David Whitwam. Sam reported to George; and it was they who, with Jack's blessing, had toppled John.

John Eser was about six months short of being able to retire with all benefits vested. Sam Bateman and George Wardeberg—and, by line of authority, Jack Sparks—were so impatient to slash and burn (they called it restructuring) they couldn't give John the opportunity to retire gracefully. They even, viciously and deliberately, may have planned to financially wound him as he left. Was his fate, perhaps, intended as an example to intimidate others who demurred in the face of fiat?

We took the Esers out for dinner once, and Edith had lunch out one more time with me. After that, before they relocated to Stuttgart, they insisted we entertain each other only at home. They were concerned that Manny should not be seen as guilty-by-association of whatever John's sin had been. Manny, as well as I, insisted this was of no concern, but John was adamant.

On our farewell evening with them, at their home, John drank heavily, perhaps deliberately, to overcome his inhibitions. Then he cried, actually cried, as he apologized to Manny for not giving him greater support when we had been in Brazil from 1969 to 1971. That was his main theme. Running through it was an even deeper strain of anguish at what an ignoble institution the Whirlpool Corporation was becoming. John Eser had put his whole life's work into something that, in the end, did not believe in him. Nor could he believe in it any more or be proud of it.

John and Edith had grown up in Leipzig; Manny, in Munich.

John and Edith must have endured, as Manny had, that post-war total disillusionment with the system that had born and bred them. Now, they were disillusioned again, in America. When you are fifty-nine, do you recover from having your cosmology, your *Weltanschauung,* shattered a second time?

When Manny and I visited Munich in 1988, we zipped over to Stuttgart on the autobahn to spend a long evening with the Esers. Our son, Curt, stationed nearby in the U.S. Army, visited them several times after that.

The last Whirlpool function the Esers attended was held at the Berrien Hills Country Club, with the Sparks presiding. It had to have been 1983 and the month was probably June. The guests were the Brazilians. Like many corporate parties, this one tended to separate by gender. I infiltrated the stag area and playfully said to Ivens Freitag, "We'll have none of that." I frequently made such gender equalizing gestures, as part of my responsibility to cultural evolution.

Jack Sparks and I had good rapport. Of course I respected him—he had risen from factory floor to CEO. The remarkable thing is that I felt the respect was mutual. Fredda was working hard and well to be a good hostess to the unfamiliar international group I knew so well. Yet these relationships never superseded corporate needs.

When Jack and Fredda Sparks traveled to Brazil to explore the industrial territory and pay their respects to the Etcheniques, Jack had sought my opinion—via his secretary who conveyed the question via Manny—about what gift would be suitable for them to give. I offered both the best suggestion I could think of, as well as the articles themselves: handmade, specially ordered stained glass Brazilian cardinals from the Weavers' Shop in Baldwin, Michigan. Brazilians who were hosted by Whirlpool at Dunrovin' were generally taken to the nearby Weavers' Shop as well. I thought they might be touched at receiving Weavers'

Shop hand-wrought replicas of one of their country's unique and most-prized birds.

Fredda called Edith for a recommendation. Edith suggested adding an expensive crystal sculpture to Helen Etchenique's collection. That is what they did. I have never been good at recognizing the value of money. Sentiment, connection, has always been more important to me. At the upper corporate level of thinking, crystal was a good gift for the Etcheniques because of its twofold status. In a country such as Brazil, racked with poverty and crime, it shows, first of all, "we can afford this" and, second, "we can afford enough guards to keep it."

Jack Sparks played a hand in John Eser's ouster, as well as in Manny's and my being forced back to Brazil. I have spent many years trying to deny this, but I know it has to be true. He veered the direction of the Whirlpool Corporation that little bit more toward ruthlessness. His design pitted David Whitwam against George Wardeberg and drew forth Machiavellian tendencies in both by rewarding their brutish behaviors.

###

In 1983, Manny led a Whirlpool foray into China, accompanied by a representative from Sears and guided by Chinese-born Katharine Yang, who was an officer with the First Bank of Chicago. He returned as quite a different person. Emerging from the chauffeured car, he strutted into the house like a huge, humorless rooster and gave me his dirty laundry as though I had been waiting for it. His behavior toward me was aloof. I had always tended to his accumulated laundry immediately upon his return from trips of any length. That time, he made me feel as though laundress, as well as walking ten steps behind him, was my appropriate station in life. I mark that day as a turning point in Manny's attitude toward me as an equal marital partner.

Manny shared details of the trip sparingly and on his terms, without regard for my need to participate in the adventure that had taken him out of my life for yet another three weeks. He always had the ability to selectively adapt to the circumstances around him and to take on the qualities appropriate to the culture. That time, he wasn't making the trip back from the host culture into his own.

In China in 1983, as in Brazil from 1969 through 1971, he was placed in positions of considerable authority. Everyone bowed before him, catered to his every whim. In those societies, wives are also expected to behave the same way. I hadn't acquiesced to that standard in Brazil any more than I tolerated it in my own country. Such sexism wasn't part of the road we had agreed, in our marriage vows, to travel together.

Manny had always and frequently hosted business dinners without my participation. Before China, he had always been considerately quiet about coming into our bedroom in the wee hours when I was asleep. No more. His typical entry changed and included normal daytime noise. He turned on the closet light and dropped his shoes loudly to the floor, belching and farting at will.

Katharine Yang explained to me she felt his new behavior was a normal consequence of his having been treated as a man of great importance in culturally exotic settings for an extended period. Drawing him back into the family psyche took me nearly a month of concentrated caring. Then, as we had achieved rapport, he left abruptly to go someplace else.

As Manny was preparing to go to China a second time in the late summer of 1984, his adaptation to Eastern culture and the role he expected to be acting in it was already in play before he left home. Even as I drove with him to the airport, he treated me like a not-that-important auxiliary to the power and the glory of his puffed-up and pompous self.

Whenever Manny went abroad, he observed a ritual of phoning me just before departing from domestic soil, and again upon his return to it. But when he called me from San Francisco before his flight to China, it was not for our usual intimate adieu. He was cool, perfunctory, and brief. At the thought of receiving another such call from this husband-turned-stranger, I left home the day before his itinerary indicated he would be back in San Francisco.

A friend from Kalamazoo picked me up and took me to her house. I left a note at home advising my life partner of my whereabouts and why I was not there. I invited him to retrieve me when and if he could get himself deflated and back onto a level plane. He called. He came. Neither joyous nor testy, our reunion was more like a void in which a question mark was imbedded. We put my suitcase into the trunk of his car and went to lunch at an out-of-the-way place in South Haven. He complained, among other things, that the prices were high, as though he had not been living royally while I scrubbed floors, paid bills, went to social events unescorted, and kept the home fires burning. However, he had come for me, and he had done so without hesitation. I could still get through to him when I really had to, but each time it required more energy and ever-heightened drama.

Again we struggled to reestablish equilibrium.

The trouble with these remissions and cures was that with each recurrence, the swing of the pendulum toward pompousness arced farther and farther. It became ever harder for me to reach him, and harder for him to feel the tenderness I bore him as I psychologically massaged him back into our relationship.

China wasn't the culprit, because he didn't go to China again. Still, his psychological distance from me and from our sons became greater with each of his trips away from home. Each time we had to work harder to find each other again.

#

Finding each other meant shutting out the rest of the world and merging our psyches in a secret space where each of us had over the other the mesmerizing power of a hundred thousand peacock-feather eyes. Recovering that space for ourselves became increasingly difficult as Manny's world at Whirlpool became harsher, and he drank more heavily than ever. Drinking in the course of business entertaining had become part of his job starting in 1963 with our transfer from Hamilton, Ohio, back to St. Paul. I did not see it as a problem then. In Brazil from 1969 to 1971, we both did a fair amount of social drinking.

Alcohol did not get out of hand until Manny's trips to Australia in the mid to late 1970s. Following the second of many trips there, Manny told me he had figured out the only way to get the Australians down to serious business was to drink them under the table. That he had done, and everything was under control—except the habit he was forming.

In a Radical Behaviorism seminar I once took with Richard Malotte, we discussed how corporate executives handle stress. Dr. Malotte let the participants put forth as many suggestions as we could imagine, but he held fast to one notion. He said, "They drink." At home, I posed the question to our family's resident expert on corporate stress. He replied, "We drink."

Manny's hosting skills included knowing liquor could not be purchased in Minnesota on Sundays. Whenever he squired guest business associates to Minnesota on a Sunday in preparation for a Monday meeting, he packed bottles in his suitcase to get his guests through an otherwise dry evening.

Bill Grimes, to his credit, set a new standard for his Whirlpool colleagues during his last year before retirement. No matter how much other drinking was going on, he ordered Perrier—showing it could be done. When Bill Grimes retired, Manny took his place as a director.

By June 1984, Manny was so into the swing of the Brazilian

projects again that he barely had time to attend the weddings of
Ed and Lori on the twenty-third and Jeff and Nancy on the
twenty-fourth. Under the circumstances of having a house full
of our own guests, we were not, at least, expected to assist in
Whirlpool's hosting at Dunrovin'. But Manny spent every day
of the week before the weddings and every evening, as well,
intensively hosting and negotiating in Whirlpool's behalf. Mentally, he was barely there with us at the weddings, even though
his sister, Lulu, had made the trip from Germany to be with us.

In 1985 I determined that restoring balance in our relationship required my taking a trip. I needed to have a great adventure all my own to counter the life he was leading, which seemed
so much more exciting. Manny understood this, wholeheartedly
agreed, and facilitated my planning in every way—even apologizing for not having thought of it first.

I needed to take a *big* trip, one Manny would be unlikely
ever to take himself. Because Manny was an escapee of a Russian prison camp and felt he was still on a border-crossing black-
list, I settled on the USSR as a place he would never willingly
go. I left early in September. Manny arranged to begin a visit
with his family as I emerged from Russia. I would leave my
tour group in Helsinki to join him in Munich. His China syndrome seemed over, or at least under control. We had a close
and wonderful time in Munich, staying nights, as we usually
did, at the Gasthaus Monopteros and spending days with his
sister and mother.

While I was in Siberia, Manny was in Mexico City on business. Staying at a downtown hotel, he narrowly survived the
destruction of a 7.8 earthquake, which toppled 250 buildings all
around him in the city center. When he picked me up at the
Munich airport, he apologized to me for having had that experience, which was probably going to steal some thunder from
mine. First I had to recover from the shock of his having had a

brush with death. Then I was touched by his embarrassment at having an adventure that, through no fault of his own, would overshadow mine—the compensatory adventure I needed to equalize my life with his.

When we returned to St. Joseph, a reporter from the *Herald-Palladium* talked to Manny about doing a feature story on his earthquake experience. Manny, though publicity prone in his youth, firmly declined. He determined—either on his own or through coaching from Whirlpool public relations personnel—that this intimately personal life-threatening experience belonged to Whirlpool. The corporation's image would have suffered were it known it placed its personnel in peril, even though the incident was totally beyond their control and responsibility.

Back home, Manny and I grew close again. In January 1986, when I rented a small hall so anyone who was interested could hear the tales of my Great Red Train Ride and see my slides, both Manny and his Whirlpool brethren were supportive and helpful. Those invited came, were attentive, and let me have my day.

Manny and I were rebuilding our good relationship. We felt like partners again. We were traveling together the road of choice.

That is how things were with us before the Whirlpool Corporation inserted a wedge between us that stuck fast and split us apart.

Beginning in November 1985, Jerry Southland, division vice president of International Sales, started sounding Manny out about a reassignment to Brazil. I was amused. The move was so out of the question that I didn't take it seriously. Nor did Manny.

After the holidays, Jerry let up on the subject, which was then pursued by Larry Kremer, corporate vice president of the

International Division—the position John Eser had once held.

At the time, I was pleased there was recognition of Manny's managerial expertise in that cross-cultural area. It was an honor, I believed, for him to be their first choice. I did wonder, however, who would be their second choice if Whirlpool were really serious about opening a holding company office in Brazil—because we were not going. I underestimated how firm a grip the corporation had on my husband.

Manny was looking forward to getting off the hardball court and retiring on his sixtieth birthday—March 16, 1987. Numerous times since his fifty-fifth birthday in 1982, he had met with Clara Dansfield, manager of Benefits and Employee Services, to determine the most economically feasible time for him to retire. For many years he had recognized his activities and associations within the corporate structure differed markedly from the "real life" he shared with his family and our friends. In fact when a fellow Unitarian asked, "Why don't we see more of Manny at the Fellowship?" Manny replied, "I find working for Whirlpool inconsistent with having a spiritual life. Maybe after I retire."

Although he said this only partially in jest, I took it seriously. Manny's remark fueled my encouraging his early retirement. As things turned out, working for Whirlpool eventually became inconsistent not only with his having a spiritual life, but even with his having a home life.

The company had no second choice for the job of vice president of *Whirlpool do Brasil*. No one anywhere in the ranks even came close to meeting the qualifications. At the time, however, both Manny and I kept saying to each other, "That's their problem, not ours."

Manny even expressed anger that the corporation had not planned personnel development to meet such eventual needs, as he had often recommended they do. They expected him, the man whose unheeded advice could have averted the situation, to play Dutch boy with thumb in the dike. Not likely. We continued making retirement plans.

Neither of us, however, was prepared for what followed. The corporation had veered toward immorality in a few instances during the thirty-three years Manny had been with them up to that point, but it eventually had always seen the light, bitten the bullet, and done the right thing by us. With our thirty-three-year track record of trust, we did not suspect we were the targets of a major *Blitzkrieg* launched with a single-minded corporate objective: "Get Von Koenig to Brazil."

The inequities surrounding our first return from Brazil in 1971 had been resolved humanely—when Manny's efforts there had been so misinterpreted within the International Division that only his direct appeal to the CEO succeeded in mitigating his pariah status. Not so in 1986, as the persistent hard-nosed pressure of any-means-to-the-desired-end was being applied. These inequities were not resolved humanely either during the subsequent years in Brazil from 1986 to 1989 or when those actions tore my family apart and led me to engage in litigation against the corporation.

Manny was firmly saying no as Larry Kremer took over the game plan aimed at moving Manny to Brazil. Larry's method was to "call Manny in," discuss with him Whirlpool's need for him to be their key man in Brazil, then pick up the phone while indicating to Manny that their meeting was over and he could leave. Manny was aware that this technique of summary dismissal was the way one might treat a faceless messenger, but not a potential vice president, and he was frustrated by his inability to counter it.

Later, Larry issued memos solidifying what he and Manny had "agreed" to, even though the understandings were unilateral and Manny had not agreed. By then, Larry was out of town and inaccessible. When he returned, he was perpetually "too busy" to respond to Manny's requests for discussion.

Larry was available only for meetings he called himself, when he was energetically prepared to bombard Manny with the next set of details to be put in place for opening the São Paulo office. After a series of such meetings had taken place in progressive, steamroller fashion, Manny went, in protest, to Larry's supervisor, David Whitwam. Dave claimed to have no authority and no control, and told Manny he would have to wait to discuss everything with Larry when he returned. How Dave must have been chuckling to himself that this plan he was master-minding was working so well.

At the time, Dave Whitman and George Wardeberg, the second and third most powerful men in the corporation, were in a contest over which of them would become successor to the most powerful man, Jack Sparks, who was both president and chairman of the board. Dave, vice chairman and chief marketing officer, was championed by Jack Sparks; George Wardeberg, vice chairman and chief operating officer, was favored by retired CEO Elisha Gray.

The stakes were high. Not only did Dave know what Larry was doing, but also he was orchestrating the performance of his subordinate, whose achievement would testify to his own worthiness to be president.

John Eser's job as corporate vice president of the International Division had gone to Larry Kremer, a younger man with a background in purchasing but, so far as I know, without experience in international ventures. He was, however, Sam Bateman's protégé, which seemed to count for a great deal.

As Dave Whitwam and Larry Kremer plotted to herd Manny toward the chute labeled Brazil, another set of maneuvers advanced as inexorably toward the same corporate goal. This plan would get Manny into the Brazilian slot by default—he was to be left with no other choice.

Richard T. Litzinger of Evansville, another protégé of Sam's and a colleague of Larry's, was recruited to move to the St. Joseph–Benton Harbor area to become division vice president of International Operations. Whirlpool's press release announced in the local *Herald-Palladium*, June 4, 1986:

> *In the new post, Litzinger will coordinate and lead a variety of international projects for Whirlpool and its affiliates in Canada, Brazil and Italy. He also will continue to direct the development and implementation of a centralized manufacturing control system for the company.*

In a sense, Litzinger was filling the position left vacant when Larry Kremer was promoted to corporate vice president. In another sense, he was taking over portions of Manny's area at the director level. From a third perspective, the umbrella view, he was working in a new position created by division restructuring, one that would absorb all of Manny's job description in both vertical and horizontal directions.

This restructuring blocked the predictable complaints in the division about failure to promote from within. It also eroded Manny's position to the point where he could be phased out of the corporation altogether on the grounds that his job had been discontinued.

Bringing Dick Litzinger in had a double effect on Manny. It effectively took his job away from him. Not all of it and not all at once, but enough of it at first, with a timetable for the rest, to strike fear, if not terror, in the heart of a man who had worked faithfully and expertly for the corporation for thirty-three years and who was within ten months of retirement.

Manny was offered no opportunity to fill out those months in any of the numerous ways his services would still be valuable. Instead, he was offered Brazil and nothing else. With that offer came the mandate to sell the family home and cars, sell or store prized possessions, sever close relationships with children and grandchildren, and somehow convince a balking wife to do the same.

When so much of Manny's job was transferred to Dick and the rank of the job elevated from director, Manny's title, to division vice president, the change made clear how much more was expected of the new man than Manny had been able to give the job. That was calculated, I am sure, to affect Manny's morale, make him even more fearful for his future, and make him more submissive and more open to the Brazil proposal.

Early in this phase I had been seated next to Larry at a Point O'Woods dinner. That such evenings were "social" because spouses were present was a fiction we all played with. Naturally, given the opportunity, I would say something intended to put my husband in a good light with his newest boss. So I began to point out how Manny's orientation differed from John Eser's. My comments fell on the biased ears of a powerful young man with incomparably less intercultural experience than Manny's and mine. I recall his responding with a knowing smile, as though to negate everything I said. "Yes, just like John," said Larry. I knew his comment about Eser did not bode well. Look what happened to John.

Manny and I had many confusing, anguished discussions about what the corporation was doing to our private lives. Personified, the corporation was David Whitwam. Larry Kremer was merely his leg man, with concurrence by the Human Resources division, which later became personified, to me, as Charlie Putnam.

A cloud hung over us constantly. Manny was told not to discuss the Brazilian speculations with anyone but me. Not even our grown children and their families were supposed to know we were considering moving away from them. I presumed such secrecy was designed to keep the opening of the São Paulo office a last-minute surprise for the Brazilians, who were not expected to be pleased by it. But secrecy also limited the number of minds deliberating on the puzzle from our side of the table. Our loyalty to the corporation on this point of secrecy deprived us of the much-needed support and counsel we should have been seeking from family, friends, and, I might add, a lawyer.

Yes, that's when I should have had a lawyer. At a preventive stage. However, a thirty-three-year history of trusting the ultimate morality of the Whirlpool Corporation precluded my doubting that they would do the right thing after all, as was their long-established pattern.

The irreversible deed of Dick's having, in effect, taken over Manny's job did not clarify the corporation's continued negotiations with Manny.

It could be argued that Dick did not take over Manny's job. Restructuring was cleverly crafted to make it appear otherwise. Therefore, the effect of losing parts of his job and feeling the rest of it slipping away was subliminal—but pervasive. It haunted our every moment, as I believe the corporation intended. Kafka could not have written a better script.

The company continued to have no other candidates for the job in Brazil. No one in the corporation but Manny had the composite skills of speaking Portuguese, knowing Brazil and the Brazilian "players," and possessing the corporation-developed management skills and loyalties necessary to open a holding company office in São Paulo.

However, Manny was not to be the "top" man, the president of *Whirlpool do Brasil*. A company officer who could make decisions on the spot and sign documents was needed for that. Manny was nonetheless the key man, because no company of-

ficer with Brazil–U.S. cross-cultural skills was capable of negotiating the tricky waters without the help of a loyal guide and
protector.

The presidents of the three Brazilian companies in which
Whirlpool had financial holdings—Brastemp, Consul, and
Embraco—were not overjoyed at the prospect of *Whirlpool do
Brasil* opening a São Paulo office, because they would then be
more closely monitored. Nor did the Brazilian government welcome further foreign intrusion. The pressure exerted on Manny
and me shows that Whirlpool felt it had to open a São Paulo
office, and that without Manny, they couldn't do it.

This new management team, from David Whitwam on
down, apparently viewed Manny as a John Eser. Therefore, in
their eyes he was an anachronism. It must have been painfully
irksome that even if they didn't like him—or me—they had to
have him—and me. It must have been additionally irksome to
them that this situation existed precisely because prior corporate planning had not provided alternatives. If this was the situation, I believe it accounts for much of the treatment we were
yet to experience.

The events of June 1986 I recall as one relives a nightmare.

Manny and I were determined to get away from it all for a
while. We planned a leisurely drive across Iowa to arrive in
Brookings, South Dakota, in time for the annual last-Sunday-
in-June reunion of my mother's people, the Bullis family, which
we had not attended for many years. From there we would drive
to my hometown of Forest Lake, Minnesota, for its biggest cel-
ebration of the year, July 4. In neither place could we divulge
and share our troubles. Hence we could not get away from our
troubles after all. We carried them within.

In the days before we left, Dave Whitwam spoke with Manny

a few times. These monologues were always nebulous, never specifying details of any announcement about the opening of the Brazilian office. Manny did not know whether, in fact, an announcement was going to be made in our absence, or what such an announcement might say, if it were made.

On the day before we left, Manny came home from the office telling me he had discussed with Dave the lack of consideration being shown our children. They might learn of his involvement with the Brazilian project through an announcement, if one were made in our absence, rather than from him. He needed the leeway to inform them before we left.

Imagine a situation in which Manny sought permission to speak freely with his own children! Permission was granted, provided they—who were neither Whirlpool employees nor spouses of employees—promised not to divulge the information before an official Whirlpool announcement.

For me, this whole series of events was surreal. I had told Manny repeatedly that I was not going to Brazil. Manny had never shown any sign he would go without me. Despite my being the key to whether or not Manny would go, no official representative of the corporation ever discussed the proposition with me. In retrospect, I realize part of a corporate executive's expertise is supposed to be the ability to "control" his wife. From the start I was seen as an item in Manny's inventory. If they applied the screws to him tightly enough, they could count on him to deal with me.

Years earlier when Manny had turned fifty-five, Clara Dansfield had invited us to her office so she could explain to both of us, jointly, the employee plan called survivor options. She explained the joint consultation and joint agreement was required by law under the Retirement Equity Act. My signature was required to certify that such explanations had been made and that I understood them.

Survivor options are important; I am glad our government mandates that the spouse, the likely survivor, has a voice in choosing the option. I believe the decision whether one should be uprooted and replanted in foreign soil is of at least equal importance. Does the corporation consult with spouses on matters that so deeply affect the spouses—i.e., treat them as mentally competent adults with equal rights—only when required by law to do so?

When Manny and I drove off to be alone together, we felt we were in a state resembling suspended animation. Our apprehensions made the trip less than joyous. I don't recall laughing much. We clung to each other for solace while we visited relatives and old friends who could not be told we were hostage to corporate dictates.

We returned to St. Joseph over the weekend to find that no announcement had been made during our absence. However, on Monday, July 7, the Administrative Center issued a bulletin with a two-page article. Its headline screamed:

WHIRLPOOL EXPANDS INTEREST IN BRAZIL; NAMES SAMUEL M. BATEMAN PRESIDENT OF WHIRLPOOL DO BRASIL S.A.

Paragraph four stated:

. . . and Emanuel (Manny) Von Koenig as vice president effective July 1, 1986.

The final paragraph, the ninth, read:

Bateman and Von Koenig and their families will reside in São Paulo.

I was livid. I had not agreed to live in São Paulo. I found this bulletin intimidating and an inhumane, unfounded violation of my right to self-determination.

Even though the bulletin was internal to the Whirlpool Corporation, it was distributed to all offices and posted on all bulletin boards. Its contents were known throughout the community by that evening. Whirlpool is the area's major employer. Most of the employees passed the news on to families and friends.

By July 8, everyone who knew me also "knew" I was moving to Brazil. Shopping for groceries, attending Sunday services at the Unitarian Fellowship, walking on the beach, even answering the phone in my own home became nightmarish experiences, because everyone told me how exciting it was that I was going to Brazil. Dozens of times I had to reply "No, it isn't—and I'm not."

At least I was certain I wasn't going to Brazil under the agreement that existed between the Whirlpool Corporation and me—which was no agreement at all. No one had even spoken to me. No one had discussed terms.

I was not averse to going to Brazil, itself. I was averse to residing in Brazil without the proper arrangements for careful management. From my earlier experience in Brazil, I knew it is a difficult place for an expatriate. Living there must be carefully managed to be enjoyed.

We had discussed the probability of an announcement in Whirlpool's bulletin with our three oldest sons, who lived in the area. We discussed only that an announcement of some kind was probable, since we ourselves did not know what would be stated in it. In late July, we went to Fort Jackson, South Carolina, for the graduation of our youngest son, Curt, from boot camp. After the military ceremonies, we discussed with him the possibility that we might be going to Brazil. At that point our going was as much a "might" as was the location of Curt's post-Camp assignment. Manny and I, with Curt, were still talking about "if" we were going, even though Whirlpool, two weeks earlier and without our concurrence, had, in its announcement, already moved us.

The bulletin stated, "In addition to the new position, he [Von Koenig] remains a director in Whirlpool Corporation's interna-

tional division." He had not agreed to that. He had insisted, first
of all, that he didn't want to go to Brazil; he wanted to retire in
ten months. With that desire uppermost, why would he even
consider accepting a lateral transfer?

There had been, as yet, no discussion of salary. Manny had
been told we would have to sell our house; he had replied we
would not. This job would be, for him, nothing but headaches
and a disruption of the personal life he wanted to concentrate
on instead.

Family values clashed with corporate values. I felt that the
corporation had crossed the boundaries of my doorstep and
stormed its way to the very hearth of my home much the way
Hitler's troops thundered into Poland—as though they had a
right to do so.

After publication of the bulletin, both Sam Bateman and
Larry Kremer felt free to call Manny at home any time. The first
time Larry called and I answered the phone, he didn't identify
himself, simply brusquely said, "Let me talk to Manny."

Sam would call, saying, so fast and so rudely I could barely
understand him, "This is Sam Bateman. Get Manny, will ya?"

One evening in July, Manny and I spent an evening with
Sam and Fran Bateman at their home, discussing if we were
going. The following week we met for an evening at our house
specifically to discuss under what conditions I might be willing
to go. When I said I saw no reason why I should give up use of
my own car and my own computer, Sam agreed my concerns
were reasonable and assured me the corporation could take care
of both those needs. I expressed concern, also, about home privacy. For example, I did not want to entertain Whirlpool engineers who would later snub me in St. Joseph—which had
happened on the earlier assignment. I wanted it understood that
the Batemans and the Von Koenigs would, in nonbusiness situations, treat each other as equals so we could "be there" for each

other if day-to-day living got tough.

That same evening Fran joked to me, "That's how Sam has always gotten me to transfer. He'll promise me anything."

I asked, "And does he come through?"

When she smiled and drawled a lengthy "N-o-o-o" in reply, I thought she was kidding.

###

Sam and Fran Bateman were leaving for Cincinnati in August for three weeks of intensive Portuguese training at Inlingua and wanted me to go with them. I declined, saying it wouldn't be fair to invest Whirlpool's money since I didn't really plan to go to Brazil. Fran, who I am sure had been instructed to work on me, said, "Oh, come on. What do you mean, you're not going!"

The Batemans' attending Inlingua gave a progressively clearer impression to the corporation that since they couldn't go to Brazil without Manny, surely he was going. As a corollary, Roz must be going, too, because Manny wouldn't go without her.

Sometime during the month of August, I heard Manny's end of a phone conversation with Larry. Angrily, Manny said, "Lay off, will you? We're still talking about whether I'm going alone."

I can understand the pressure Larry was under to impress both Sam and Dave. I can understand the pressure Sam was under to impress Dave, George, and Jack Sparks. Most of all, now, I can understand the pressure Dave was under to get this Brazilian office opened up so Jack and the Board would be more impressed with him than they were with George.

However, none of these corporate-invented stresses justify, in any way, the abuse to which I was subjected.

As an executive, Manny was entitled to biennial check-ups at the Mayo Clinic. If I was going to Brazil, I was supposed to have one, too. We made appointments for both of us, on the grounds that Manny's check-up was corporation-paid-for, one way or the other. If I did not reach an agreement with the corporation that I would actually go to Brazil, we would pick up the bill for my examination.

We made appointments for Monday, August 25, 1986. The Saturday before, I made an absolute positive irreversible decision that I was not going to Brazil.

The Batemans and the Von Koenigs had met only twice; once at their house when nothing was accomplished in my behalf, and once at our house where only two of the four items on my agenda were conceded: the car and the computer.

We had not discussed the sanctity of each other's homes nor the four of us relating as psychological equals during this assignment so we could help each other through rough times.

Sam Bateman was a manager from the old school. He blustered, cursed a great deal, avoided eye contact. Fran was a good golfer, but beyond that, she seemed in my eyes to take pride in appearing empty-headed and in having a husband who knew how to buy big cars.

Sam epitomized the "Doonesbury" cartoon of March 5, 1987, in which the old bull-o'-the-woods says, "I'm from a different generation. Our wives were raised to be empty vessels for our ambitions." In the same strip, he says to the man at the computer, "I understand you're still married, that you still have a family life . . . that makes me wonder about your commitment . . . maybe this business isn't for you."

What Gary Trudeau knew I had not yet integrated. Sam appeared at least moderately cautious about submerging his own wife in breaking-point situations, but neither he nor his colleagues cared what they did to other people's families.

Fran had never, to my knowledge, been out of the States before. Sam, I believe, had acquired his first passport for business purposes a year or so earlier. Though Fran Bateman represented herself to me as not being a rank-puller, my later experiences with her in Brazil showed she was more expert than most. In St. Joseph I could avoid her and her type. I knew that in São Paulo I would be trapped—and I was.

In addition to what I considered to be their shortcomings, the Batemans knew little about the decades of Whirlpool's history in Brazil or about personal relationships with specific Brazilians. They did not know, for instance, that John Eser, who had lived and worked in Joinville, Brazil, for four years as president of Consul, was still a close personal friend of the Freitags, Consul's founding family, and that they privately still wondered what had happened to John's career.

The Batemans did not know about the subtle divide-and-conquer strategy of Miguel Etchenique's social politics and would not believe us when we tried to fill them in. To the Brazilians, Manny knew too much. To Whirlpool, he knew too much they didn't want to hear about—even though it was also the reason they had to have him in Brazil.

Whirlpool seemed to do business ahistorically, as though history could be erased, as though factors that didn't fit their theory could be ignored. From our previous experiences in Brazil, I knew enough to be thoroughly frightened, not so much by Brazilians, several of whom became my close friends, but by the combined ignorance and arrogance of upper-echelon Whirlpool personnel. They would be providing our life-support if we went to Brazil, and, if they felt like it, they would be pulling our strings from 7,000 miles away.

I pointed out to Manny, who did not disagree, that if we went to Brazil and stayed until March 1989, as Whirlpool wanted, we would again be on Etchenique turf, which was like shifting sand. Our lifeline to our own culture would once again be through Whirlpool, this time in the person of Sam Bateman, whom I perceived as insensitive, uninformed, brusque, self-cen-tered, and ruthless.

What was to be my role in relation to Sam's wife? Fran's characteristics were the opposite of mine. She was a gregarious, big-spending up-stager. She was not likely to heed any experi-entially acquired philosophies I might try to share with her, nor was she one on whose shoulder I could cry if things got tough.

I'd been through some of that before. From 1969 to 1971, when Manny worked directly for Mike, the Etcheniques had cut us out when we needed them the most. I'd been through Whirlpool's taking Mike's word against Manny's. I'd been through John Eser, who, even with all his cross-cultural experi-ence, had failed us when we needed him most, apologizing only many years later. Sam Bateman represented far less security as our Whirlpool guardian than we had during our first assign-ment in Brazil.

Manny still could hear my voice when I told him, "No, I won't go." We still had a solid partnership marriage at that point, and there was no question in his mind that if I wasn't going, he wasn't either. If it meant Whirlpool would be retributive and let him go seven months short of vested retirement—an action bear-ing similarities to John Eser's exit—then, we said, so be it.

The next morning, Sunday, Manny went over to the Batemans' house and told Sam in person we were not going to Brazil. With light hearts and unburdened minds, we flew that afternoon to Rochester, Minnesota, and checked into the Khaler Hotel for our appointments over the next few days at the Mayo Clinic.

On Monday, after full enemas and without breakfast, we underwent the first rounds. The telephone light was blinking in our hotel room when we returned. The message was for Manny to call Sam.

Manny called. Apparently Sam had gone to the office that

Monday morning, conferred with his superiors, and was authorized to offer Manny an internal promotion from director to division vice president, South American Operations. This position had incalculably more substance to it than the indefinable title of vice president of the undefined *Whirlpool do Brasil*.

The unspoken catch was still, of course, "provided you go to Brazil—otherwise there's no job for you at all." This episode exemplifies Whirlpool's goal was not only "get Von Koenig to Brazil," it also had been to "get him at the lowest possible cost," the way you treat somebody you don't like. They upped the ante only when necessary.

I heard gossip, later, about what a hard bargainer Manny's wife was. That she had held out and had, in effect, "held up" the corporation. Not so. I just plain didn't want to go, not at any price.

We never did get around to discussing "under what conditions" I would be willing to go—other than the car and a computer. To Whirlpool, everything was materialistic, and nothing was important unless it had a dollar value. I wanted to talk about the safeguarding and welfare of my soul. There were conditions under which I would have been happy to return to the land of the gentle Rainbow People, an expression referring to their skins of all colors, a people whose cuisine and music are incomparable, whose climate is mellow, whose art and lives are surreal. With terms not complete, however, I still said no.

Manny, though, was swept up and away at the thought of becoming a real division vice president. That was one rung up from the highest to which the immigrant youth from war-torn Germany had ever aspired.

He seemed not to notice that no one had discussed a salary adjustment. Nor did he notice that Sam had not said "check with Roz and let me know," even though he knew how adamantly opposed I had been just the day before.

I had been the winner one day earlier, on Sunday, when Manny went to Sam's home to give him our final "no." I reminded Manny he had agreed we weren't going.

For Sam and Manny, everything became "rush-rush." Deliberately so, I now realize. Sam's having no more time to talk to me was cut from the same cloth as Larry's not having had time to talk to Manny—part of steamroller tactics.

Sam insisted that having wasted so much time already, he and Manny get down to Brazil right away and start setting up an office. When the two of them left for Brazil on the twenty-eighth, I was still saying, "Whoa. What about the assurances of privacy and egalitarianism that are still on my docket?"

My marriage started to break up right then and there. Already I was out of the loop. No discussion. Just action deliberately contrary to my expressed wishes. The effect on me was numbing. Later I debated whether I should have continued to trust my up-to-then trustworthy husband of thirty-five years or whether I should have continued to refuse to go, even though Manny, as soon as he'd hung up the telephone, was in a sense already gone. Distrusting him would have been as out of character for me as his disregard for my self-determination would be for him. Empathically, I was still hanging in with my husband. All my hesitation and apprehension came from a gut-level mistrust of the corporation, based on my experience during our assignment in Brazil many years earlier when the corporation failed to understand the scenario in which they placed us and failed to support us, their expatriates.

By promoting Manny to division vice president, Sam had taken him to the mountain top and made him feel like one of the good old boys in the ring of real power. Sam convinced him that among the old boys, written contracts were not necessary; they did business according to gentlemen's agreements. Certainly a contrary wife was not a problem.

By design, Sam did not speak to me again about our unfinished agreement. Nor, leaving as he and Manny did by the end of the week, did he allow Manny time to do so.

Manny wanted so much to say yes at that point that he took it upon himself to assure me everything would work out. He emphasized that we had a verbal agreement to mediate, and if things got bad, he could quit and we would come home.

Part of his old, honest self really believed that, but another part, which was to grow larger, had already slipped into Sam's way of living: promise her anything to get her to transfer, whether or not you intend to deliver.

As Manny said "I do" to the Brazilian assignment on August 25, no formal, published corporate policy stipulated the terms of expatriate employment. Even if such a policy existed, both Manny and I would have understood that it did not apply to us, given the conditions I had been articulating. At the time, no Whirlpool employees lived and worked abroad. In anticipation of the need for a policy that addressed the relationship of the corporation to its expatriates, a formal statement was in the process of being iterated. Manny had explained to me something about the work he had been doing in helping Whirlpool formulate its expatriate policy.

This policy, which I knew was being drafted and which I knew Manny had been consulted about, was understood by us as becoming applicable, at some future date, to employees and their families as Whirlpool developed the need to send more people to live abroad. Manny and I understood we would be treated somewhat as laboratory guinea pigs. As problems arose for us in Brazil, as they surely would—problems of a cross-cultural nature which could not be anticipated in the sterile, passive environment of the policy theoretician—they were to be worked out to our satisfaction as well as Whirlpool's. What Whirlpool's theoreticians would learn by working through problems with us *in situ* could shape new or additional principles for the overall policy.

As far as both Manny and I knew on August 25, 1986, the expatriate policy was still a work in progress. Manny had been assured, and had assured me, whatever its stage of iteration at the time, that it did not apply, letter for letter, to us. Manny's was a one-of-a-kind assignment. We were going to Brazil on the terms of a "gentleman's agreement," and we were showing a tremendous amount of faith by so doing.

Manny's assignment, we understood, was to be under a grandfather clause. That's because he was an experienced expatriate who could aid management by helping work the bugs out of their rough-draft policy through trial and error, and because he was doing them a favor by going at all when he preferred to retire.

In reality, the Whirlpool Corporation, acting with what appears to me deliberate deception, had completed—to its unilateral satisfaction—a publishable expatriate policy. Not until after Manny said "yes" on August 25 did they inform him of its completion and of their intention to hold us both to its terms. But I did not know this.

It was three years later that fate put into my hands a letter dated August 26, 1986. It was a two-page letter addressed to Manny from Mike Simeck, staff vice president, Human Resource Services, on the subject of employment in São Paulo, Brazil. One section read:

> [A]ll . . . *expatriate policies as stated in the Company's International Compensation Policy will apply to you and members of your family. Such policies may be changed from time to time by the Company, at its sole discretion.*

How did I come across this three-year-old letter? It was left behind by my ex-husband when he moved out of the house after our divorce.

Manny had received that letter almost as he was going out the door to meet Sam and catch a flight to Brazil. I recall his being outraged by some correspondence he'd received from Whirlpool, details of which he did not share with me. I had known nothing about this letter or its contents, but when I found it, it did much to explain my frustrations and anguish during the intervening time.

I would not have moved to Brazil had I known the move was going to be under the condition that any and all policies could be changed any time at the sole discretion of people whom I had no good reason to trust.

I did not know about that letter.

But Manny did, and he kept it from me.

Manny knew his corporation had violated his integrity as well as mine by slapping on him at this eleventh hour a set of policies to which he had not agreed.

Manny knew I wouldn't go under those conditions, and he knew he had to go. He didn't want to go without me, so he didn't tell me. It was a terrible thing to do, but he was in a double bind. He was damned either way.

Sam and Manny left for São Paulo about a week before Fran and I joined them. During that week I went to New York. Months earlier, I had been invited by a fellow member of the American Sociological Association to room with her for the ASA annual meeting in New York. I had declined, but with a move looming, the timing fit. Attendance helped me hang on to my self-esteem and professional dignity, at least for those last few days before surrendering my identity to the insatiable and wasteful demands of the corporation. I felt like the proverbial immovable object being propelled, as Manny was, by a huge, irresistible force.

I left the ASA meeting early, on September 4, to meet Fran Bateman's plane coming in from O'Hare. Together we flew over-night to São Paulo for our necessary house-hunting functions.

Our husbands met us in the morning and took us to our quarters in the Maksoud Hotel. The hotel was within five minutes of the Sumaré area where Manny and I, with our four sons, had lived before, and where I hoped we might live again.

At the start, the Batemans had agreed with us that it would be good to live in different areas of the city so our home lives would be distinct from office interference that could threaten our personal privacy.

Santo Amaro, thirty or more minutes south of the Loop, was the residential area preferred by the Americans, British, Dutch, and Germans. It was upscale and newer, but not any safer. Finding accommodations was easier there, especially for executives in a hurry.

The high-rises were characterized by lavish tastelessness. No matter what the cost, they were still without warmth or charm. The upper-class Brazilian families who lived in them knew foreigners were temporary, "migrant labor" so to speak. They did not waste much time on us, and that added to the chill.

Yet that is where we "chose" to live. Once Sam and Manny had surveyed the automobile situation, they decided our families' living across the street from each other would facilitate their being transported to and from the office together by the company driver. I was not even allowed to see the old-world penthouse apartment in Hygienopolis that Manny had told me earlier he was sure I would love. Nor, mysteriously, did there seem to be any dwellings available for me to consider anywhere but in Santo Amaro.

During the week of house-hunting, the fact surfaced that the amount authorized for the Batemans' rent was double what would be paid for ours. It later became clear that if we flew anywhere with the Batemans, we all flew first class. Unaccompanied by them, we flew club class. Such a matter was small, but it did set the tone for whose opinions would carry more weight in supposedly equal-discussion opportunities.

The Von Koenigs' housing decision was made first, giving me a free day at the Maksoud while the other three made a final determination for the Batemans. The Maksoud is about as macho a hotel as I've experienced anywhere, except for one later experience in Rio. High-priced call girls frequent the Maksoud lobby restaurant "feeling up" their clients before going upstairs.

My instructions for the day were to stay put. Sam wanted it that way, although the dictum came from Manny. They didn't have time to waste by anybody getting into trouble. That was all right with me. I was too depressed to argue about my right to roam and unable to muster enthusiasm to plan anything, anyway. I ordered lunch from room service and ate it gazing out the seventh-floor window at police helicopters periodically circling. They were monitoring a workers' protest a block away on Avenida Paulista.

That demonstration occurred September 7, Brazil's Day of Independence, similar to our July 4. Our housing decision had been so quick it had taken only two days, September 5 and 6, to accomplish. These Whirlpool men were in a hurry to get on with what they perceived as important business.

When Manny returned to the hotel, he told me he had run into our friend Trude Hauptmann at the Congonhas Airport. She was, naturally, offended to learn I was in the city and had not called her. Eventually, I created an opportunity to explain to her that the conditions under which I was there were oppressive. I had not wanted to involve her. I had hoped to overcome my negativity, to rise above the situation, and, later on, to have called her in high spirits. That didn't happen. To this day, I believe she neither understands nor has totally forgiven me.

One morning at the Maksoud, for some reason I don't recall, Sam and I had breakfast alone together. He said to me, "I've been listening to how well you handle yourself in Portuguese,

Roz, and I don't know if I can justify the expense of having you at Inlingua for three weeks."

Manny's Portuguese was relatively fluent, mine less so, but showing promise. Sam's capability did not extend far beyond reading signs; Fran was nearly mute.

I replied, "Don't be silly. Of course I'm going to Inlingua. Back in August, it was taken for granted, by you as well as everyone else, that I would." I did.

An announcement of Manny's promotion was made in Whirlpool's in-house publication, the *Full Line News*, on September 5, 1986. This time when Whirlpool said, "Von Koenig and his wife, Rosalyn, who have four grown sons, are in the process of moving to São Paulo, Brazil," it was closer to being true than it was when they had made a similar announcement on July 7. But it wasn't true yet. I was still holding out hope for a miracle.

When the four of us returned to the States at the end of our exploratory week, also on our plane was Ivens Freitag, the new president of Consul, and his wife, Yvonne. Sam invited them to join us on the Whirlpool jet, which would be picking us up in New York for the flight to Benton Harbor, Michigan. Other Brazilian executives were already in Benton Harbor, and all were invited to a Sunday dinner at the Point O'Woods Country Club.

There my acquaintance with Mike and Helen Etchenique resumed. One of their sons was in Benton Harbor on a Whirlpool management training program, and another son was there on a visit. Diners were seated strictly by rank at one or the other of two tables. The Whitwams, Wardebergs, and Batemans (second, third, and fourth top-ranking corporate executives) sat with the Etcheniques. Manny and I, the eldest in age and the only Americans present with a history of Brazil–U.S. relations, were seated with "the children"—the Etchenique sons and their wives, the Freitags, and the Kremers.

Larry Kremer was young, but having taken over Eser's job, he was Manny's boss. I had to keep reminding myself of that fact and to control my tongue as Larry's contributions to the conversation centered on his wife's inability to understand football. Football is not a Brazilian sport, so our guests could not be expected to understand it nor to care who else did or didn't. The guests may or may not have noticed, as I did, that his comments denigrated his wife, who seemed not to mind.

During the brief cocktail time that preceded dinner, both David Whitwam and George Wardeberg introduced themselves to me. Only Barbara Whitwam engaged me in anything resembling a real conversation. But no one offered me a "welcome to the team" or "thank you for the service you are undertaking."

Yvonne Freitag and I shared comments later about the graceless seating arrangements and fast-food pace of the whole evening. She wondered, also, why Julio and Gloria Caicedo hadn't been invited. During the year that she had lived in St. Joseph with their small children while Ivens trained at Whirlpool, the Caicedos had assisted them far beyond the call of duty. They had become close friends, and the Freitags would have truly enjoyed their company.

I tried to explain office politics and protocol as I understood them. But I realized that Yvonne didn't grasp the concepts, because two years later, when I was her guest for a day in Joinville, she asked me essentially the same questions. Yvonne, however, was a bright spot in my Brazilian life. She warmed my heart with her common sense.

The day after the dinner at the Point, Dee Wardeberg called to invite me to a Wednesday luncheon for Helen Etchenique and her daughters-in-law. I did not attend, telling Dee simply I had other plans. I had no particular interest in helping entertain, again, the wives of the Etchenique children, nor in fawning over Helen, who had not said good-bye to me when I left

Brazil in 1971. Nor could I muster any expression of delight over returning to Brazil to live under similar employer-imposed protocols. No way could Dee, standing at the edge of the pool, understand the overall game plan, as I did from my previous total-immersion experience.

I was still in St. Joseph when Manny left for Brazil again. A Whirlpool executive in the legal department called to say he had been out of town when Manny left, so couldn't say farewell. Would I do this for him so Manny would know he wished him well? I agreed to do so, but I was dismayed that neither this man nor his wife, both of whom I had worked with on community projects, added ". . . and you have a good trip, too, Roz."

The International Division held a farewell dinner for Manny at Schuler's. Perhaps it was for us; at least I was invited. The focus, of course, was on Manny, as it should have been. Department anecdotes highlighted the carefully staged "impromptu" speeches.

Sara Shine's presence got me through an evening in which my role was that of chattel. My gut sensation of the event felt the same as when, years before, the St. Joseph Township's property tax notice came addressed to "Emanuel Von Koenig & Wife." I took the notice to the issuing office and waited, with reigned-in anger, while the clerk made the appropriate substitution of my name for "wife."

Sara was leaving the corporation for employment that offered the career advancement promised but not delivered by Whirlpool. Having worked for a Brazilian company many years earlier, she and Manny publicly exchanged satiric toasts about Whirlpool in Portuguese. These remarks were understood only by them, the Caicedos, and me, none of whom, of course, would tell. We had a drink in the bar with Sara before the dinner, and again after.

The farewell dinner underscored that Manny was going to

Brazil, and his "wife," whoever she might be, was accompanying him. The house in St. Joseph, which we jointly owned, had been taxed in his name solely, with acknowledgment that his wife, whoever she might be, had some responsibilities, too. Brazil was being hailed as some kind of marvelous opportunity for Manny. His wife was going too. He would be the one to have experiences in Brazil. The wife, whoever she might be, would just "be there."

Manny and the Batemans moved to Brazil in October as our son Curt was coming home on furlough before reporting for duty in Germany. Sam was in such a hurry to go that Manny was compelled to leave the day before Curt arrived. This denied us our last opportunity to be together as a family.

Leaving was much simpler for the Batemans, whose house was to be under Whirlpool guard and maintenance during their absence. We had been asked, almost ordered, to sell our family home of fifteen years. For me, selling it was out of the question, and I had adamantly refused even to discuss the possibility. Jeff, Nancy, and one-year-old Sandy would house-sit in our absence. Because they would bring furnishings of their own, I had to send some of our things into storage and sell off others.

No address change at the Post Office was necessary, because Jeff was going to sort through our mail and take to the Whirlpool International Division only the pieces he knew would be of interest to us. Whirlpool would then forward our mail to us by pouch or, when business trips were being made, in person.

Not wanting to go to Brazil at all, I dragged my heels in the hope that, perhaps, something would intervene. I delayed for several events.

Ed had married Lori in 1984, the same weekend Jeff married Nancy. The boys' Aunt Lulu, in Germany, invited Ed and Lori to honeymoon in Munich as her guests, with Jeff and Nancy to come the following year. In 1985, Sandra Rachel was born to

Jeff and Nancy, postponing her parents' honeymoon until 1986. How could they follow through on their plans if I did not take care of little Sandy, as I had promised?

I had joined with thirty-four other Berrien County residents in organizing and becoming a charter member of the Berrien United Nations Association. In addition, I was deeply involved in planning and implementing programs scheduled for October 26 and 29. I would not leave before then. Nor should I have been expected to.

The last thing I did was sell my car, as Manny, at the last minute, had sold his. Whirlpool's internal travel service supplied me with airline tickets to Cincinnati, then Phoenix, Miami, and São Paulo. I began my three weeks at Inlingua on November 3 on a Whirlpool expense account, keeping detailed daily records.

I had become a ward of the corporation and of my husband. Our finances were so complicated we were not expected even to try working them out ourselves. Ernst & Whinney, under Whirlpool supervision, calculated our taxes for us over the next few years.

Cincinnati was nice. I had familiarized myself with it during our Whirlpool year in nearby Hamilton. Ironically, literature in my hotel lobby included an article about the attention and considerations corporations should be giving to the spouses of employees they are transferring. Whirlpool was doing none of the things recommended.

One Saturday, my Inlingua tutor and I—speaking Portuguese all the while—drove out to Hamilton so I could take pictures of the house where Edward had been born.

For comfort, in my fancy but lonely hotel room, I sewed— on a machine I rented by the week. I had brought with me a pattern and material for a dress. I finished the dress in time to wear it one evening in mid-November to a Cincinnati Opera performance of Puccini's "Girl of the Golden West." It is a dress I still wear for comfort and courage. I wore it to court on May 21, 1990, when I stood, unrepresented, before the judge to plead my case.

November 22, I flew to Phoenix to spend a few days with friends. While there, my body broke out in hives. The weather was cool so my skin was fully covered by clothing. My friends didn't need to know.

We drove north to explore the Grand Canyon and Sedona before they left me in Payson with Dennis and Shirley Brisson—the dear friend from first grade who had been my matron of honor and who, with her husband, had sponsored Manny's immigration thirty-four years earlier.

I was with the Brissons for Thanksgiving and the few days after. Each succeeding day, as the Brazilian experience drew closer, I had more hives than the day before. They came and went, but with each appearance there were more and they were more virulent.

No matter about the hives. I had to leave Phoenix and move on. Airports are exciting. I always enjoy them. I spent my waiting time in Miami checking out the shops, watching the people, sipping espresso, avoiding the awareness of what came next: which plane I would be boarding, where I was going.

The time came when I had to rise from reverie and blend in with the people moving toward the Varig departure gate. Once on the plane, I felt incredibly relaxed for the duration of the ten-hour flight. Everything was, thenceforth, to be completely beyond my control. I felt powerless.

L-R: Jeff, Roz, Ed, Manny, Doug, and Curt (in inset; not born at the time of this 1963 family portrait)

Part Two

Value Conflicts with the Corporation: The Brazilian Years 1986–1989

The account I give in the following pages is as factual as I can make it. Whatever I say that may seem critical of Emanuel Von Koenig is not so intended. I am the one who crumbled. If I had not the strength to endure the gantlet, how can I fault him, who had so much more to endure?

###

I came through the customs crush—it couldn't be called a line—at São Paulo's Guaruljos Airport the morning of December 1, 1986, to be greeted by Manny, Sam, and Fran. They wore the most welcoming expressions I ever would see on their faces. They had been in Brazil one harrowing month, and all three greeted me as if they believed everything would be better, now that I was there.

This attitude did not last long. They expected that my showing up to complete the quartet would wave away all the "ow-ies" like a magic wand. Not so. I came, literally, with "ow-ies" of my own. The attacks of hives that began in the States continued to plague me. Ironically, these appeared only on the parts of my body covered by clothing. Like the perfect corporate wife, I hid my stress so other people couldn't see it.

My arms, legs, and back were covered with red spots—all five-foot-four of me. Yet I could put on a bathing suit and robe and head for the pool on the ground level of our condo, and by the time I arrived, I could remove the robe and the hives would have disappeared—only to reappear later under clothing. Manny was the only witness, as my secret affliction persisted over the next six weeks.

There was no point in seeing a doctor, who would simply tell me what I already knew: my hives were stress-related. If my desire not to be in Brazil was really so intense, the medical expert would say, perhaps I should go back to the States.

Unfortunately I wasn't going back; I couldn't go back, because I had been unable to keep myself from leaving in the first place. Although I took the matter of my psychosomatic rebellion seriously, I also knew my body would give up eventually and settle down. It did, at least on the surface. Manny appreciated my positive attitude and effort, as well as the fact that at age fifty-six I was still slim and pretty.

However heavy and stressful my load in Brazil would become, Manny's would always be heavier. He had taken the job unwillingly and only because the corporation held ransom his pension benefits and his retirement status. Their deliverance could be assured only by his compliance with the corporation's needs over the next several years. The job fell to him because no one else in the corporation could do it. Not even he could do it while maintaining his own health of body and mind—and his family.

Sam, as an officer of the corporation, sat on the boards of all the Brazilian companies affiliated with Whirlpool. His signature, on the spot, could authorize many things. Manny sat on the boards with him. In addition, Manny was the designated office manager in charge of anything that came up. In many ways, but at a much more responsible level, this duplicated his position with the U.S. Armed Forces Post Exchange in 1951–1952 when he worked as liaison between the American Occupation Force and its German employees.

Shortly before my arrival, the Brazilian government ordered a price freeze. Producers then withheld goods from the market rather than suffer inevitable losses as the rate of currency inflation rose each day.

This had strange effects on day-to-day life. Meat was scarce. Household furniture and accessories were hard to locate and purchase. In contrast, fine restaurants exceeded even their own already superlative standards for the few people who still could afford to be patrons. I understood and empathized with the Batemans' confusion and frustration. I found it frustrating, too, but was less confused because I had known similar Brazilian experiences in 1969–1971. I could draw on these for understanding that some kind of order lay behind all the apparent chaos.

Whirlpool do Brasil ordered two company cars, which, due to economic conditions, would not be delivered for many months. During the interim, the company rented a car and hired a driver. Marcus picked up Manny first, then Sam, at 7:30 and took them to the office. At 5:00 or later, he brought them back. Between 8:30 and 4:30, his services were available to Fran and me.

With the help of Olga, a decorator who knew where to find things that couldn't even be gotten, Fran had about completed purchase of her household furnishings by the time I arrived. Olga's services were transferred to me, and we drove with Marcus around São Paulo, sharing his time with Fran. Even with

Olga's connections, deliveries ran late. It was June of the following year before everything was in place.

In December, the furnishings in our condo were few. A built-in table with benches took care of the kitchen, and Manny had bedroom furnishings made-to-order by one of Olga's craftsmen. I tried sleeping with Manny, but we have different lights-off habits. He needed the bed more than I, to be fresh for the daily challenges of Brazilian business.

So that first night, and for several weeks thereafter, I slept on a sheet spread out on the bare dining room floor. I did not fail to see the humor in the situation: fifty-six years old, the big-shot wife of a big-shot executive, on an exotic assignment in a far-off land—for which we were being paid extra big bucks. Why was I sleeping on the floor? Olga also saw the irony and used it to spur on her suppliers.

From the start, Fran and I had problems sharing our daytime use of the single car and driver. In an unguarded moment, she revealed her impatience with my need of the car and with Olga to complete furnishing our apartment: "If you had gotten down here with the rest of us, you'd have been finished a long time ago."

Not that I went beyond half-time use. On the half day I had the car, Olga often urged Fran to come along rather than sit in her apartment with nothing to do. The few times she did accompany us, she was a sullen and resentful companion who showed no enthusiasm for my project.

She saved her enthusiasm for her new friends who lived either in the same complex as the Batemans or in the other elegant one nearby. They were all, like Fran, wives of CEOs of their companies' Brazilian operations. Status consciousness, I could see, was going to be a problem. I can be a supportive friend and am even reasonably good at playing second fiddle, but I do not genuflect. Fran and I were not meant for each other, but there we were, cast by Whirlpool into incompatible roles.

Sam was less than fair in the matter. Too often, Fran prearranged that Marcus, after delivering the men to the office, would return directly to the Batemans'. On at least one occasion, with Manny's approval, I was ready and waiting with him for Marcus's morning pick-up. When we stopped to pick up Sam, he was surprised to see me in the car. He quickly deduced the reason. If possession had become the law, then prior occupation was the only way to access transportation, short of begging. We needed groceries. My trip didn't take long. Fran could have the car for the rest of the day, if she liked.

Like Fran, I joined the American Society and the Newcomer's Club. We shared transportation to commonly attended events in the company car that served the basic life-support and social needs of two families, as well as the business needs of *Whirlpool do Brasil*. Fran would "invite" me to join her in "our" car and "then we'll pick up Cindy and Diane." Even though Cindy had a car of her own and was accustomed to driving in São Paulo traffic, we might make a stop to pick up her dry cleaning or to go grocery shopping if Diane needed toilet paper. Fran and both her friends acted put-upon, however, if Roz wanted to swing by the Romano Center for a few pots and pans that she didn't have.

These were mere social inconveniences. Political and security issues were yet to come.

Whirlpool do Brasil's business needs included frequent evening restaurant entertaining, both of Brazilian colleagues and of Whirlpool associates from the United States. Fran and I were generally included, with Marcus chauffeuring the four of us. Otherwise, Sam and Manny worked at the office late into the evening and spent some time there even on weekends.

I told Manny that Marcus, who daily spent an additional two hours on his motorcycle making the round trip to the office where the car was garaged, was becoming dangerously tired. If he returned us at midnight and picked the men up again at 7:30, he not only had two hours less sleep than his employers, but, in addition, no time at all with his wife and children.

My remark seemed not to influence *Whirlpool do Brasil*, even though I was appealing to enlightened self-interest by pointing out that *we* were in danger being driven by such a fatigued person. Finally I said if the three of them chose to persist in such exploitation, I could choose not to be a part of it. I told Manny to keep Marcus out of my sight unless conditions were altered; I would learn to get around by taxi and bus. Marcus's schedule was lightened.

For the first several months, we lived out of our suitcases, using what we had been able to hand-carry to Brazil. For me this meant that I had nothing appropriate to wear when the Etcheniques invited us to their home—a gathering followed by dinner at the Jocuei Club in honor of Charlie Putnam, Whirlpool's executive vice president of Administration and, as such, head of the Human Resources division.

I scurried through store after store trying to find something elegantly understated, bordering on casual. The best I could come up with was not very good. I tried not to let that interfere with my psychological functioning. My recollection is that I behaved well that night, being an alert and appreciative guest, solicitous of others' well-being.

Charlie Putnam's behavior, on the other hand, was pompous and self-serving. At that time, I was unaware of his role in Human Resources, unaware he was among those ultimately responsible for the deceptions that took out of my hands control over my existence.

Since he was the first stateside representative to arrive, both the Batemans and we had asked him to bring a few things for us. When Manny picked him up at the airport, Charlie handed him a bill, saying, "This is what you owe me." Not until days later did he give Manny the items for which we had been billed. We were left wondering, in the interim, if we were going to get the vitamins, medications, and wash cloths we'd asked for. Wash cloths, for some reason, couldn't be purchased anywhere in São Paulo.

Charlie and Sam were not only current working peers, but also friends from many years before. During cocktails at the Etcheniques', Charlie grandstanded on the subject of what great support service the corporation gave its expatriates. As an example, he told how he had gone out of his way for Fran, having his secretary pick up her prescription glasses. On the other hand, he had not yet given Manny the few things we hoped he had actually brought for us. Nor did he remember having met me before, even though he had, in a small intimate group at the home of mutual friends. I was given the impression that should we ever meet again, he still would not remember ever having met me before.

Manny and I deserved better than that for what we were doing for the corporation—postponing retirement to make the opening of *Whirlpool do Brasil* possible.

Ed Dunn was vice president of Human Resources, sandwiched between Charlie Putnam as his superior and Glenn Youngstedt, his subordinate, whom I would later subpoena. When Ed, whom I had never met, came to São Paulo, he requested a visit to our apartment so he could see Whirlpool's investment. I allowed it, but I considered it an invasion of privacy.

Others in town at the same time were Dick Litzinger, who had taken Manny's job at the Ad Center, Sam Pearson, and Tony Mason. The final evening of the group's stay, at a home dinner given by Brastemp president Cesár Bonamico and his wife, Maria Angelica, Dick finally said, "If there's anything my office can do for you, just let us know." It sounded insincere, and it surely was, because the conduit that ran through his office continued to supply the Batemans at the expense of the Von Koenigs. Tony Mason, one of Whirlpool's most inventive engineers, whose wife later became my valued friend, was the only visitor that evening with whom I felt truly comfortable, and I was grateful for his company.

There is some evidence that Human Resources' failure to counsel me, failure to have even *one* face-to-face conversation with me prior to my moving to Brazil, was not an oversight, but deliberate.

That evidence exists in Tony and Nancy Mason's experience. Starting early in 1986, Whirlpool and the Masons had been negotiating a transfer to Brazil. As a result, starting in September 1986, the Masons went for a series of three-months-at-a-time assignments on tourist visas rather than as permanent residents. "Permanent residents" defined our status—for the second time. (How many times can a family "permanently" immigrate to the same country? As many times as it takes to get around the country's laws that attempt to protect indigenous development.)

In the Mason household, Nancy, not Tony, managed their funds and financing. When Human Resources met with Tony to negotiate a foreign assignment compensation package, he informed them they really should be talking to Nancy, because she handled such matters. He couldn't answer most of the questions that came up. After several more such attempts by Human Resources, Tony said to them, "Look, you're going to *have* to talk to Nancy, whether you like it or not." They finally did.

From this it appears Whirlpool not only lacked a policy of obtaining informed-consent of employees' spouses going along on foreign assignment, but even moved in the opposite direction of not dealing with them unless absolutely necessary.

###

Our apartment telephone alternated between crackley and comatose. New phones were not to be had. As they gradually came back onto the market, Olga said she could get me one if Manny would "let" her. I knew what he was doing. He was trying, as manager of not only the office but also, in a frighteningly real sense, both homes, to maintain control of all situations at all times. He was basically allowing me—yes, his position gave him that authority—to do nothing except furnish the doll house, and that, only under his ever-watchful eye. The home phone was not high on his long priority list.

Phones at the office worked, and the home phone was not seen as a big problem until it interfered with business—as it did when a change in schedule occurred. Men from the home office were traveling from São Paulo to the Amazon city of Manaus on business. The Benton Harbor office called São Paulo with the message that the departure time of the company plane, which was to pick them up, had changed; please notify them. Despite all of Manny's close-to-neurotic care in handling their arrangements, the detail of where the men were staying had slipped past him. Sam left town for the weekend, leaving Manny with the order to "find them."

They seemed not to be at any of the predictable places, from the five-star Hotel Tropical on down. For hours, Manny bellowed into our phone, as though the sheer volume of his voice could reach Manaus in spite of competing static. After he had been inconvenienced, phone replacement advanced in priority, with a better one installed early the following week.

Olga called me a few days later to tell me she had located two identical, good quality television sets, one for the Batemans, one for us. I bypassed office approval by responding, "Get them!" Fortunately for me, everyone was grateful. I had not taken initiative earlier in the matter of the phone, because I would not have dared. Although these might seem domestic matters, they weren't. I was only nominally in charge of supplying my house-hold. Sam controlled the most minute details, often acting on whims, and these were executed by Manny, often dictatorially.

Because I had neither word processor nor typewriter, in December I asked Manny if Sandra, the office secretary, could type three paragraphs of a Christmas greeting for me to photo-copy. I wanted to prepare Christmas cards that the Batemans could take back to the States and mail for us. Manny kept tell-ing me Sandra was too busy, wait a few days. When I found Sam had done a similar project for Fran, Manny said, "Well, OK, I can do it now. The way Sam's been pushing, I didn't think he'd want us taking time for that." I had to stay up most of the night to get the cards ready by the Batemans' flight time.

This is the text of the note I sent out in December of 1986:

> *Whirlpool has asked us—for the second time—to work in Brazil. Since direct mail is frequently lost, this note is travel-ing to the U.S. in an American's suitcase, even though we know you would like a Brazilian stamp and postmark. If you write to us, please send the letter to our home in Michigan. Jeff, Nancy, and Sandy live in our house and forward all mail via the cor-poration; we would not like to miss a message from you. Our card is enclosed for your information.*

> *Our lifestyle here is comfortable and the results of our work-a-day efforts gratifying. But we miss family, friends, and snow. Even though Rio de Janeiro hotels are booked solid through the end of the year, we hope to find a way to spend New Year's Eve at Copacabana Beach to participate in the Yemanja Festival. What can we say? We're here—we might as well go with it.*

The Batemans went back to the States for the last two weeks of December because Sam had to attend year-end board meet-ings. This meant the Batemans could be back in St. Joseph in their own house with family and friends over the holidays. For us, it meant holding the fort at the office and planning a party appropriate for its three employees: Marcus (whose monthly salary was under $300); the bilingual secretary, Sandra (whose income more nearly approximated what U.S. secretaries are paid); and the cleaning woman/coffee server, Antonia (I shudder to think how low her income must have been).

I bought toys for Marcus's children and a food basket for his family. Manny presented gifts of some kind to the other two staff members. With Manny, I presided over an "office family" lunch at a moderately priced restaurant where we hoped no one would feel awkward.

It was strange. I was 7,000 miles south of the Berrien County Youth Fair Grounds where I had observed, from a disassociative distance, how Fredda Sparks played the part of First Lady for the oddly disjointed Whirlpool "family" whose father was, apparently, the CEO. Due to the absence of the Batemans, I was an understudy playing the role of First Lady (and "mother"?) of *Whirlpool do Brasil*. The role was unwritten but presumed. It never was played out by the person whose role it was by "right," because the Batemans would never be in São Paulo over the holidays. This *Whirlpool do Brasil* traditional event spiraled into 1987 and 1988, becoming ever stranger.

On Christmas Eve our children and grandchildren would be driving through snow and cold to gather, as usual, in our house. Jeff and Nancy, instead of us, would be the hosts. We, on the other hand, would be experiencing Brazil's hottest time of the year. Manny and I were prepared to drink large quantities of wine the night of the twenty-fourth and pretend we weren't separated from the joys of our lives.

We were saved from that by the mercy of Cesár and Maria Angelica Bonamico, who insisted we be part of their family that night. We went with them to the home of Cesár's sister, where dozens of relatives of all ages gathered for a sumptuous buffet dinner that extended to midnight, when presents from under a tree were distributed. They had even purchased presents for us. People with a true feel for family, the Bonamicos were similarly kind to us on other occasions.

From the States came Whirlpool's 1986 official Christmas card signed by everyone in the division Manny had left. The card, one in a series of Native American images commissioned from St. Joseph artist Michele Gauthier, featured a stately, elderly woman telling a story to her two grandchildren. The inscription read, ". . . honors the Wyandotte matriarch who continues to transmit knowledge, tribal traditions and clan membership to her descendants."

How ironic this should come before my eyes! I, the matriarch, the grandmother, who had been whisked away from the life of my own clan by the more pressing needs of the corporation. With one hand Whirlpool honored the spiritual primacy of the clan mother, while its double-dealing other hand had tricked me—also a clan mother—into accompanying my husband to Brazil in the belief that any issues would be resolved in an honorable way. When such issues did arise, the corporation's ignoring my pleas for help suggested that my words were not worth hearing, traditions of communication had no value, and I had no knowledge worth being transmitted.

With the *Whirlpool do Brasil* office closed between Christmas and New Year's, Manny and I realized our wish to spend New Year's Eve in Rio by boarding a tour bus as part of a group that included a retired police officer and his wife, and two young Amazon Indian sisters who had assimilated into city life. A short, slim woman named Flavia was our guide. Associating with the retired police officer and his wife was pleasantly educational. We had heard about Brazilian police brutality, but these were delightful people. Familiarity can dispel prejudice.

We stayed at a hotel one block off Copacabana beach. It was adequate, except for one thing. The first time Manny and I walked out the door together, the doorman called him aside. When Manny returned, he said the doorman told him if he wanted a "better woman," it could be arranged.

This, in itself, did not surprise me. São Paulo has innumerable motels that rent by the hour, serve free "executive lunch," and exist for the purpose of convenient, presumably illicit, sex.

What surprised and frightened me was that he relayed this in a tone devoid of embarrassment, suggesting satisfaction that, as a man, he was recognized as a superior being who deserved, perhaps, the Girl from Ipanema. He seemed to have no cognizance of what this made me, nor of how I would feel to know he and the doorman had formed a bond of conspiracy.

Any time I had to pass by the doorman, I felt myself diminished and demeaned. To him, I was even less than Whirlpool's "just a wife." My Whirlpool executive husband, instead of apologizing to me for the doorman's effrontery and reporting him to the manager for having insulted us both, indicated, by his lack of indignation, that the doorman's attitude was at least somewhat justified. The doorman, unscathed, stayed at his post to continue assaulting other marriages.

This uncharacteristic behavior and several other occurrences in our relationship during that week, Manny's and my fourth week together under expatriate circumstances, alerted me to the troubled state of the "democracy in the family" that I so prized. I did not see how these changes in Manny's behavior could derive from anything I had or hadn't done, because I had arrived only December 1 and had not been around to contribute to their development. But I could attribute these new behaviors to Manny's elevated role within the Whirlpool Corporation and the fact that we were living in an environment which values men over women even more than the States does.

###

Another change I became aware of was Manny's avoiding being alone with me. Starting with that trip, and carrying over into all the other trips we were yet to take together, he arose early and went to find other members of the tour. In the evening, he did not go with me to our room; he said he would "be up later." He seemed to have no trouble being my partner in public, even if we were alone in the sense that we were not with a group, as long as people, even though total strangers, milled around. But he seemed, by his pacing and general nervousness, almost panic stricken when absolutely alone with me within four confining walls.

He lacked respect for my conversational space, too. Still feeling my way into actual (as opposed to classroom) use of Portuguese, I pondered my responses before uttering them. Over lunch at a pleasant outdoor restaurant, the retired police office and his wife were being particularly gracious to me, asking how I found Brazil so far. Since their query began with "a Senhora," there was no ambiguity about who was being addressed. Manny, sitting next to me, lunged into the pause with, "Oh, she . . ." and gave a complete description of how he supposed I felt. Confused, I let it go.

Another time, I came down to breakfast alone; Manny had made his escape from my presence half an hour earlier. I was standing in the lobby having quite a lively discussion with the Amazon sisters. Manny, unseen by me, approached from behind and greeted the young women loudly and jovially, breaking up our conversation by cutting me off in mid-sentence. He did not deliberately interrupt me. It was worse than that, since he didn't even notice I was speaking. His entire focus was on himself and on how others would perceive him.

As with most tours, problems arose that had to be imaginatively dealt with on the spot. Manny bonded with Flavia almost instantly. Any problem she had was his. She was a "jolly good fellow," not a temptress, a tiny little thing next to Manny's six-feet-two.

It did not seem unnatural that she would accept any help offered, but it progressed from strange to weird that this German-American, who had come back to live in Brazil only three months earlier, should be obsessed with helping her. Why not the retired police officer? Presumably, he could have been of much more assistance than Manny, but he didn't have a chance to move into space already occupied.

Our bus developed a mechanical problem as we drove into Petropolis. Flavia directed us all to the museum, asking us to guide ourselves through it while she and the bus driver sought attention for the bus.

Manny said to me, "I have to help Flavia."

I said, "No, you don't. The bus is *her* business. *Your* business is to see the museum."

He paused to reflect on this. I could see how he struggled within himself. Finally, he came with the rest of us to the museum.

Manny seemed to derive his vibrancy, even his will to live, by feeding on another manager's menu. His identification with the group crystallized around Flavia, the tour leader. A number of times he disappeared from my side saying, "I have to help Flavia."

Manny's identification with the travel group and his presumed responsibility toward it was analogous to the situation I saw developing between Manny and Whirlpool. Both were abnormal.

His quickly established sense of identification with the tour group seemed to override his memory of why we were there, specifically for the New Year's Eve Afro–Brazilian ceremonials honoring the sea-goddess, Yemanja, on Copacabana beach.

On December 31, Flavia was instructing us where we should

all meet to go together to the bleachers, which were strategi-
cally positioned to view the midnight fireworks display as well
as to avoid the very sights Manny and I had come to see. Already, the megaphoned voices of Christian fundamentalists
could be heard up and down Copacabana urging the faithful to
ignore the Afro–Brazilian candomblé rituals, which began at
dusk.

Tugging Manny away from the bleachers—away from Flavia
and away from the tour group—took all my wits. We had come
for the rituals and would have seen nothing of them had we not
freed ourselves of our conservative companions in order to roam
the length and breadth of Copacabana.

Manny is glad my will prevailed that evening. I have frequently heard him tell people about that numinous experience.

Candomblé priests and priestesses, dressed in white, led
circles of devotees in trance-dances. Samba rhythms were everywhere, because this was the true beginning of Carnaval.
Worshipers of all colors and stations in life constructed altars in
the sand, either by building up or by burrowing down. Delightful little sand tables were set with roses, champagne, and cigarettes. A multitude of people walked far enough into the water
to place little boats on the waves in hopes these would make
their way into the bosom of the sea goddess, who would then
grant their wish.

The midnight fireworks, which could be seen from anywhere, not just the bleachers, were the most glorious I ever experienced, or could even imagine. Whereas many things in Brazil
"don't quite work," this—and Carnaval—are two that do. As
we stood enraptured by the cascading display coming off the
high-rise at the north end of the beach, rockets flared behind us.
Almost simultaneously, more flares burst from boats stationed
for that purpose out at sea. Others exploded directly overhead.
This grand-scale outdoor theater was participatory, a happen-

ing. The best part was simply being in the crowd of wall-to-wall people, each so gracefully deft of foot and body that there was still, always, space to maneuver.

###

The Batemans returned, and word was out that Fran needed a maid. Everyone of any means at all in Brazil has at least one maid. I came to view this as a necessity when I lived in Brazil the first time in a household with four children. Even living in a smaller unit, I saw it as a social responsibility, as a way to put some money in the hands of a person who desperately needed it. So I hired Idalice, an attractive, intelligent, dependable woman about thirty years old, to come in on Tuesdays and Thursdays. I paid and fed her well, and sympathized with her complaints about the employer for whom she worked the other days. Still, I could tell she hated me for my wealth, leisure, and general uselessness. I did not blame her. Life was as unfair as she thought it to be. Before long, I couldn't stand having her around two days a week and cut her down to Tuesdays only, even though I paid her just as much. Still, she resented me. Oh, well.

When Fran needed a maid, she, like me in 1969, had no idea of how to deal with that aspect of Brazilian culture. Neither Olga nor Marcus wanted any direct involvement in the project, which was almost guaranteed to get messy somewhere along the way. I had been through it in 1969 and realized, as they did, that painful experience is the only training available to the novice employer. They had participated in sending out the word, but that was as far as their good judgment let them go.

What was Fran to do, alone in her apartment one afternoon, when Maria, the sister of a driver for another family in the Batemans' building, showed up at her door babbling in Portuguese? She frantically called the Whirlpool office for help. What could Sandra do? Her job was at her desk and her job description did not include interviewing maids for the boss's wife.

Sandra frantically called me, suggesting I go immediately to *Senhora* Bateman's apartment to interview the prospective maid for her.

I give Fran credit for understanding it was not my responsibility and for not calling me directly. She may have been constrained because she found my bicultural competence threatening and irksome to her position as "First Lady." We experienced quite a bit of this ambivalence—"I need your help but I hate having to ask for your help"—up until the time our relationship ended.

Sam was in a similar but much deeper dependency on Manny's bicultural expertise. However, this did not bother Sam: it was the very reason he required Manny's services in Brazil.

That I had a B.A. degree in human and animal behavior and an M.A. in educational psychology did not help. I could analyze the situation, although not dispassionately because I was a participant in it. I had little power to alter the structure within which the abuses to my dignity were institutionalized. Oh, if only there had been *real* psychologists in the Human Resources division, not just "industrial" ones. They could have identified Fran's and my difficulties as structural. Much of our dyadic thrashing could have been prevented.

I helped Fran with the interview, although I didn't jump in response to the summons. Sandra called Fran, who put Maria on the phone so Sandra could instruct her, in Portuguese, to return the next morning at ten o'clock, at which time *Senhora* Von Koenig would be present. Maria was hired. As months wore on, she and Fran did not get along too well. But then, neither did Idalice and I.

One particular Catch 22 episode in my relationship with Fran followed a Newcomer's lunch. Fran suggested—and her groupies and I, in that order, agreed—it would be fun, maybe even profitable, to go to a sale in the exclusive Chacara Flor district. The sale was offered by Americans who were returning to the United States. Such sales meant the availability of desirable items not for sale in Brazilian stores, even in the best of times.

I was amazed at Fran's shopping expertise, how focused she was as she scanned the hunting grounds before zeroing in on her targets. With Cindy and Diane as allies, Fran soon had accumulated so many trophies they overflowed the capacities of the trunk. Considering the circumstances, I confined my purchases to items I could hold on my lap.

Heaters for sale brought back memories of the uncomfortably cold winters in Brazil during 1969–1971. With no central heating, we had been grateful for the self-contained gas heaters—at that time produced by Brastemp—we had spread about the house. Manny had asked me to be on the alert for purchasable heaters, for both the Batemans and us.

I had discussed this with Fran who, in turn, discussed it with Cindy. Cindy, whose opinion soon came to far outweigh mine, scoffed, telling Fran São Paulo wasn't cold at all. Well, perhaps it hadn't been during the one winter Cindy had been there. I hoped her judgment, based on a favorable one-season experience, accurately predicted the weather to come.

In an irony of ironies, Cindy came rushing to me from another room to advise me she had seen six top-quality electric radiant heaters I could buy if I was interested.

She did not similarly advise Fran because Fran, due to Cindy's own comments, saw no need for them. My mission, in collaboration with Manny, was to supply both households, not just ours. Should I? Could I force heaters on Fran (in the Whirlpool family spirit of being in the same lifeboat) in the very presence of Cindy, the force opposed to their need? Cindy, apparently, thought I should have heaters if I felt I must, but she would have been grievously offended if Fran had gone along with the purchase of heaters for the Bateman abode.

If I bought heaters, even for us alone, how would I get them home in a car already filled with Marcus, Fran, Cindy, Diane, me, and a trunkload of kitchen gadgets? Fran's purchases reached a point where she was mumbling about sending Marcus back for a second load. I could have piggybacked on that, but how? She was the commandant in charge of the expedition. What kind of attitude and comments could I have expected about transporting heaters that she thought, thanks to Cindy, were a silly idea anyway?

I thanked Cindy for the information but let it go. Both households managed without heaters for the duration. Fran, anyway, did not stay for Brazil's coldest period, June to August. The closest she ever came to admitting that Manny and I might have "known something" on this issue, was to say, "I have to admit, Roz, that electric blanket you insisted we bring felt pretty good." For us, heaters also would have felt good. Manny and Sam had both winter heat and summer air conditioning at the office, but our homes did not.

I recall how Princess Grace had been ridiculed by the American public, and by me along with them, for taking with her to Monaco whole planeloads of American merchandise that she could not live without. Most Americans living in Brazil have that same mentality—or they quickly develop it. Not until a friend told me she was still—two years after returning home from Brazil—living on the supply of U.S.-purchased lingerie she had desperately hoarded in Brazil, did I realize that after four years, I was still drawing on my similarly acquired stash of pantyhose.

During the period from 1969 to 1971, we had met our expatriate needs through the goodwill of John Eser, Frank Livingston, and Julio Caicedo acting as carriers. And we had attended sales of the Chacara Flor variety. For the 1986 assignment, which overall was so odious we fought every-which-way to avoid it, we had thought that one of its few favorable features would be an open supply-line to the States. After all, most of the men who would be making frequent trips between the States and São Paulo had been working directly with Manny for many years. They and their wives were our friends. Surely they would be happy to deliver whatever items we had Jeff buy and bring to the Whirlpool office.

In reality, they would have been glad to perform this favor for us, but Sam, who was the boss, imposed so many lists on them from Fran, that each time they made the trip from the States, they were loaded with full shopping bags for the boss's wife. We backed off, said nothing, and did without.

About mid-February 1987, the Batemans' daughter, Lisa, came for a visit. Fran was so excited she could talk of nothing else for weeks preceding the visit. I told her Manny and I wanted to meet Lisa and to assist in entertaining, but realizing Fran would have many things to show her, we wanted to avoid being preemptive. My unique contribution would be to make plans to do totally without use of the car while Lisa was there so Fran could have it always at her disposal. Fran said she appreciated that.

As they had no plans set for Friday, the day after Lisa's arrival, I told Fran I would be at home the entire day, and they should drop in, at their convenience, for tea.

All day Friday passed without a word from them until 5:30, when Fran called. She was sorry they hadn't stopped by, she said, and then catalogued for me, with almost manic delight, all their day's activities, including having found American-style doughnuts they could take to other American friends the next day. They had started a game of Scrabble when, having forgotten me all day, she suddenly remembered. I didn't know what to say.

Something similar occurred at a later time at Nancy Mason's first Newcomer's Club coffee. Fran ran off for a minute to do something, telling Nancy she'd be right back to join her. The next day she called Nancy to say, "I'm so sorry, but I just forgot all about you."

The week of Lisa's visit passed with both Marcus and Olga giving me strange looks, questioning why I had not yet met Lisa. This embarrassed me, because I didn't understand why, either. Fran invited me to join them for a trip to the zoo on Wednesday but then changed her plans to something that did not include me.

On the last day of Lisa's visit, Fran called to tell me what a good time they'd been having all week. I bit the bullet and said, "Look, whatever else you have planned, be advised that, once again, I will be at home the entire day, prepared to serve tea."

She assured me they would come. Morning and afternoon both passed with tea service set to go at a moment's notice and me in a transcendental state seated on the balcony staring off into space. At 5:10 they called. At 5:30, they came. Could it have been more under the wire? I was treated to a running account of how they had spent their exciting day. This time, at least, it was in person.

At 6:30, Manny walked in, hardly knowing how to deal with this odd situation. At 6:40, the phone rang. It was Sam, for whom no note had been left, trying to find his wife and daughter. He, too, had to have recognized that for the "Second Lady"—me—the week had been strange.

###

Having experienced the Afro–Brazilian New Year's Eve in Rio, Manny and I were excited to learn that Carnaval had grown since our 1970 acquaintance with it to become a major event in São Paulo as well as in Rio. Carnaval was a festival also grounded in the religion practiced by the Yoruba people of Nigeria. At Olga's invitation, I was able to attend an extremely informative February lecture on the hows and whys of Carnaval, which ran that year from February 28 into the morning of Ash Wednesday, March 4.

As in Rio, São Paulo tickets for the grandstands were expensive and limited. Still believing cultural assistance was part of our duty to the Batemans, we invited them to go with us for one of those all-through-the-night experiences. To become better guides to the event, Manny and I participated in an earlier all-night, as well.

During that night, in the bleachers among multicolored natives enthusiastically samba-twisting to the pulsing drums, we alternated between sitting and standing to grasp the vibrating pipe handrail that additionally transmitted through our bodies the throbbing rhythms of the parading dancers. We were unable to last beyond two A.M.; nonetheless, the experience was extraordinary.

Fran and Sam were good sports in that they were willing to go at all. I thought they showed faith in us by letting us be their guides. In retrospect, I think it was naïveté, not faith. I think they did not know they needed to be guided, shielded or protected as they entered into this deeply other-culture reality. They wore their own reality and acted totally themselves, as though they were going to a grandstand event at the Berrien County Fair. Sometimes that's all it takes to be an Ugly American.

They did nothing wrong, but, at the same time, they did nothing right. We were in the stands for less than an hour when the uniformed courtesy attendant, a refined and educated young Brazilian woman, came to us, iron fist in velvet glove, to escort us to another section "where we would be more comfortable."

She meant "where we would be safer." On the night Manny and I had been there alone, we had blended in. With the

Batemans, we all became intruders—by dress, postures and body language indicating lack of empathy and involvement with the true spirit of Brazil manifest in Carnaval. The attendant noted those around us were becoming restless, even agitated, by our presence.

I remained so absorbed in the blend of the earlier night's experience that I was partially unaware how Manny's and my chameleon properties were overpowered by the contradictory signals given off by the Batemans. We, too, wore their color.

It is a national characteristic of Brazilians to be soothsaying diplomats, but I lost my ability to blend and couldn't go along with the attendant's polite charade. I knew precisely why we were being moved, and some demon within me—uglier than any Ugly American—wanted it out in the open. As she pursued with grace her theme that "we would be more comfortable," I pointed out the stand to which we had been taken lacked the refreshment facilities of the other. She lost neither composure nor time in replying, "We will send you a waiter."

I persisted. What I suppose I wanted, irrationally and unrealistically, was for her to finally say, "Look, the appearance and behavior of your two friends here made it obvious to those who observe Carnaval as a religious tradition that you are all just tourists contaminating their devotions. I am placing you in a section where the people don't care much and won't turn on you." But of course, she did not see me in the holy and holier-than-thou light in which I saw myself.

Sam spoke up, changing the subject. The relieved attendant responded to him, adding, "Thank you. You are a good psychologist." And he was. I blew it that time.

Again, we lasted until about two A.M.—a shame, because being there when units are still parading as dawn breaks, which we managed to do in Rio the following year, is the peak of each twenty-four-hour cycle. Fairly sure in advance we wouldn't make it, we followed our preset schedule of doing what we understood society-level Brazilians do. We went to a fancy place for breakfast. Our choice, the restaurant in the lobby of the Maksoud Hotel where we had all lived the first week of September, was not a good choice. The atmosphere there was almost American, with no Carnaval fervor whatever. Fran and Sam were gracious good sports about the whole evening. I was the one out of step for even thinking immersion into such an intense Brazilian tradition was something the four of us could successfully accomplish.

Around this time, Manny was seeing a doctor about aches and pains. I marveled that the Brazilian doctor, like the ones at the Mayo Clinic, did not ask him whether he drank too much. But then, what is "too much," if stress is the cause and alcohol relieves the symptoms? Short of being told to abstain from alcohol, he was advised to do sensible things I could totally support and encourage. Each day rather than take the elevator, he was to climb the seven flights of stairs to our apartment and, again, the seven flights to his office. The doctor said even that much exercise would help him tremendously.

He followed this regimen for less than two weeks. I watched, helpless, as even his exercise in the pool deteriorated from a few yards of swimming to standing still and splashing a little. He wouldn't listen to my "nagging."

I introduced Manny to the world of Embu, the suburban artists' colony where I had gone frequently with Olga in the name of household decor. Hilly, twisting streets, unexpected eateries, every alley and plaza an art fair—Manny enjoyed it. He was unpleasant about those trips only when I scheduled them in a way that did not include a huge lunch or huge dinner with the attendant drinking.

In trying not to be an enabler, I quit buying beer, wine, and scotch. I put Manny through the physical experience of buying his own, but his anger at this arrangement, when he saw the frequently short supply, cowed me into returning to the old system. His wrath, I believe, had something to do with his questioning what else I had to do with my time but supply his needs.

Sam Bateman made a sudden trip to the States in March, leaving his wife in our care. He did not offer to take anything up for us or to bring anything back. I found it astounding that Sam, living as he did with Fran's never-ending needs, was blind to the fact that we, who were in precisely the same boat, had similar needs that were in no way being met.

One difference between the Von Koenigs and the Batemans was how our mail was being handled. Because our son Jeff and his family had a clear understanding of what we considered important, they removed the chaff before taking our mail to the Whirlpool International Division to be sent on to us. However, the Batemans' mail was being forwarded directly to Whirlpool in St. Joseph–Benton Harbor, where the International Division secretary, not knowing what the Batemans did or didn't want and mindful of Sam's high rank in the company, forwarded everything that came for them. All mail went by twenty-four-hour service pouch, because regular mail was both undependable and expensive. The Batemans soon realized that receiving the Sears catalog that way was a bit much. They and Manny, as office manager, worked out a sorting process whereby all items over a certain size would be sent regular U.S.–Brazilian surface mail, under the theory that if the mail didn't make it, nothing much was lost.

Sam and Manny gave the head office secretary instructions to follow that policy with our mail, too—without consulting me. I blew! Had Manny forgotten our mail was already being screened by a son intimately familiar with our priorities? No, he had not forgotten, he said, but how could he insist that policy for us be different from the one Sam was applying to himself?

Read my lips, I told him. "Because, even with the new policy Sam is applying to himself, their mail will still contain some junk, whereas ours has been and will still be as clean as a whistle." Before Manny got all our mail back on the pouch track, an $8^{1}/_{2}$" x 11" catalog of African art, carefully hand-constructed by our friend Barbara Paxson, had been diverted to the junk route and arrived a full month after I had expected to receive it. I never knew what else might have been sent that way and possibly lost, because the home office kept no records.

Issues of the *Brazil Herald* and the *International Herald*, subscribed to by the office, were read first there, then by Fran, then me. Sam had these third-hand copies with him on the morning run to the office, and Marcus got them to me during the course of the day.

One morning at 9:30 as Marcus came by to drop off newspapers, he went on to Fran's. At 9:45 he was back, explaining that the maid, Maria, had asked for a salary advance. Fran had only partially understood what Maria was talking about and asked Marcus, who understood little English, to interpret. He explained to me what Maria wanted and pleaded with me to call Fran to make sure she understood. Marcus did not want to be involved. Neither did I, but I had to do it.

Friday mornings we shopped for food at the open market, the *feira*. It was colorful and exciting, the kind of scene Hollywood puts in movies, but Fran didn't like it. After she hired Maria, Fran stayed home Friday mornings but invited me to go with "her" driver and her maid to the *feira*. I tried that once, but the personnel dynamics overwhelmed me. Both Maria and Marcus had seen how Fran treated me, and tended to look down on me with the same disdain. After all, everyone deemed me subservient to my husband's boss's wife. Suddenly I was supposed to manage two servants who acted as though I were subservient to them, as well, because they worked primarily for the superior woman. Having been a maid myself, I knew from both ends of the car—the front with the employees and the back as the chauffeured employer—that Maria's manner was glaringly inappropriate. Instead of being deferent and inclusive, she engaged Marcus in loud, lively conversation, the content of which made clear that she was unmindful of my presence.

I handled successive Friday mornings by staying home. I didn't get to the *feira* again until months later, when I had my own car.

Fran used the Newcomer's Club as a setting in which to be cliquish. She and her two best friends, also wives of CEOs, clustered into a tightly knit unit. I was welcome in it to the extent that I stayed in my place, which called for a bit more genuflecting than I found comfortable.

The day we lunched in a Japanese restaurant somewhere on Avenida Paulista, I excused myself from the group for a little while to pursue my purpose for attending such events, which was to meet some of the world's most interesting people. I settled opposite a softly beautiful young woman who, in America, would be called black. I thought she might be from somewhere in Africa or some exotic island republic. As it turned out, she was from the United States. We liked each other, exchanged phone numbers, and later saw each other a few times.

When I rejoined Fran and her friends for light shopping, Fran asked, "And how did you get on with the little colored girl?" Ignoring her tone, I replied matter-of-factly, "Her husband is with the French Consulate, and they keep a house outside Paris."

Use of the car was one of the numerous things that tied the home to the office, intertwining the two households. Another way was the manner in which we supplied our households with local currency. Because of rampant inflation, it was imprudent to have more salary paid into a Brazilian account than was actually going to be used. The dollars were converted into cruzados through a procedure at the office that involved covert use of the black market.

This meant that periodically Manny took my checkbook to the office for replenishing, and Sandra took over the balancing of my personal accounts. It was the most practical way, but it had the effect of stripping me of a very intimate area of responsibility and of exposing my spending habits to the staff.

The office and home were at times indistinguishably intermingled, with Manny the manager who handled affairs for both. Sometimes supplying the Batemans with their cruzados, a function of the office, took place in the car, the garage, the elevator, wherever, and sometimes involved Manny's advancing money from his own pocket to be recouped at the office the next day. Sometimes the money for Fran came out of my pocket, also to be recouped by Manny at the office the next day.

Against that backdrop, Fran set me up for further humiliation: when I was at lunch with her and two of her friends one day, she handed me a wad of counted-out cruzados, saying, "Now, that makes us even, doesn't it?"

Thinking of the several thousand still outstanding, I had to reply, "Well, no it doesn't," and I mentioned the figure.

Fran laughed broadly and said loudly, "Oh, I gave that to Manny the other morning. Doesn't he tell you anything?"

I was, as she anticipated, embarrassed. Not because my husband didn't tell me anything, but because she made it appear he didn't.

Manny made his first business trip back to the home office in Benton Harbor on April 13, 1987, after I had been in São Paulo for a little more than four months. He had not made such trips during our first assignment to Brazil, which I now believe was because John Eser did not think dependents should be left to fend for themselves on foreign soil. A good idea if there ever was one.

Manny's trip seemed normal to me at the time. I was not alone. Sam and Fran lived just across the street and would be looking out for me. In Manny's absence, they assumed an almost real sense of family responsibility for me, calling me at least once a day, inviting me over for a Fran-cooked dinner one evening, and taking me out for pizza another time.

With Manny still gone, the Batemans had a dinner party for friends on Friday, April 17, the eve of my birthday. The next morning Fran called to tell me about how Sam had slipped on a rug at their party and been taken to the hospital emergency room for treatment of a shoulder injury. Through *Whirlpool do Brasil,* we had all been pre-registered at the city's two best hospitals, and we had test-driven the routes from our homes to each of them. His guests took Sam to one of these. Even with such a minor injury and even though it was treated at the best hospital, Sam's succinct report was: "Don't get sick in Brazil."

In spite of Sam's accident and Manny's absence, the Batemans were going ahead with their weekend plan to go out of town. If anything happened to me, I'd simply have to take care of myself. I thought, "Happy Birthday to you, too, and I'll be extra careful not to slip on a rug."

Manny and I had agreed he should spend Saturday, the eighteenth, my birthday, with our kids and grandchildren rather than hurrying back to be with me. Manny called me Saturday from our house where the family had gathered, and I had a chance to talk to each one. It was wonderful to be lovingly remembered by so many dear people. At the same time, I was haunted with loneliness in my still, dark, cold São Paulo apartment, feeling like the only child not invited to a party.

Sunday morning—it happened to be Easter—I drove to the airport to pick up Manny. He brought back a VCR and other littler things I had asked for, but he was tired and brusque. He did not express any joy at reunion, told me no more family stories than had been shared on the phone the day before, and showed no personal tenderness.

His entire self-centered focus was on resting up for the important work he had to do the next day. I could take little joy in his homecoming other than the rather sick security that things were back to normal. If my own attitude seemed equally self-centered, it was because so little fire glowed within me in support of the great work of the Whirlpool Corporation. The company already had drained me of more than I had been freely willing to give.

A Brazilian government order severely restricted, if not entirely prohibited, the import of foreign-made computers. Problems inherent in the Brazilians' developing the technology for themselves, plus the price freeze, meant computers were no more available than cars. The wait was lengthy, but finally in May 1987 we acquired two identical computers, one for the office and one for me, as had been promised by Sam.

Sam had never used a computer, wasn't quite sure what it was good for, and didn't want Manny wasting his office time on it, beyond setting Sandra up to use it. This technological lag of Sam's had gone undetected in the Benton Harbor setting where his usefulness to the company was based on his use of data rather than on his assembling it. But in Brazil, after a full day at the office, Manny would bring home his disks to do work for Sam, for the office, and for Whirlpool—work that had to be done, but which he was not allowed to do at the office, because his boss did not understand the place of computer technology in the 1987 international business world.

I understood Manny's dilemma: as a good company man, he could do little else. I also understood that my privacy, my home life, my marriage, were being unreasonably impinged upon. Because I had no other social companion, Manny's companionship was lost to me on the many evenings that he worked long hours on the computer. Moreover, when Manny took over the computer and my study, he deprived me of their use and of productive ways in which I might have spent those lonely hours. Added to my lonely days, those dreary evenings with my over-worked husband did much to increase the ennui into which I already had drifted.

The office computer led a life more cushy than my computer did. It resided in a climate-controlled environment optimal for its function. Mine experienced all the vicissitudes of tempera-ture and humidity, as well as suffering from the dust that blew through our open windows. Every few months it went into dys-function, with each descent taking out varying amounts of my hard-written prose.

I have nothing but praise for Manny's patience with both Sam and me during this computer-crisis phase. He drew gener-ously on the good will he had earned and stored up with a col-league from the 1969–1971 years who was then the computer manager for a large enterprise. Through the graciousness of this friend and through Manny's perseverance, skilled computer technicians sat at my desk many times to study the immediate problem. Usually the solution was to replace a drive.

Manny soon decided that whenever my computer went down, switching it for the one in the office was the simplest thing to do. Repair people responded more quickly to an office call because the problem seemed more urgent.

When the computer was functioning at all, Manny did not seem to have the problems with his spread program that I was having with the Brazilian-supplied version of my word process-ing program. We did not rule out the possibility that something in the Brazilian translation of the program was contributing to the computer's trauma.

By the time our son Doug was expected to visit in December 1987, so many of my disks had deteriorated into gibberish that we asked him to bring his copy of the American original. He installed it. We'll never know how well it might have worked in the long run because, one day shortly after Doug's departure, while Manny and I were both at the computer, in less than centered mentalities, we inadvertently executed a function that destroyed Doug's input.

We had not the strength to request the program disks, arrange for them to be delivered to us, and insult the patriotism of a Brazilian technician by asking him or her to reinstall the American program. We gave up.

My boredom evolved into catatonia. One evening when Manny came home, I was sitting on our beautifully textured handcrafted couch staring blankly through the sliding glass doors at our charmingly furnished little terrace.

He asked, "What did you do today?"

I looked up and said, "Nothing."

"Nothing?"

I replied as blankly as before, "Why? Was there something I was supposed to do?"

There was nothing I was supposed to do. Except to be quiet and not cause trouble. To be a Stepford wife. It is even easier to be a robotic wife in Brazil than it might be in Stepford. Why, then, my husband must have wondered, couldn't I do it?

Manny's chameleon-like shift into the upper-class Brazilian mind set became even more evident when I purchased a sewing machine. Brazilian "ladies" do not sew. Each household has a *costureira,* or seamstress, on call. Olga, graduate of an American university and versed in the ways of Americans, had not thought it strange when I asked her to help me purchase a sewing machine, even though she herself had a *costureira.*

Manny stroked his chin and asked, "Why did you get a sewing machine?"

This was such an unusual and unexpected question that I

turned to him as I would to a not-too-bright child and answered: "Because I have sewed ever since I was twelve years old, because a sewing machine was the first piece of furniture we bought after getting married, because I have always had one and even had one here in Brazil the first time around, and because I need one, if not for necessary articles, then at least because I am comforted when I sew."

He was upset that I was behaving outside of socially correct boundaries. Fran did not sew.

Another change was in our custom of cutting my hair. For many years, Manny had been trimming my hair in the back, and I cut the front myself. Each such grooming had been the occasion for a little petting and closeness, much the same as that engaged in by primates when they groom each other. No more. When I set up the chairs in the utility area off the kitchen and announced that all was ready, Manny came and mechanically performed the brief ritual, barely touching me, and left.

###

On Sunday, May 10, the Whirlpool corporate jet was scheduled to arrive bearing six people: the newly elected CEO David Whitwam, and his wife, Barbara; the corporation treasurer Jim Samartini, and his wife, Irene; and the vice president of the International Division Larry Kremer, and his wife, Diane.

Fran started mapping daily itineraries for the women. Practicing benign exclusion by not conferring with me in any way, she moved in the direction of aggressive exclusion by informing me of her plans for the first day: "There won't be room in the car for you, Roz, but maybe you could join us for lunch."

Manny was nervous because he wasn't being consulted either. By the Wednesday prior to the guests' Sunday arrival, he had been given no information at the office.

I called Fran, who said, "Oh, don't you have a schedule? I'll tell Sam to be sure to give Manny one." It made us wonder who was second in command at *Whirlpool do Brasil,* Manny or Fran. Manny was then given a schedule.

Full responsibility for planning the social schedule was assumed by Mike Etchenique, president of Brasmotor, a holding company similar in function to *Whirlpool do Brasil,* and chairman of the boards of Brastemp, Consul, and Embraco. The schedule did not affect Manny's working days, because he was expected to be closeted with Jim Samartini anyway. Neither of them was going to Joinville, where Consul and Embraco are located, when the other men went there later in the week.

The schedule included evening involvements for both of us and daytime responsibilities for me. I was included only in the two days of sightseeing in São Paulo. Mike made sure "there was room for me in the car" by placing a van, rather than a car, at our disposal. Mike, who knew me and my abilities well, needed my services, because those would be difficult bilingual days in heavy city traffic, with cultures at cross-purposes. We would also be tailed by security guards, who would place more emphasis on the fact that, with so much top brass aboard, we were in danger.

With us would be Ruth Bertola, wife of the president of Embraco. Even though I had known Ruth since 1969 and had entertained her in St. Joseph as she had previously entertained us in Brazil, she had not, during the period from September 1986 through April 1987, called either the Batemans or us. Manny knew, but I learned only later, this was probably because her husband, Rudolpho, had hoped to become president of Brastemp, rather than of Embraco. When the politics of business are disharmonious, social noses get out of joint. Maria Angelica Bonamico, wife of the man who did become president of Brastemp, was also scheduled to be with us, but "had a headache," no doubt for the good reason that Ruth would be aboard.

Apparently Diane Kremer had not been briefed nor done any preparatory homework. As we shopped at a sportswear store, she dumped each selection she made on Ruth Bertola, saying brusquely, "Here, hold this." Only later did Diane pull me aside, point to Ruth, and ask me, "Who is that woman, anyway?.".

My explanation included the word Embraco, but Diane seemed not to have heard of it, so I put it this way: "Her husband was featured in *Fortune* magazine a few months ago."

Helen Etchenique was returning from a six-week trip to China and could not join us until Tuesday. At the Jocuei Club where we all had lunch, I found myself alone with Helen and Ruth in the ladies' room. Helen asked Ruth in Portuguese where she had taken everyone for lunch the day before. "Oh, you could have done better than that!" she admonished. "Here, let me fix your hair in back; it looks terrible." If I hadn't known already, this exchange would have clarified that Helen's husband outranked Ruth's, just as my being the one for whom there had initially been no room in the car clarified that my husband was outranked by Fran's.

Of all the women, American or Brazilian, who were involved in the São Paulo events, I was the only one excluded from the part that I felt would have been a just reward for my services. My name was not on the list for the excursion by corporate jet to Joinville. There, as the men worked, the women would go on to visit one of the world's greatest wonders, the Falls of Iguaçu.

Neither Manny nor Jim Samartini was going, but Irene was. Mike was not going, but Helen was. Manny empathized with my outrage but said he could do nothing about it. As office manager and coordinator of almost everything else, he was over his head in work. Besides, I think he had by that time essentially quit defending either himself or me. The daily opposition was too overwhelming, and resistance to it so energy draining.

If Manny wouldn't stand up for me, I'd do it myself. I asked him to make an appointment for me to see Sam. I went in the next morning.

Sam protested that he had no control over Mike's social arrangements. I pointed out to him the obvious: there were no social arrangements; it was all business. He shouldn't expect me to believe he had no control over that, or we might as well have all gone home.

I left Sam with a bottom line. Either a new list came out the next day including me in everything or they could jolly well go to Joinville and discover when they got back that I had returned to the States. I didn't intend to be a Cinderella who didn't get to the ball.

During our discussion Sam said, "We assume the wives always agree with their husbands." I told him this was quite an assumption, and it had nothing to do with the relationship Manny and I had with each other.

Somewhere along the way, he said, "Roz, you're a very private person." He said it judgmentally, making it sound as though something were wrong in being that kind of a person. I was being declared wanting in qualifications for some kind of hypothetical job with Whirlpool that I didn't know I had, as though I had applied for it, wanted it, and accepted it under false pretenses. Nothing was further from the truth. Throughout all of 1986, my queasy premonitions about such scenes had contributed to my not wanting to come to Brazil at all.

I told Sam the problem was one of many that had been accumulating. I pointed out that the problem with the following week's schedule was one that had to be dealt with and resolved right then, but I wanted to talk with him about other problems I had with him and Fran before he left for the States in a few weeks.

Although I won inclusion at that particular ball, I later lost practically everything that mattered, including my husband.

###

The evening the Whitwams and others arrived, the Batemans hosted cocktails at their condo, with Manny and me assisting. I had no problem with that. Fran had even acted on my suggestion to serve caviar appetizers.

Manny had cautioned me, "These are social events. I don't want you trying to discuss your problems." What a caveat! David Whitwam did give me an opening by asking me how things were going. I hesitated too long, remembering that I had been admonished. I just said something polite.

Even without Manny's prohibition, I think I would not have voiced my woes to David Whitwam. I was intensely aware that he was the very man who had spirited me into my situation, against my wishes and without talking directly to me about the transfer. He, above Manny and Sam, was the one who had initiated the deteriorating course of my life. I felt it deep in my gut.

Later when the emperor and his court had gone back to the States and I groused about not having had an opportunity for consultation, Manny—showing the first clear signs of corporate Machiavellianism—said, disingenuously, "Why didn't you bring it up when you had the chance?"

After cocktails at the Batemans', we dined at the Ca' d'Oro. Dave Whitwam had Helen Etchenique on his right, and he insisted I be seated on his left, as though, I thought, Sam had said something to him about my complaints and he was trying to smooth things over. But he turned all his attention to Helen. With Sam on my left, you can believe conversation was scant. I did not feel noticeably better about anything.

A few days later, the Whirlpool "party" moved to Joinville via the company plane and was checked into the leading hotel. I roomed with Irene Samartini. The men went directly to the factory offices. Yvonne Freitag, whose husband, Ivens, was president of Consul, took the ladies to lunch. We were entertained that evening at the Freitags' home.

Manny and I had a secret in common with the Freitags. Like them, we maintained our close friendships with the Esers, who, in retirement, had moved to Stuttgart, Germany. John was a pariah whose name was never mentioned publicly. Larry Kremer operated as differently as he could from how John had operated.

Thursday morning was business as usual for the men. The women boarded the jet in anticipation of flying to Iguaçu. But the clouds simply would not clear away; the trip was not to be. The hours spent on the plane waiting gave me an opportunity to watch corporate wives throw their husbands' weight around.

Fran accosted the pilot, in full hearing and view of all us passengers, to inform him that the "cleanliness of the toilet was simply way below standard." She added, "Would you please get it cleaned up immediately?"

On the other hand, I found it totally appropriate for Barbara Whitwam to announce, after a morning of waiting, her decision for us to give up, as waiting longer made no sense. Each incident was a not-so-subtle example of how corporate wives have rank just as if they worked for the company.

During the Whitwam-Samartini-Kremer visit, much was made of poor Fran's loneliness and unhappiness in Brazil. This, even though she and Sam had been home for two weeks for the holidays after only ten weeks in Brazil and even though their daughter had come to visit in February. When the group left on the seventeenth to spend the summer in St. Joseph, Fran would return with them.

The Samartinis had planned to fly out Friday morning, so Irene was not included in the other women's last-day plans. But their flight was canceled and Irene came back from the airport to join Fran, Barb, Diane, and me in the lobby of the Maksoud

Hotel. I can still hardly believe what happened next.

Fran announced it was just too bad for Irene. There wouldn't be room for her in the car. I was startled to hear the very phrase that had applied to me a few weeks earlier being directed at the wife of the corporation's treasurer. Nevertheless, Diane quickly agreed with Fran that Irene's problem was her own. How could we be expected to make such a last-minute accommodation?

Before the matter went any further, I called Fran aside. I was sure we could rent an extra car and driver for the day from the line of vehicles stationed across the street. Manny had provided me with a big wad of money for emergency use.

Fran agreed with my suggestion that I find Marcus and have him help arrange it. Within twenty minutes, we were off for the *feira* at the Pacembu Stadium, Irene and I in one car, the others with Marcus, all followed by a cadre of security guards. They had been contracted according to Whirlpool insurance requirements, and our instructions were to spread out whenever we were out in the open, not to stay hunkered together in a tight package easy to attack. Manny had emphasized these precautions to me. Even though Fran pooh-poohed the precautions, I guided Irene's and my path so we separated from theirs. I was startled that the wife of the president of *Whirlpool do Brasil* treated so lightly the judicious suggestions of the vice president— Manny.

We shopped at a gem and jewelry store across from the Ediﬁçia Italia. We were treated to the spectacle of police helicopters scanning the area trying to apprehend robbers who had just held up a bank.

As we lunched in the Restaurant Manhattan's garden court, one of the visitors raised a typical first-timer question, "What is it like to have a maid?" The question was directed primarily to Fran. I, too, was curious to see what she would say. When she got to the part about English-speaking expatriates agreeing to hold the line on the demands for salary increases made by the maids, I had to speak up. I would have liked to remain silent, but to do so would have implied agreement with what she said. Even though Fran was right in a way, I had to object and state my sympathy for maids, drivers, factory workers, and all of the other exploited, undervalued people in Brazil. It can be argued that foreigners have no right to upset the local way of life by paying domestics excessively more than the going rate. This makes it difficult for Brazilian householders to maintain staffs they can afford. Still, I spoke up to counter the impression that we, who lived here in such wasteful lavishness, were being taken advantage of by the maids.

An earlier incident at the Joinville Hotel is something of a case in point. We all had our doors open and were scurrying back and forth as we packed for departure. The Kremers had more to carry than their suitcases would hold and no one seemed to have an extra tote to lend them. A maid was called and asked if she could find a plastic bag for them. The look on her face indicated the request might be something of a problem, but she would see what she could do. She was told to hurry.

In the maid's absence, a solution was found, bags were shouldered, and everyone disappeared down the elevator. Not unreasonable behavior, under the circumstances, but what about the maid who was hurrying to comply with the foreigners' wishes?

I waited for the maid, who soon arrived with the bag. I thanked her and tipped her. Maids are people, too. I had been one. As a maid, I had experienced a few awkward moments, but never what maids in Brazil suffer with regularity. One of my Brazilian friends often spoke of her two live-in maids as "the one who can't read and the one who can, but isn't allowed to"—illiteracy making it easier to exploit them.

When the corporate jet left at dawn on May 17 with its six

visitors plus Fran, Manny and I were there to see them off. Manny remained at the airport to meet a commercial flight coming in with other Whirlpool personnel aboard, and Sam drove me home. As we coursed along the marginal of the city, we had the type of conversation Sam had been avoiding—about politically sensitive office matters that are not supposed to concern wives. When I brought up how different things were from "the Eser days," Sam, whose input had been disciplined and sparse up to that point, became engaged.

Sam told me about being in Frankfurt for an international trade fair with John Eser and others. John was so opposed to the strategies being plotted by the new team (Sparks, Whitwam, Wardeberg, and Bateman), that his protests bordered on violent. Sam's exact words were: "I thought we were going to have to kill him." He didn't mean this literally, of course, but "as the only way to calm him down." It was shortly thereafter that the chain of command was reordered, with John's being told he would report to George Wardeberg. Instead, John cleared out his desk and left.

Sam's final note on the subject was the most telling. Unprompted, he added, "Now it has turned out John was right."

This vindication of my own assessment gave me some strength to go on. But it would not be enough.

Between the time the Whitwam group departed and Sam was to leave, Manny and I smoothed our feathers and soothed our nerves by indulging in a weekend at the Falls of Iguaçu. The elusive Falls—they are so often able to cast a misty shroud over distant airports that few visiting Whirlpool personnel have ever been able to find a window of opportunity through which to fly.

At our take-off point, Guaruljos, on the edge of São Paulo, we met the young German couple who lived in the apartment adjacent to ours. They were round-tripping to Iguaçu on the same flights as ours. We explained we had taken a cab to the airport, afraid our car might be stolen from the parking lot. They laughed over having taken the chance themselves, and they offered to give us a ride back home—providing their car was still there when we returned. About a year later, we saw them right before they moved back to Germany. They were laughing hysterically: "It happened! Can you believe it? This close to going home, and our car was stolen!"

Manny tended to be standoffish with fellow Germans, especially those of the generation following ours. His explanation was, "You have to remember there were good reasons for my leaving Germany. If I wanted to be with them, I could have stayed." He was much more comfortable among our Jewish friends, of whom Trude was one. They liked him, too. I always thought this spoke well of him.

Manny was using alcohol to drug his emotions. Sometime during the first part of our stay in Brazil, Fran asked if Manny always drank so much. Yes, he did. In many ways drinking was part of his job. After years of doing business with the Australians, he drank more heavily than he had before. Since relocating in Brazil, he drank even more.

I told Manny about Fran's question, hoping his awareness of her observation would help him to see that my similar comments on that point, which he brushed aside, were valid. The result was that he drank less in the Batemans' presence for a few times and then resumed his overindulgence.

A few months later, when Fran was in the States and Sam, Manny, and I were out for dinner, Manny noticed Sam was drinking only water and joked, "I have to drink because I'm driving." I didn't think it was funny. Sam, the commander-in-chief, knew Manny drank more than most, but did nothing about it.

By the time the Batemans had been long gone, leaving Manny in sole charge for three months until the arrival of the new First Family in September of 1988, all my attempts to communicate with Manny seemed to be through some kind of alcoholic haze. I could get responses, but they were impersonal and disconnected.

I tried creative drama in attempts to get through to him—I mean really through—like the time he'd come back from China and found my note instead of me. After having gotten through to him that time, I had told him it was getting harder to reach him each time. I asked, "What am I going to do when I can't reach you any more?"

He was serious, concerned, and realistic in his answer, which was, "I don't know."

At one point in São Paulo, I was so desperate I calculatingly took one, then two, brand new wine goblets out of the cupboard and hurled them onto the tiled kitchen floor. He looked up from his newspaper for a moment, but that was all. I wasted no more wine glasses. Instead, I thought hard about what to do.

Somewhere underneath the thick hide he had developed, I knew some sense of reality still existed. One day he stared trance-like into space and muttered, "I hate to think what you're going to do to me when we get back to the States." It was reminiscent of his "I don't know" response to my question of how to reach him. Deep in his psyche he knew that by American standards (family, that is, not corporate), and even by German standards, he was being chauvinistic, domineering, undemocratic, and unfair. Within the corporation and within Brazilian culture, however, these were the only ways to treat me that fit in with everything else he had to do. Under the conditions of our existence in Brazil, he was seemingly incapable of reaching out to me. All his energy went into survival within the corporation. And deep in his psyche he knew, as I did, that I was putting up with his

altered behavior only because I had to. Once out of this con-
straining situation and back in the States, what would I do? I
hated to think of it myself.

During a period of loneliness earlier in the year, Fran acquired a Siamese kitten. During the approximately eight weeks
she would be gone, none of her friends could (or would?) care
for it. Knowing the finger would eventually point to me, I pretty
much at the last minute "volunteered" to house and feed Gigio
and clean its litter box.

The Batemans took to calling Gigio the Corporate Cat, and
via small-talk during intercontinental phone calls, his antics became as well known at the Administrative Center in Benton
Harbor as at the *Whirlpool do Brasil* office. Engineers, when they
came to Brazil, packed sacks of kitty litter in their luggage.

During the next few weeks, Sam made no move to discuss
with me all of the other problems I told him were lurking below
my surface. My adrenaline was not running high enough to
mount another strike. We invited Sam over for dinner the night
before he was to leave. Even then, he provided no opening for
serious, problem-solving communication. The next day Marcus
brought Gigio and all of his apparatus over to our place.

The two notes I received from Fran during the summer were
mostly about Gigio. She called me once from St. Joseph. Initially
I was thrilled; then that, too, turned out to be just a query about
Gigio.

Two cars, Santanas, identical except for color, had replaced
Whirlpool do Brasil's one rental vehicle. Santanas were the favorite target for thieves. We were in constant fear of their being
snatched. Whenever Sam and Manny had no need of Marcus
during the day, they made him available to me, insisting I use
him rather than drive myself. They didn't want him dawdling

around the office with nothing to do. But going out with a driver is a far cry from being on one's own. I felt I had to dress better, plan time better, be more formal, be pleasant, talk.

I had discovered a new low-calorie restaurant, so one day I invited Helen Etchenique and Maria Angelica Bonamico to join me for lunch. Sure, it was fun to see each of us driving up in her own chauffeured car. For me, it was a lark; for them, a way of life. About that time, I realized neither of them knew how to drive. "Being driven" was a right of the privileged, but I didn't care much for the loss of privacy. Chauffeurs, generally speaking, work for the man of the house. If called upon to do so, they report all his wife's movements. The pedestal is narrow.

One day when my own Marcus-imposed boundaries were grating on my nerves, I had him drop me at home, go for his own lunch and pick me up again two hours later. The minute he was gone, I jumped into my own car and drove a few miles to the nearest McDonald's. You and your chauffeur cannot have lunch together at McDonald's, or anywhere else, nor could I have him waiting outside with the car while I indulged in a passion seemingly beneath my status.

Always super cautious while in traffic, once in the safety of the condo underground garage I relaxed my guard. But I relaxed too soon. Pulling into our designated stall next to a cement pillar, I cut the turn too short and gashed the passenger side of the brand new Whirlpool-owned Santana. This was no casual side-scraper between husband, wife, and the insurance company. Things being as they were, I had to answer to Whirlpool as well. Sam and Manny, who had provided me with a driver for God's sake, each asked, "How could you do such a dumb thing?"

Using the same tone of voice, or maybe louder, I answered, "I don't know!"

#

Sam returned at the end of June and was due to go the States again for meetings beginning August 2. He did not discuss with me his plan to take Manny with him. He should have, because Manny's going—and Fran's already being gone—meant I would be alone in São Paulo with no other Whirlpool representative anywhere in all of South America.

Manny felt honored to be needed at these higher level meetings and shushed me when I raised the question of the wisdom— the legality, even—of leaving a lone dependent 7,000 miles from home base with no buddy system support and no emergency contingencies. Brazilian counterparts were not even alerted, because we were not their responsibility—as we had been in 1969–1971.

Sometimes Tony and Nancy Mason spent three-month stretches in São Paulo as "tourists," but they were not in town at the time Sam and Manny left. If they had been, it would have been all right. Their presence would have constituted a buddy system.

When the Masons did come down again a short time later, the need arose for Tony's boss, Sam Pearson, to talk with Nancy about the possibility of Tony's being sent back to Benton Harbor for a few weeks. He told her she would have to stay in Brazil without him because company policy would not pay for her accompanying fare. Even though at the time others of us were there to "buddy" with her, panic struck her heart. I am sorry for her having that experience, but knowing that my own reaction was not isolated has been somewhat comforting. At least Nancy had been forewarned. She pleaded with Tony not to do this to her, and he didn't. He stayed with his wife, regardless of what his boss preferred.

But Manny abandoned me, too far gone into over-identifying with his job and with the company. He abandoned me because Whirlpool told him to. I mark this event as our marriage's point-of-no-return. Where there is no trust, can there be love? Manny's behavior toward me, from then on, began to parallel more and more the powerlessness he himself was experiencing.

I have no doubt that Sam Pearson's broaching the subject with Nancy Mason—of leaving her in a foreign country while sending her spouse away—stemmed from behind-closed-corporate-doors discussions of what should be done about me. My abandonment represented the first case of this nature. No clear policy existed. Because of the naïveté of all of us, this was the type of problem arising on the spot that I had insisted on having the right to help solve. Before I left St. Joseph, I believed this contractual right had been granted.

Adding to Whirlpool's desire to set policy on this issue were other corporate needs that dictated my staying behind in São Paulo. Manny, speaking as office manager rather than as husband, "told" me to use Marcus, to find something for him to do every day. I was also supposed to make random visits to the office to keep Sandra on her toes.

Ordinarily, Manny discouraged my dropping by the office on the grounds that my presence was disruptive. His wanting me to stop in there during his absence was not a loving gesture motivated by concern for my isolation, trying to help me fill up my hours. It was a corporate assignment.

In addition to being abandoned against my will, which I had fiercely opposed, I was also to be the coerced, unpaid, and unrecognized manager's stand-in.

There was another reason my presence was needed in São Paulo. Who else would clean the Batemans' cat box?

So Sam Bateman and Manny Von Koenig left me alone in Brazil. They left me alone in all of South and Central America. Except for the cat.

Even though I like felines in general, I did not relate well to this one. Our interactions had the same overtones and undertow as my relationship with the Whirlpool Corporation. Tense and alert like a perpetual hunter, Gigio would not hold still to be petted or caressed. He seemed always to be tracking and attacking. If I didn't shut him out of my room at night, he would awaken me in the morning by sweeping one forearm and paw across the bedside bench, crashing everything on it to the floor.

I learned through experience that my loneliness had to be borne for what loneliness is—a solitary burden. When I mentioned my predicament to a Newcomer's Club associate, she reacted in horror that any company would do such a thing—as Nancy Mason had reacted at the thought it might be done to her. Suddenly I felt disloyal for having "squealed"—a paradoxical feeling not unlike what a child might feel on revealing that her father was molesting her. This twisted loyalty was further isolating.

Marcus brought me newspapers from the office every day, Monday through Friday, and took me shopping, whether I needed anything or not. I haunted the various malls—El Dorado, Iguatemi, Morumbi, Ibirapuera—where I could enjoy an espresso at a coffee bar and exchange a few pleasant words with a stranger without being tempted to divulge my pain.

Remembering Sam's comment to avoid having to go to a hospital in Brazil, I was compulsively careful not to fall. Maybe Marcus and Sandra would take care of me if I had an accident during office hours, but my evenings and weekends were devoid of linkage to a support system of any kind. For two weeks, I took down nothing from the higher kitchen shelves—I didn't touch the flower vases or the fish poacher—because I feared the danger inherent in using the two-step ladder set on a slippery tile floor.

During that time, I did not drive the car. An accident was too probable, both because traffic conditions were life-threatening and because I suffered some destablizing effects of anxiety.

We already knew of three families in our condo whose cars had been stolen. I did not want to chance either an accident or a theft while on my own. Dealing with police was not high on my list of things to do.

One welcome diversion was hearing from an old friend. Leland, with whom I had corresponded since we met in 1977 at the Associação Alumni language conference, invited me to join him and a friend of his on Sunday at the Praça de Republica for the weekly art fair. I dressed "down," studied the city guide, and figured out how to get there by bus. The day was typically bright, sunny, and languorous.

From a bus stop on the lower edge of downtown, I took a stairway that wound its way up an embankment through semi-dense foliage. A rest area near the summit featured a beautiful old fountain that spewed water into a surrounding basin. Two dirty little boys—urchins—free from the civilization barely visible through the low-hanging boughs, laughed and played in the sun and the water as they laundered the filthy ragged T-shirts they had removed from their bodies. They flitted about like birds and we chirped greetings at each other as I moved through their space. I tried not to worry about how they took care of the rest of their needs.

At the appointed time and place, I met Leland and his friend, Lutch—a Russian from Australia. We spent several hours ambling about the Praça, one of my favorite pastimes since my earliest visit. On Sundays, this larger-than-a-city-block area is filled with the most exotic varieties of art, crafts, gadgets, stamps, coins, food, and people. We went to the nearby Japanese sector for a simple but unusual lunch, after which my friends drove me home.

I still had five days of emptiness to hang through. I spent as much time writing as I could. Writing was getting harder and harder for me, not only because of the computer problems. The protagonist of my novel was a strong woman with whom I was no longer able to identify. I had been working in a fictional form to elucidate a truer nature of Helen of Troy than that set forth by Homer. But the passiveness enforced on me by a patriarchal structure in the twentieth century C.E. handicapped me in setting Helen free of hers in twelfth century B.C.E.

Our condo's pool area was nice, and certainly convenient, but I used it infrequently, thereby avoiding any need to guard my feelings if I encountered one of the few business people living there. I had been able to speak freely only with Leland and Lutch, academicians who were not part of the corporate madness. In the condo, I could think of nothing I would dare to say.

I felt that the choice Manny made in leaving was a negative one in many ways. He chose not to destroy us financially. He chose not to rock the boat that would have thrown us overboard. But he overestimated me and the cumulative effect of all the isolating and depressing experiences I had been having. He thought I would be strong enough to get through the nightmare, and everything would be all right again, as it had been eventually after we came out of the darkness of 1969–1971.

As a matter of principle, I wouldn't spend several thousand dollars of our own money to go with Manny on a business trip to the States. But with a budget of nearly the cost of one round trip to the States, I planned a journey for myself to Machu Pichu, not that far from São Paulo. Manny had been there as a side venture on one of his business trips to Colombia. From the office, through which all deals flowed, I received literature about tours.

Manny understood and agreed when I told him how much it would help me get through those weeks alone if I could look forward to a fantasy escape for myself on his return.

My anger prompted me in part to book a tour of two countries considered to be even more dangerous at the time than

Brazil—Peru and Bolivia. In doing so I realized I wasn't afraid of being in Brazil with Brazilians, any more than I feared Peruvians or Bolivians. I was afraid of the power held over people by the uppermost ranks of the Whirlpool Corporation. If they had the power and lack of scruples to leave me stranded far from home in a country known for its social unrest and denigration of women, what else might they do?

I planned the nine-day trip to begin August 7 so as not to be in São Paulo the day of the Batemans' return. I did not want to face my tormentors. Manny returned August 2. Our business-like reunion lacked tenderness. He thrust unexplained papers in front of me with the order to sign them. I demurred. He told me they were "just a formality" and I "had no choice" because the Whirlpool Credit Union had already taken the action my signature would, retroactively, authorize. It concerned a perk Manny was receiving from the corporation in the form of favorable stock options. While Manny and his boss had been together in the States, Sam, making another Whirlpool payment for Manny's soul, encouraged him to pick up the stock options. To raise this large sum needed for an even larger return, my husband placed a mortgage on our house. A half-owner of a property cannot do this without the prior consent of the other owner. Not, that is, unless the first party is a vice president of a company that operates its own credit union and, in addition, is backed up by a member of the corporate board, Sam, who assures the credit union that it's all right. All that these men wanted from me—Manny had become "one of them"—was my signature. Otherwise, I was to "shut up."

I was reminded of a cartoon in which a husband says to his wife, "I don't want you to be happy. I just want you to be quiet." Culturally I was not alone in my martyrdom, but I felt alone in every other way.

I signed. What else could I do?

While in St. Joseph, Manny also had talked to Marv Fuller, an associate at the Unitarian Universalist Fellowship, about doing an evaluative inspection of our home. Marv told me, when I was on home leave a few months later, that Manny basically wanted to know whether the house was worth fixing up.

His words hit my panic button. Manny's negative approach to "our home" signaled his desire to dispose of it and thus to strip me of a major source of my sense of stability—hence, of power. I loved that home—even if strangely built and old—where we had raised our children, where I had felt safe and secure no matter where in the world he was or what eerie political flurries swept through the community. Although I was conscious of leaving on my trip in time to avoid having to greet the Batemans, I was less aware at the time that another purpose of the trip was to put distance between my traitorous husband and me.

Leaving the damn cat with Manny, I said, "Ho, ho, ho. Maybe cleaning the cat box for your boss's wife is part of your job description."

A travel agency representative met me in Lima and at each subsequent destination, guiding my tour until delivering me to a boarding gate for my next departure.

In Cuzco, all incoming visitors were sorted according to the language they understood and which sub-tours they chose. For each of the tours, I was with a different group of people.

On the day of the ascent to Machu Pichu, the English-speaking group consisted of only a fellow American named John and me. Our guide put us on the train with instructions to disembark at the obvious place and get in line as quickly as we could for the bus going up. John asked me during the train ride if I had heard about the bomb planted on that very train the week before. It had killed the several people for whom it was intended. No, I hadn't. Even with that knowledge, I still felt safer than I

had felt when left alone in São Paulo under the "wings" of Whirlpool, whose corporate logo is the eagle.

Chaos reigned at the transfer point, with people jostling for
access to the buses. I don't jostle well, and John seemed tired.
Spotting a knot of aggressive young German backpackers who
seemed to be making progress, I led John into their wake. Like
barnacles on whales, we boarded the bus when they did.

An Inca guided my group through the Cathedral. He railed
against the Catholics who had destroyed the native temple to
raise a house of worship for the competing god of the victors.
Later, atop the Fort of Sacsayhuaman looking out over a vista
that seemed to be the guide's more natural setting, the perfect
opportunity arose to photograph him against that background
as he lectured to his semicircle of tourists. Several of my traveling companions shrank back as though I should not have done
that without having asked his express permission. The Inca cast
a stern look in my direction, but missed not a beat of his presentation. What passed between us was his knowing that if he ob-
jected, I would report to his employer what he had said at the
Cathedral. I knew his anger. I felt it and respected it; and I wanted
a picture of it to take with me. His anger stemmed from his sense
of the injustice perpetrated against his culture. I felt the same
sense of injustice at what the Whirlpool Corporation was per-
petrating against my culture—represented by my marriage and
my family. With pain equal to his, I respected the Inca's anger
and deserved the picture. I was not just a tourist, but a pilgrim
in quest of a way to deal with my own anger.

Although my hives had long since disappeared, when I later
wrote about the incidents detailed above, they welled up again
on the undersides of both forearms.

I rode the train to Puna, boated across Lake Titicaca, and
bussed into La Paz. The next day I flew Aero Peru back to São
Paulo, where I had only one week of *Whirlpool do Brazil* to en-

dure before taking off for the States for an early start on home leave. I was hoping to be present for the delivery of a grand-child. Close. I arrived in Grand Rapids the day after Benjamin was born to Ed and Lori.

Back in St. Joseph, I moved into the upstairs back bedroom of what, for the interim, was Jeff's, Nancy's, and Sandy's house. This room looks out over the river. I like that. I opened the sew-ing machine and worked pointlessly on unnecessary things. Sewing was pacifying therapy.

Jeff and Nancy had a floater car I could use, a little blue Chevette. I maintained, or think I did, a façade of normal cheer-fulness within the family circle. I enjoyed seeing Doug and Jo, but missed Curt, who was still in Germany.

Before leaving Brazil, I had insisted Manny make an appoint-ment for me with Whirlpool's Human Resources office. Some-thing had to be done about my intolerable living and working conditions. On August 31, I had a meeting with Glenn Youngstedt, who called in Jerry Sorenson and Bill Gargiulo to help him hear me out.

At the close of my afternoon's full confessional, I felt much better. I felt I had gone through proper channels to call full at-tention to a situation which, when thoroughly understood by the corporate mind, would undoubtedly be redressed.

The second week of September, I took a bus to St. Paul, want-ing to feel the familiar countryside and to gain strength from it. I rented a car and drove out to Forest Lake, where I stayed with Ronald and Lanora, my brother and his wife. They accompa-nied me to my fortieth high school class reunion. It was good to be back among my roots.

I shopped at Dayton's in St. Paul for clothing for the coming year, having by then a better idea of what I would be needing.

September 23, I flew to Miami, stayed at the airport hotel, and did some sightseeing. Manny arrived on the 25th as coldly matter-of-fact as if spending time with "the wife" held no more significance than any other routine item on his business calendar.

We went to Disney World because every upper-class Brazilian we knew already had been there. We stayed a day in the Ft. Myers area and then went on to Punta Gorda to be the guests of Manny's one-time boss, Dick Devine, and his wife, Pat, my one-time associate at Lake Michigan College.

Our friendship with the Devines strengthened in me the dim memory that Manny and I developed a few true friendships within the corporate framework. I felt something was definitely abnormal about the Batemans' strictly hierarchical cutoff line. Our problems with them, mine especially, were not all my fault, as my "superiors" would have it seem.

Returning to St. Joseph, we stayed at the Boulevard Hotel. More than one evening I spent watching television and retiring early, while Manny was at the bar with the Whirlpool "guys." He would come in late, having drunk too much, and pass on to me greetings from a few of them.

Our suite was on the southwest corner of the hotel, picture-windowed in both directions. It was the most perfect spot imaginable for watching the sun sink into Lake Michigan. We used to do that often—drive to the lake at sunset and become transcendental through the visual experience.

One evening I called to Manny in the next room, "Oh, come! The sunset is magnificent!" Indicative of our failed rapport, he shot back, "I saw it," as though one fleeting glance paid the same homage as did observing it for the duration. He went on shuffling papers. He did not want to be close to me. He no longer could sit euphorically facing into the sunset with one arm around me and his other hand cradling mine. Nor did he have time to recognize this was a problem and to deal with it. He had more important work to do.

The second weekend in October 1987, we turned in our rented car at the South Bend airport to begin our long triangular route back to Brazil—via Minnesota to touch in with my relatives and then Germany to visit Manny's family. Because my previous journeys on this eighties' tour of duty had been first with Fran, then alone, this was the first time in eighteen years that we were making the trip to Brazil together.

At the luggage counter at South Bend's airport, something—I don't know what—nudged Manny into a display of irrational behavior. Needing to fill out two tags for each of our four suitcases, Manny possessively grabbed all eight instead of each of us completing four of them. He fought my efforts to be of any assistance in this routine clerical task, in full view of an amazed luggage handler. Manny seemed obsessed, as though he had to establish control.

With such signals, would this have been a good time to jump ship and refuse to go back? Yes and no. Much as Manny was showing he didn't need anyone for anything, I knew otherwise. I loved him, I understood him, and he did need someone. I was the one he needed. Because I had been to Human Resources, I expected we would get help—a round table discussion, counseling, *something!*

Jeff and Nancy had been expecting their second child to arrive any day, and we had hoped to be there yet for the occasion. However, we had to leave and were in Minnesota at my sister's house when Jeff called on October 12 to say Nick had been born.

This was home leave, and Manny's sense of home included his mother and his sister. We flew directly from Minneapolis to Munich to visit them. Germany was also where we would find our youngest son, Curt, stationed at the Army base in Schwetzingen.

Curt was the frequent Munich visitor. His grandmother doted on him, calling him her "little Manny." How good it was that she could have her "son" back with her in that form! His aunt spoiled him. Six years later, when Lulu died in 1993, Curt grieved the most, saying, "I was the one who knew her best." He was right, I'm sure. I was happy to have had such a fine son to share with her, to have made possible for her an experience very near to mothering.

It had become a tradition, starting in 1971, for Manny's mother, *Mutti*, whom we also called the Queen Mother (*Königen Mutter*), to put us up at the Pension Monopteros bordering on the English Garden near the Haus der Kunst.

Curt, on a weekend pass, came by train and was supposed to meet us at the Ratskeller, a cellar pub burrowed under a corner of the Munich courthouse. Together with Manny's old school friends we were there practicing *gemütlichkeit*—the cozy, genial good-natured camaraderie so uniquely German that it defies translation. Principal among them were Peter Glück and his wife. I had known Peter since 1951. His wife and the others I was meeting for the first time. We were all speaking in German.

The flow of wine transported the men reminiscently to earlier years, making them boys again. The other woman and I, not having been part of those years, were tolerant of them and kindly attentive to each other. We heard my husband gleefully saying, ". . . and then I went to the States and got married so I could go back again." I was hit by that stray bullet. The other woman hurt for me and along with me. Peter, and perhaps one other man, glanced in my direction with expressions that read, "Oops! Did she notice that?"

Back at the Monopteros, seeing Curt's gear stashed in our room, we knew he would be back shortly. He had not been able to find us at the jam-packed Ratskeller where we had been tucked away in a back corner. If Curt had been with our group at the Ratskeller, would his father have said what he did?

After Manny sobered up from the previous night and before German family life took over, I raised the issue. How, I asked him, after thirty-seven years of what had seemed to me and to most observers a quite successful marriage, could he have implied to his cohorts, even in jest and even if it had been out of my presence (which it wasn't), that our marriage had been one of mere convenience—to become an American? How could he have so denigrated my importance to him and to his life by publicly throwing it into my face? How could he embarrass me like that?

What could he say? A man who loved his wife and who had all his faculties intact might have leaped to span the chasm between us at that moment. Loving me still, but impaired, he kept himself turned away from me and widened the gap by sputtering, "Oh, don't be silly. That was just talk. You know I couldn't possibly have meant that."

So I should stop being silly—not, he should regain some sensitivity. He refused to see that his "just talk" was a dagger to my heart. If he hadn't meant it, then why didn't he wipe it out by protestations to the contrary? We both knew he had wanted to emigrate as a youth. We also both knew I wanted a marriage that would take me into a different culture. There had been times when we had both joked, publicly and in each other's presence, about both of us having married for those ulterior motives, to which there was some truth.

But his saying what he did in a context without consideration of my perspectives became an issue of control. Mistakes make one vulnerable, but corporate men don't make mistakes. They can't afford to; therefore, they don't. Records, written or verbal, are altered to make sure no evidence exists of any mistake having been made.

It follows that if no mistake is made, there is never a need to apologize. Manny brushed aside this personal matter, proving to himself his invulnerability and showing a thicker layer of the shell that he was using alcohol to help him build around his poor, lonely soul.

I saw the need, then, to start consciously growing a shell of my own.

After the weekend with Curt, as we drove him back to his base we revisited beautiful, romantic Heidelberg, which Curt knew intimately from his many off-duty hours spent there. He proudly photographed his father and his mother against the castle background and sent us a framed copy for Christmas.

After a night at the local hotel in Schwetzingen, Manny and I drove to Stuttgart and spent a long healing evening with John and Edith Eser and their daughter, Harriet Phillips. Curt was not with us that evening, but at their invitation he spent a weekend with them later.

We returned to Curt's base, saw him at work, and met his buddies and bosses. Curt took leave on the twenty-first, and we whisked him off to Portugal with us. I laughed at the analogy to a scene from "Private Benjamin," where her parents came to "take her away from all this."

In Lisbon, both the weather and the accommodations were luxurious and the language so close to Brazilian that we felt almost at home. Some sightseeing the three of us did together, but occasionally we split: Curt and I taking the castle tour while Manny checked out the harbor. After four noticeably tense days, Curt flew back to Germany; we, to Brazil.

During most of that home-leave month together, Manny was distant and cross. Our relationship had deteriorated so badly that I had last-minute thoughts of jumping ship, right up to the moment I actually boarded the flight to São Paulo.

I saw no way of getting out of the situation. Our house in St. Joseph was occupied, and Manny controlled all our assets and income. Strangely, uppermost in my mind at the time, the eleven boxes of files and all the reference books for my novel-in-progress were in São Paulo. I was all too familiar with the hostage concept and could not leave them to that fate.

###

My respite from the Brazilian scene was over. I was back to walking gingerly over psychological fields strewn with hidden mines.

On the phone the day after my arrival, Fran wanted to know how my interview with Human Resources had gone. She confided to me that Sam had been quite worried. "Aha!" I thought, "Perhaps I did make a right move, and relief will be forthcoming."

Sam need not have worried. Nothing was done that had any positive effect on my daily life. September turned into October into November without a follow-up note, call, or letter of any kind from Human Resources in relation to our meeting on August 31. If I were helping them to "improve their human resource service in the future"—one of their goals stated to me in their letter of July 24—they were doing nothing to help me in the present.

Millie, a dear friend since 1971, came to visit. Manny's altered personality alarmed her, and she expressed her concern to me. She found him, as I did, unreachable and remote. He went through all the expected host motions, but so mechanically that it was as though no real person was motivating the gestures.

November 6 was Fran's birthday. Nancy Mason's birthday was five days later. Nancy suggested that she, Fran, and I have lunch on the eleventh to celebrate both their birthdays. We did, within the context that Fran and Sam were making plans to be in the States from mid-November through January 6. Any time I talked to Fran, I was extraordinarily cautious not to mention the word "cat." The hugeness of the favor I had done for her in caring for Gigio during June and July had not resulted in her treating me any better than she had before, so I saw no value in investing further effort in the cat market.

As if to drive that point home, Fran regaled us, during lunch, with the plans she and Sam were making for a "Thankmas" party they were going to give the next weekend to show gratitude to all the people who had been "so helpful" to them. It was not lost on Nancy and me that the Masons and Von Koenigs were not included, nor were Olga and Tony Lyra, who had been a virtual life-support system for them.

Marcus chauffeured Fran and me to and from that luncheon. On the way home, she said the word I had been avoiding. "Roz, while we're gone, Marcus is going to take care of our cat. Would you be willing to be back-up in case something happens to him? It's just back-up. Not as though you'd ever actually have to do anything."

I managed to convince her that the situation was more complex than she thought, and we should not continue the conversation in Marcus's hearing. He understood more English than he let on, especially when his name was embedded in it. We agreed to let him deliver us to our homes, then I would go over to her apartment so we could discuss the matter more fully.

Manny had told me the Batemans had checked kennels—or rather, had Sandra do so—to find that the daily rate was $14.00; more than they wanted to spend. Because Marcus had watered plants for them during a previous absence, they apparently reasoned that, in a pinch, he also could take care of a cat.

When I had originally lived in São Paulo, a Brazilian friend of mine ordered her husband's company driver to take her poodle to the vet for shots. He flew into a rage and said he wouldn't. He did, but only after the woman's husband told him the company would fire him if he didn't. That was about how much Marcus did not want to take care of that damn cat.

Marcus's attempt at avoidance was to ask Manny how much

vacation time he had coming and if it would be all right if he took it in early December. He advanced the reasons that the Batemans would be gone and the Von Koenigs seemed to prefer driving themselves around. Marcus thought he could escape cat duty by being off-duty.

Manny agreed that the need for Marcus's driving services would be minimal during that time and granted him vacation. But because Manny had "betrayed" Sam by letting Marcus take vacation, Sam had to find out through Sandra whether Marcus would be leaving the city or staying home. Unfortunately for Marcus, he told the truth about staying in the city, and Sam made him an offer he couldn't refuse without putting his job at risk. As a result, Marcus essentially lost his vacation time that year; his boss commandeered the time and chopped it into unusable slices.

These injustices were too much for me. If Manny would not protect me from the Batemans' rank-pulling, and if Sam would not invite me for the step-two interview I had requested, then I was on my own. I, not quite as helpless as Marcus, was not going to take care of that damn cat again.

I arrived at Fran's apartment, and she poured coffee. I explained Brazilian machismo to Fran, and how Marcus's vacation timing was an indication of how badly he did not want to cat-sit. I acknowledged that what was done was done, that Marcus would be taking care of Gigio, but I thought it was unconscionable exploitation for which extra money was insufficient compensation.

I also emphasized that I had considered all of this none of my business until she asked if I would be Marcus's back-up. My answer was "no," I would not back up an exploitive set-up of which I disapproved.

Fran interjected, "But he has to do it. He's an employee!"

I responded, "Come off it, Fran, when was the last time you

were able to order a driver at the home office in Benton Harbor to clean your cat's litter box?"

I had been witness to her ordering a pilot to clean the plane's toilet, but there must be limits, I thought. Was this why the Batemans treated Manny and me as they did? Because they thought of themselves as first-class executives and of Manny and me as "just employees?" In my reality, both Sam and Manny were "just employees," unless there existed at Whirlpool some divine master class about which we mortals did not know.

Moving off the exploitation theme and back to machismo, I pointed out to Fran that if I were to be Marcus's backup and he knew I was, he'd be outta there.

I was concentrating so hard on carefully phrasing the thoughts I wanted to communicate that I didn't notice how Fran must have been getting angrier and angrier. It's possible no one ever had talked to her that directly before, and she knew she didn't have to put up with it. I admit I was quite surprised to hear her say, through clenched teeth, "Will you please leave?"

I put down my coffee cup, rose, and walked to the door. She closed the door almost on my heels and rapidly turned the lock behind me. We have not spoken since.

Manny empathized fully with my position. I won the battle of the cat, as I had won the battle of attending the ball, but I lost the war. I lost my husband. I lost the father of the family we created.

And I lost the civil lawsuit I later filed against the Whirlpool Corporation. In countering that suit, Whirlpool mocked my agony by citing the cat episode as evidence of the triviality of my case.

Not a single word passed between Manny and Sam about the untenable situation that existed among the four members of Whirlpool's team in Brazil. We were *Whirlpool do Brasil's* first and second "families." To extend the analogy, any reasonable mothers in this situation would have called a council of resolution. But mothers are without voice in the patriarchal corporation. Fathers call all the shots.

The difficulties I had told Sam on May 8 I wanted to discuss had grown into a crisis—the result of his not wanting to talk about them. I felt that Sam was directly responsible for all the inhumane family-related decisions imposed by the Whirlpool Corporation in Brazil.

Mercifully for me, the Batemans left so Sam could be in the States for the corporation's end-of-the-year meetings, and incidentally, could be home again for Thanksgiving, Christmas, and New Year's.

Back in the seventies, Manny used to say of his Whirlpool colleagues, "Nobody wants to rock the boat. They want it to be on an even keel when it sinks." Although he had not talked that way for a long time, I still did. And in the part of me that continued to be what he had been, he could still see his old self. That part of him—the part with which I was soulmate—was nearly dead, but he did not strike out to kill it in me. In me, it would die of its own accord if Operation Bootstrap—my effort to help myself—was not successful.

As the holidays approached, the Bonamicos insisted we again spend Christmas Eve with them. This time we firmly declined their generosity, explaining we had family coming to visit us on the twenty-seventh and that would see us through. Nonetheless, on December 24 we did the same thing Doug and Jo said they had done their first Christmas Eve away from home and family, and without close friends in Hawaii. Manny and I bought one huge bottle of wine, and we drank it.

Life looked much better on December 27 when Doug, Jo, and three-year-old Jonathan arrived. They accompanied us on our second annual pilgrimage to honor Yemanja on Copacabana beach on December 31. I could not understand Manny's quarrelsome behavior en route. The drive was only six hours, even though we took the long way. He complained of being tired and of how much was demanded of him, but he would not let anyone else drive. He never did.

When we stopped for lunch, he attempted to herd us into the dark interior of a restaurant whose only appeal was a charming verandah overlooking the ocean, where I insisted we be seated.

This had become a pattern. He could let Whirlpool responsibilities tire him to the point where he had no energy left for me, yet, if official entertaining called, he would be instantly alert and ready to go again. I think he was not so tired as he was tired *of*, and I didn't know what to do about it except to stand my ground. Was he tired not only of me, but of his family as well?

As we entered the city, Manny lost his orientation, questioning aloud which way we ought to be going and frantically engaging Doug in a glove compartment search for the map. I knew where we were as well as how to get from there to Copacabana; and I advised, from the back seat, which turn to take. He would not listen, but kept directing his entreaties to Doug. I stated again, clearly and firmly, where we should turn. Manny seemed unable to tolerate that I knew something he didn't. Where did this come from? The halls of the corporation? Brazilian custom? Both?

Doug practiced neutrality by producing and studying the map and then announcing, based on his perusal rather than on trust in me, "Mom is right. Take the next left."

When I fled Brazil thirteen months later, Jo succinctly summed up her impression of Manny's and my interrelating during that period with, "I'm surprised you didn't come back sooner."

We checked into our beachfront hotel, had dinner, and then

napped, because it was a long way yet until midnight. Amazingly, the only person not tired enough at that point to lie still and cool it for a few hours was Manny, who, so far as I know, spent the time pacing the lobby.

By 11:30 P.M. when we headed for the beach, the gentlest of warm rains was falling. Only Manny complained, as though his memories of the year before had washed away. I was able to push his darkness aside in my eagerness to induct the others into the wonders of this night. I am overjoyed that what Jonathan remembers of his adventure in Brazil when he was only three is his going down to the water's edge with Oma to help her launch a little wooden boat bearing a rose. He remembers the boat was not sent back by the waves. Yemanja had accepted our offering.

Manny went back to work. The rest of us packed off on January 7 for Manaus, in the Amazon. Doug, Jo, and Jonathan returned to the States from there. I went back to São Paulo, but only after the Batemans had returned, to avoid the awkwardness of their homecoming.

For one week in January, Dick Devine, Sam's once-upon-a-time protégé and Manny's once-upon-a-time boss, came to stay with us with his wife, Pat. They were entertained for a weekend at the Bonamicos' ranch and, of course, wanted to see the Batemans. Without giving away the secret that Fran and I weren't speaking, Manny arranged for the Devines to go over to the Batemans one afternoon without us.

Late in January I spent an evening at the language school Leland directed and helped him guide his teaching staff through a culture simulation game he had learned as a student of mine in 1977. For those few hours I experienced a bit of my true self set amid the surreal madness that was my corporate life. It was my personal Switzerland set in India, affording a brief respite.

Shortly after, Tony and Nancy Mason came back to São Paulo to put in another three-month stint for Whirlpool with Brastemp. We, the Masons, and the Batemans had all previously made reservations for the American Society tour of a samba school.

To be fair to Nancy, I told her why we three women wouldn't be having lunch together again, and alerted her to the tensions that might affect our evening. The Masons thus became participants in an awkward and stressful event that started with all of us waiting around together for the chartered buses. Sam made a point of coming over to our group and chatting for a "polite" few minutes.

The Batemans were already seated on the bus, Fran on the aisle, as we passed them to take available seats further back. I looked at her as I approached and passed and would have said hello, had there been even the slightest invitation for me to do so. There wasn't. She looked firmly and purposefully in the opposite direction.

Fran and Nancy remained in contact. No reason why they shouldn't.

The time Manny and I spent with the Masons had been good for us. Tony and Nancy practiced "democracy within the family," as I faintly remembered it existing in our family. Unlike Manny's, Tony's childhood and adolescent years had not been shaped by the Nazi party, followed by limbo. Unlike Manny, Tony had not been manipulated by their common employer into a box from which even Houdini could not have escaped.

I see the Batemans' silence about our conflict as an example of Whirlpool's tendency to sweep things under the rug. When there is so much under the rug that it's difficult to walk across the room without stumbling, it gets to be high time someone wrote a book.

Valentine's Day fell on Sunday. Manny was at home, sitting on the living room couch reading the paper when the back doorbell rang. Answering it, I was handed a floral bouquet by one of the condo's attendants. Genuinely surprised, my startled eyes moved from Manny's signature to his smiling face.

But no, he wasn't actually smiling. In his eyes lay not one trace of the smitten devotion that filled him on that same date in 1951 when he first brought me roses. What I saw and felt was more of a self-satisfied smirk. These flowers were not a token of love, they were a trophy for himself. It seemed to me as if the card had read, "See? Even though I am more important than you have ever known me, and busier, I'm able to remember such a trivial thing as Valentine's Day. That should satisfy domestic requirements for a while and keep you off my back so I can concentrate on work."

I thanked him and gave him a quick kiss on the forehead, which, in his eagerness to get back to the paper, was all the acknowledgment he needed to seal his triumph.

Then came Bob Collins-Wright, CEO of Inglis, Whirlpool's Canadian affiliate, and his party of four. I was expected to entertain them for a day. It was Sam's expectation, made known through Manny. The only reference to their wives not being on speaking terms was Sam's asking Manny, "How is Roz going to know where Fran took them the day before?"

Manny, still proud of my ability to cope, although I knew that ability was waning, claims to have answered, "Don't worry about Roz." What he meant was "She'll be able to handle it." I would like him to have meant, sarcastically, "You don't seem to have been worrying about her so far. Why should you start now?"

The day spent with Bob, Yvonne, and their guests was one of my darkest in Brazil—in terms of my doing coerced slave-labor for the corporation. Weeks earlier during Pat and Dick Devines' visit, the appearance that all was well at *Whirlpool do Brasil* could be kept up simply by my being passive. But the

bizarre situation with the Collins-Wrights required an overt demonstration by me to these outsiders that everything was all right.
Well it wasn't—and there was nothing I could do about it. I
hadn't wanted to do this "work" for Whirlpool—but I had no
choice.

I took them to lunch atop the Edifiçia Italia, where we
laughed, told stories, and strolled the terrace to view São Paulo
stretched out below in all directions. They were delightful companions, treating me in the collegial fashion I had hoped for
from the Batemans. They renewed my faith in myself, as de-
serving to be treated that way, and my belief that some top-level
executives are actually okay.

Still, for me, the day had been a charade. I had not been able
to utter one word of truth about the reality of my life; I had not
been able to call out for help.

When the Batemans moved back to the States in April of
1988, the Bonamicos invited us to a farewell dinner for them. As
a matter of form, I initially accepted the invitation, knowing that,
of course, we couldn't go. Since Fran was not speaking to me, it
would have been awkward for both of us for me to be honoring
her with my presence. Perhaps it could have been pulled off to
the satisfaction of the politically correct, but I had no desire to
participate in sweeping unresolved issues even further under
the lumpy rug.

The day of the dinner, I called Maria Angelica and lied about
having a bad headache. I believed this to be something she did
from time to time, so she may have understood my message.

Manny had no problem with my sentiments and gladly sat
out the event himself. He knew what I was doing was right. He
felt, I think, empowered by my courage to defy the absurd.

When I left Brazil myself, I did so without saying farewell to
anyone associated with the corporation, except for Marcus. The
only Brazilian associate I have seen since is Maria Angelica,

whom I encountered shopping at Rimes in downtown St. Joseph one day in June 1989.

I explained to her why I had disappeared as I had; that I had divorced Manny. She had not known that. I expressed how much I appreciated her many kindnesses to me while I was in Brazil. She said I was welcome at her house if I ever returned. Unlike my need to tell Nancy Mason of Fran's having booted me out of her apartment, I chose not to mention the event to Maria Angelica. Such knowledge would not have improved the quality of her life.

Toward the end of my tenure in Brazil, I was having trouble controlling my weight. Frequent kilo notations on my calendar indicate how much of a preoccupation this was for me. On my birthday, I recorded 61 kilos or 135 pounds, fifteen pounds over my normal weight. This is the inevitable outcome of too much drinking and eating in an attempt to be happy.

Mike Etchenique hadn't been to our home yet, and he said he wanted to. Helen had been there in the company of other women, but I had never thought to invite Mike because I didn't consider our home any big deal. No discredit to Olga, who had done the best it was possible to do with a bare box. Nothing could have given it the charm and warmth of the house Helen had helped Manny select for us in 1969. I had felt pride in that house on Rua Grajau because it had such "heart."

So Mike wanted to call on us. I decided that a good time for his visit would be when my friend Ruby was expected to visit in May 1988. She had the Ph.D. in sociology that eluded me. In addition, she later earned an M.B.A. and went to work as a consultant in Quality Statistical Control.

Manny called Mike, suggesting he might enjoy meeting our visitor. Helen was out of town, but Mike accepted our dinner invitation. Since Quality Statistical Control was the newest, hottest specialty in manufacturing at that time, Mike added that maybe he should do more than meet my friend—he should probably try to hire him. Manny corrected him, "No, Mike. Her."

We also invited Tony and Olga Lyra, who had not been as fully informed about Ruby's background as had Mike, who was coming specifically to meet her. The Lyras had been invited, on this particular occasion, because Mike's son worked for Tony and because, under any circumstances, they are charming company. We viewed Mike, Ruby, and Tony as people who had a great deal of business background in common and could probably communicate easily from that base.

Perhaps either Mike alone or Tony alone would have been all right. Did some rule of Western civilization dictate that they had to be macho to impress each other? They joined forces and treated Ruby "like a woman," seemingly determined not to let her open her mouth all evening.

Insufficiently forewarned, Tony launched enthusiastically into a discussion about this "new thing," Quality Statistical Control. I turned to him, beaming, and with an open-armed gesture that pointed to and psychologically embraced Ruby, said, "You are in great luck. That is Ruby's specialty."

Tony's demeanor changed abruptly. Flustered, instead of looking expectantly at Ruby for words of wisdom, which she surely could have supplied, he looked down at his plate until he could find the switch to de-rail the subject and change our train of discussion.

It was a graceless slip with an awkward recovery that, more than any other discriminatory situation in which I have participated, gave away how men demean women's intelligence and accomplishments.

Mike did nothing to help. During our autopsy of the evening, Ruby called my attention to the fact that Mike, who had arrived early, downed two quick double scotches before socializing even began. True.

Nor did Olga do anything to help. Brazilian women at all levels accept that men have the right to be puffed-up centers of attention. Still, I think Helen's being there might have made a difference. She retained a spark of independence I found to be rare among the upper-class Brazilian women I knew.

Back in the States, Manny, as host, would have acted on this slight to Ruby and would have driven a wedge into the conversation through which she could have entered. But he was so far gone into the Brazilian system that he didn't even notice.

Several times I managed to create a brief space for her, but it was essentially a lost cause. Neither Mike nor Tony—who was actually an American but so Brazilian-enculturated I tended always to think of him as a Brazilian—was up to having a fair conversation with a woman.

Added to the list of Manny's credits, and he had many, he persisted in scheduling for Ruby the tour of the Brastemp manufacturing plant he had promised her. Viewing his efforts, I could see that his peers were giving him no cooperation. When the tour had finally been arranged, Ruby and I, both dressed professionally in our business suits, could feel the resistance of the male department heads beneath their pasted-on smiles, made obligatory by Manny's presence. They were being forced to share with a woman their fraternity secrets of manufacturing techniques.

At the May Newcomer's Club luncheon held at the Golden Dragon, I heard Joyce Mitchell speak. A black American, she had immersed herself in the African religion of her forebears, which she discovered in Brazil. I so admired her skill in explaining macumba to this audience that I sought to meet her later. We did not connect until August.

At our first meeting, she spoke enthusiastically about friends

of hers who had developed a computer program based on attributes of the African pantheon of deities. They were promoting it at the book fair being held at the Ibuapuera exhibition
hall. I went, alone, one afternoon, leaving a note for Manny next
to the hall telephone. I should have put the note on the refrigerator door, or, better yet, taped it on the scotch bottle, because
he came home after dusk and didn't turn on the hall light. When
I came in about eight, he was in a panic and one stage short of
falling down drunk. Since I was "always there," he had imag-
ined the worst. Nearly in tears, he moaned, ". . . and I wouldn't
even have known how to start looking for you."

He had not worried at first and imbibed his usual first few
drinks, thinking I would return at any moment. But when he
became concerned, rather than eating he employed his usual
method of dulling pain by continuing to drink.

I fed him.

One lone, snuffed-out cigarette lay in a saucer on the kitchen
counter. It was a fiction between us that he didn't smoke any
more. He smoked, but never in my presence, so I wouldn't
"know." The next morning, he was seriously disturbed by his
theory that someone must have somehow come into the apartment while we were out—a maintenance man, probably—and
left this butt behind. He had no recollection of having done it
himself, which of course he had. Nor did he long remember how
shaken he had been by my disappearance on that particular
night.

As a management couple, we had been holding the fort alone
in Brazil for more than three months. Even before Sam left, his
vice president/acting president had shown acute signs of dete-
rioration. I could do nothing, even though as he weakened, so
did our marriage.

June 2, 1988, is probably the date that best represents the
beginning of my total undoing. Two really wonderful people

arrived in São Paulo, courtesy of the Whirlpool conduit, to check out housing suitable for the next First Family of *Whirlpool do Brazil.*

I had never before met either Jim or Pamela Doan. I saw them as innocents coming into the slaughterhouse, yet in welcoming the Doans to Brazil, I was forced by circumstance to join in the deceit I felt sure Whirlpool was practicing on them, as it had on us.

Jim was the boss who had told Sara Shine, after her two hopeful years as a Whirlpool accountant, that the company had no development plans for her. She left Whirlpool to found her own consulting firm. One of her first clients was Clark Equipment in Campinas, Brazil, just outside São Paulo. Her first job out of college had been working for them. They liked her; they trusted her; they hired her back as an auditing consultant. She was there when the Doans arrived.

We attended the Bonamicos' dinner for the Doans on their first evening, a Thursday. That weekend, even though Sara Shine was our house guest, we were obligated to squire the Doans through the Sunday Praça de Republica experience. Laughing, Sara called to us as we left, "Say hello to Jim for me!"

She and her friend Marco were going to the Praça also. Sara thought what fun it would be if they should encounter the four of us. They didn't, and I was glad. Unexpected catastrophes were already abundant; I had no taste for planned ones.

Jim had risen to become comptroller for the corporation. Then, through restructuring, the title and its job description had bitten the dust. Jim wandered around the halls doing a bit of this and that until he felt so insecure and vulnerable that when he was offered this "marvelous opportunity" to become president of *Whirlpool do Brasil,* which a number of men already had declined, he was not about to say no.

Did Jim's situation bear a similarity to how Manny had been

maneuvered into *Whirlpool do Brasil?* Yes, though not quite as dastardly. Doan was considerably younger; he could have gone out on the market, although his having had a job written out from under him would have aroused suspicion about his capability.

Sara, knowledgeable about Brazilian culture and fluent in the language, had been in Campinas earlier that year to work at Clark. Sam, having learned by experience the value of these qualifications, had pondered, "Who was the fool who let her get away?" I wonder if he ever learned that the fool who had let her get away was the man who came to pick up his own reins. It didn't take long for Jim Doan, himself, to say, "If only we had Sara."

Tuesday, June 7, we dined with the Doans at the Etcheniques' exquisite home. How many times had I been there, all told, since 1969? I had long since overcome the feeling that I was acting within the set of some lavish Hollywood film. I relaxed and watched Jim and Pam begin that experience, partially calculated by the hosts to be deliberately overwhelming. It catches the novice off guard and gives the home team an advantage. If the visiting teams change personnel frequently enough, this advantage is considerable.

The best that Manny and I had ever been able to do by way of reciprocal entertaining was as part of the host group at Whirlpool's lodge, Dunrovin', near Baldwin, Michigan. That was good, very good, but anyone would have to admit it couldn't hold a candle to what the Etcheniques offered.

###

Manny brought home from the office a videotape of David Whitwam's address June 16, 1988, to the Twin Cities salaried employees who still had jobs following the extensive corporate restructuring that he had mandated. The tape was still on the shelf as I packed to escape eight months later. I took it with me. I become apoplectic when I think of it.

Whitwam first thanks everyone for coming, recognizing that "Evenings are an important time, away from work, to be with family." Right. Perhaps for many people, but certainly not for us who were more in exile than in expatriation. For us, there was little difference between home and office, and practically no respite from the corporation.

He remarks on the fierceness of competition, saying it is "no longer cutthroat" but "all out warfare."

When I first watched the tape in the isolation of my seventh-floor apartment 7,000 miles south of the home office, I talked back. "So what if there are a few fatalities, if a family or two bites the dust? Are there any really civilized standards in warfare?"

The tape shows him saying there would be "no more decision by committee," but "we will conduct ourselves with open communication." Really? I couldn't get anyone to two-way-communicate with me here, there, or anywhere, but then, my status within the Whirlpool "family" was unclear, except there I was in São Paulo, apparently because I fit into that family somehow.

Dave continues on tape, "There are going to be people in this organization who are not going to be able to accept [the new operating principles] and . . . if there are those of you who find you just cannot be comfortable, it is so important for your own well-being, for your own health, and that of your families, that if you really do not believe you can be a part of this coming together—you might want to look at other alternatives."

In other words, quit. Manny had tried to quit, and they wouldn't let him.

On tape, David Whitwam states, "No one at Whirlpool will ever be asked to do anything unethical or immoral, and each of us has the responsibility to report any practice which violates this unwavering standard. We must all believe there is no right way to do a wrong thing."

This, after David Whitwam himself immorally squeeze-played Manny into the Brazilian assignment over the objections of his wife. It was a wrong thing, there was no right way to do it, but he had done it.

Toward the end of the tape, he says, "I went over these questions with my wife." What a touchingly appropriate irony for me to hear. Dave's emissaries had rushed Manny off to Brazil so he could talk no further with his wife about the big questions still hanging over their lives. As I listened to that tape in late June of 1988, having been in Brazil for more than a year and a half, I was still being kept in the dark as to the conditions of the assignment. I, who was dramatically affected by it, was still unaware of the publication of an expatriate policy that governed us—even though neither of us had agreed to it.

The tape concludes with Dave's inviting people to stop by his office anytime, followed by the audience laughing long and hard. I would have been laughing, too, except I was so angry and hurt.

Manny and I needed a vacation. July 30 we took a one-and-a-half-hour flight to the city of Campo Grande in the state of Mato Grosso do Sul, gateway to the vast wetlands of the Pantanal. Called for at the airport by a van from our host-ranch, Pousada Caiman, our drive of about four hours took us farther and farther away from urban life.

The isolation of the ranch setting, along with the anonymity, impermanence, and small size of the supporting cast, acted as a dye on the fabric of Manny's and my relationship. It brought out a strange color and pattern I had never seen before. Lifeless as a rhythm gone dead. Hues and shades eroded through bad human chemistry, beyond resuscitation.

Manny did what he had done in Rio over New Year's 1986–1987. He played to this new cast of about a dozen as though it was his audience. He shaped himself before their eyes as important, interesting, and genial. He was first at the lounge bar, the first to offer drinks, the first to initiate conversation, the first and foremost to augment the hospitality of the hosts.

He was accompanied by what must have seemed to them a lackluster wife who did not appreciate her husband's giftedness, who lacked social skills of her own, who was mismatched with this man of greatness. What a shame! What a burden for him to bear, this millstone around his neck. That was how I felt myself perceived.

When I appeared in the lounge or the dining room, Manny rushed to my side to appear appropriately attentive. His stage behavior was meant to illuminate his role, not mine. Nothing passed between us; the action was all between him and them. I did not like my part but distanced myself from the disgrace of it as best I could and played it through.

As in Rio, the only time he spent in our bedroom was sleeping time. He left early and returned late.

Both mornings that we spent at the ranch, we drove out to the marshes in a Land Rover. It was equipped with high rails so we could stand to see out over the grasses. We saw the most marvelous creatures: immense stork-like jaburus who, walking in the distance, looked like bent old men; toucans; roseate spoonbills; even the bird I most wanted to see, the Brazilian cardinal, both genders colored equally in red-white-blue; and monkeys in the wild.

The first afternoon, we set out on horseback on a lengthy route that, upon our return, brought us face to face with a magenta sunset. Silhouetted against riotous color, we saw a dozen huge long-tailed blue macaws fluttering to their night's lodging in the upper reaches of an immense palm tree.

I saw this sight from a position near the end of the line of nose-on-tail horses. But Manny saw it from the very front. He had carefully noted landmarks on our way out, scheming even then to lead the group back. At first when he assumed the lead position, our ranch host loudly called out a general directive about how we should all stay behind the ranchero who was guiding us on the trail. The ranchero made several discrete attempts to resume his lead position, but he gave up when it became clear that "O Senhor" considered himself in command.

Yes, I was embarrassed, but, more than that, alarmed. We had not raised our four sons to be self-aggrandizing superimposing boors. How could their father be acting this way? What had happened to his internal wiring? How could I help him in any way, considering he treated me as some kind of wind-up doll? How could I help him when I couldn't help myself? Whirlpool did not believe anything was wrong with our situation or with Manny. To them, I am sure I was the only problem, and I did not matter.

After dinner, in pitch dark, we were taken to a nearby bridge to watch a multitude of jacare (caiman alligators) lying in the river waiting as fish tumbled down the rapids into their open mouths.

The following afternoon, Manny, and what was by then his entourage, toured without me. Alone, I enjoyed the soothing effects of the courtyard pool. The next morning was occupied by a long, dusty ride back to the airport.

I had become a little ill—slight headache, a little nausea. It could have been from the combination of dust, heat, and motion, but I believe I was psychologically sick of the situation. Manny attended to my disability by staying close to me, not wandering off to have a drink with the other departing guests, as he might have. I appreciated that, even though it was done without feeling, as if by an automaton. His personality was in repose. The curtain had rung down, and he was between plays, on hold for a new cast.

###

Ed, Lori, and one-year-old Ben came in early August to visit parents who were essentially estranged. None of the three spent much time with Manny, and I think I may have been responsible for arranging it that way. It did nothing for my morale to have further witnesses to our discord.

One time Ed raised an eyebrow and asked, "What's with him?"

Because Ed and Lori have missionary hearts, I wanted them to experience the *favela* (shantytown). This visit was arranged through Trude, who, having retired as Director of English courses at the Associação Alumni, volunteered her energies to the Communidade Monte Azul. Even though Trude termed Monte Azul a luxury *favela*, the conditions of poverty there brought tears to Lori's eyes.

###

Early on, I had asked Manny if there were any problem with my doing so much exploratory driving. I knew gas was expensive and some kind of Whirlpool-negotiated formula put most of the expense on their side of the ledger, presumably on the assumption that most driving of both cars was primarily business.

Manny's command, "Drive all you want to," may have been in retaliation for Sam's concurrent slight of refusing to take Manny along to top-level meetings with Brazilian government officials and business leaders. Manny reasoned that since Sam would be leaving Brazil before he did, to be replaced by someone as yet unknown, Manny might garner insights from such meetings, and that knowledge would be close to indispensable for *Whirlpool do Brasil*'s functioning during the changeover to Sam's replacement.

At any rate, my authorization to drive all I wanted was never rescinded. The only time I did not drive at all was when I was left alone for two weeks and did not dare to risk an accident, either to the car or to myself.

My major source of pleasure became *O Guia*, the 371-page guide to São Paulo's streets and attractions. It was a master-piece of accuracy and thoroughness. In this, the second (or third) largest city in the world (depending on the source of informa-tion), I could reach every street, even if only one block long and located in a seemingly unassailable maze of twisted one-way streets, by carefully following *O Guia*.

I set out in my lonely but eager explorations of this great and fascinating city with the same intent held by long-term pris-oners in solitary confinement. They devise daily routines while bound by surreal surroundings. They count or journal or do any-thing that keeps their minds sharp and normal, toward the day when there will be release. I got myself into and out of numer-ous peculiar and potentially dangerous situations. This was pref-erable to the scenario in which Manny, upon returning at the end of his vibrantly busy working day, would ask what I had done that day and I could only say, "Nothing."

August was a stellar month, because I caught up with Joyce, whose speech to the Newcomer's Club about the African dei-ties, the orixas, I had enjoyed so much in May. She came to my home on a day when Idalice was there. Idalice, also black, beamed with delight that her "Senhora" had a black friend. In the long run, this did not alter our basic relationship, but she did seem, after that, slightly less hostile.

Joyce's eyes scanned my walls and settings, trying to find something complimentary to say. When she couldn't, she kept silent on that potential subject. I appreciated her integrity as well as the confirmation of what I already knew. In no way could I have given that place a soul.

We had lunch on the balcony of Manny's bedroom, looking out over the pool and across to the compound where the Doans soon would live. By the time Idalice brought coffee, we were soulmates, sitting on the bedroom floor littered with various little personal treasures I was sharing.

We were still talking, by then sitting at the dining room table, when Manny came home from the office. They met, and liked each other, and then Joyce left.

Early in September the Doans returned to Brazil, this time to stay as immigrants. They brought, as a dependent, their twenty-three-year-old daughter, Angela, who had recently graduated from college and had been convinced by her parents that beginning her career in Brazil could be a wise move.

Jim was there, ostensibly, to begin functioning as the new president of *Whirlpool do Brasil*. After his job as comptroller for Whirlpool had been erased, he had done highly valued work for the corporation in Europe, financially evaluating the Phillips Company in which Whirlpool was acquiring major holdings. Coincident with Jim's arrival in Brazil was Whirlpool's consideration of whether to acquire Phillips subsidiaries in Argentina, Chile, Colombia, and Venezuela. So instead of allowing Jim to settle in and have Manny start training him to take over the Brazilian operation, the home office sent him off, accompanied by Mike Etchenique, to all those various countries to do assessments.

The Doans moved into the same complex in which the Batemans had lived, but in a building closer to ours. We could wave to each other from our balconies. Whirlpool life was getting cozier and cozier.

Pam sewed. She sewed even more than I did. So in Manny's

eyes, either my sewing was no longer strange or Pam's behavior was equally inappropriate. I don't think he had time to notice such things any more.

Olga went to work helping Pam decorate. This was a good occupation for Pam and Angela, who had in essence been shipped to Brazil and then abandoned. As they were alone on Angela's birthday, Manny and I took them out to dinner. Off and on, when Jim was in town between countries, all five of us dined together, out of mutual choice either at Tomatto's or at a nearby Chinese restaurant. We were compatible.

On one such occasion, over the Brazilian national drink to which we had all become addicted, *caipirinhas*—a concoction of lime juice and sugar cane liqueur—I overheard Jim and Manny commiserating about the untenable situation in which they found themselves. It seemed to have just occurred to Jim, who said something about "once you've agreed to that contract and you're out of the U.S. you have to do whatever they say." Manny nodded a brooding agreement. They were talking about the expatriate policy, which had been slapped on Manny after he agreed to go to Brazil. I did not know what they were talking about at the time. Now I do.

September 14, Manny and I were dinner guests of an older couple named Aida and Arnauldo. He was an architect trying to win Manny's vote for an assignment to some *Whirlpool do Brasil* project.

Never before nor since have I experienced such perfection in planning and execution—and hadn't I worked as a maid? Hadn't I been a visiting queen at the St. Paul Winter Carnival? Hadn't I dined with the Etcheniques' at their home and at their club? Hadn't I seen many movies?

Eight guests in all, as there should be, had been selected with compatibility in mind. The distinguished German couple and we were clearly meant for each other. The canapé tray, whenever offered by the maid, was completely restocked before each pass.

Two attendants served at dinner, each side of the table simultaneously, from silver platters exquisitely filled with beef roast *en broche* and accompaniments. Second servings had the same fresh, unmarred appearance as the first.

Inwardly, I squealed with delight at the inclusion of a special cheese course. To cleanse the palate, of course. Topped off with something chocolate. Liqueurs and coffee in the drawing room. Even an "only for our special friends" tour of their perfectly appointed dwelling.

I wrote an effusive but nonetheless sincere thank you in which I expressed with honest sentiment my doubt that even the Duke and Duchess of Windsor could have hosted with more grace and elegance.

Aida called me the following week to say how much the distinguished German woman had enjoyed my company and that the three of us must have lunch soon. Arnauldo did not get the contract, and we ladies did not lunch. I would not have carried it that far, anyway. The mere thought of staging a reciprocal dinner at our place would have driven me insane.

My weight, noted on the calendar, was up to 63 kilos, or 139 pounds. A sign I was not a happy camper. I was feeding that sinking feeling in the bottomless pit of my stomach.

On September 28, Sam Bateman arrived, followed by Larry Kremer on the twenty-ninth. We made no effort to see each other.

On the thirtieth, a Friday, the Doans went with us to a Newcomer's Club party at a member's home. After a few drinks, Jim cozied up to me and shared his concerns about a report that had come in from the port in Santos that day. Their shipment of household goods had arrived and been damaged en route. He was going to keep the bad news from Pam until Monday so as not to ruin her weekend. "She's had enough problems."

Well, so have I, Jim, in case you hadn't noticed. I didn't need to be hearing that, either. In despair, I saw that my charade was going too well; Jim viewed me as a set of strong shoulders he could lean on. Not so. Having almost no one to lean on myself, I was precariously close to falling over. Inside, I was collapsing into a depressed gray ball. I wondered how I would cope with the Doans' expectations that I would support them as the new First Family of *Whirlpool do Brasil*. My energy for supporting First Families had been drained by the Batemans, and almost nothing had occurred to replenish the exhausted supply.

Since their shipment would not make it up the escarpment from Santos to São Paulo for at least another week, Pam and Angela did not have appropriate clothing to wear to the following Monday evening's Brastemp-sponsored event, a performance by the Chinese Opera Company. Putting on my politically correct face, I "volunteered" to take them to shops recommended by Sandra, the office secretary.

The Doans were still staying at the Maksoud, and Marcus and I called for them there. Manny drove separately to pick up Jim for a visit to the Brastemp installation in Rio Clara. Joining them for the excursion and assembling with all of us for a moment in the hotel lobby were Dick Litzinger and Larry Kremer, both of whom barely said hello to me and chose not to look me in the eye.

The next evening was the event for which Pam and Angela had needed new dresses. They looked divine and felt good about themselves. Pam's, as I recall, was a soft celery color—a favorite of mine. I was comfortable in a swirly French silk abstractly printed in black and white.

David Whitwam arrived in time to preside over an elegant private-dining-room supper for our Whirlpool "family" before we went to the Chinese opera. Dave sat across the table from me and a bit to the right. I anticipated he would make some pretense of interest in my welfare and was prepared when he called across the table, "Well, how are things going, Roz?"

I gave him my practiced look, calculatedly cool, and replied, "Leveled off and holding. And you?"

Later, both a van and a car were required to transport our party from the hotel to the National Theater. I was the only woman to ride in the van, which I entered after Dave was seated. Although he had a vacant seat next to him, I moved on. Seated that close to the man I perceived as "Iago" in my personal Othellian drama, I could not have maintained the pretense of civility required to pull off another "don't rock the boat" event.

I sat instead with Steve Holmes, and we talked about his recently purchased house in St. Joseph.

In the lounge area of the opera house, I was aware that Ruth and Rudolpho Bertola, whom I had known so long and thought I knew well, snubbed me. Manny explained later that it was business related. They were snubbing everyone that evening— for reasons I didn't need to know about. "That I didn't need to know . . ." seemed familiar.

The final event of the Chinese week was the circus, which apparently nobody important wanted to attend. Manny got tickets for us and for the office staff and their families. I sat in the bleachers with Manny on my right and Marcus on my left. The performers were great, but the experience was a hollow one for me. Manny did not even notice I was speaking to him when I addressed my first few delighted-with-the-show remarks to him. I was forced to turn to Marcus for repartee.

All the American visitors were gone by Friday, October 7. Manny and I packed our bags for suburban Embu and retreated into our friend Joyce's world for the weekend. What a different world it was, and soothing to both of us. We were accommodated in separate suites. Breakfast consisted of coffee, fruit, and pound cake. Joyce does not cook, so we ate out in one mysterious cavern after another. In each, Joyce was well known. We experienced a deeper Embu than had been visible to us before.

The following week, with Manny beamed back into his office, Joyce and I drove to Aparecida for an overnight with Brazil's patron saint. We stood before the black, 15^1/$_2$-inch-high statue in its niche above the elevated causeway, which spanned the width of the Cathedral above and behind the altar to Christ. Joyce glowed in epiphany.

"It's Oxum," she said breathlessly. "The attendants know this. See, they have placed flowers in her colors, white and gold, on either side."

Oxum is the Nigerian-Brazilian deity who is the goddess of rivers. Blacks would know that this statue, which had emerged from the nearby Paraíba river, was the river itself.

Joyce was a devotee of Oxum, sister goddess to Yemanja, who is commemorated each New Year's Eve on Copacabana beach, and sister to Oya, goddess of precipitation. I was coming to identify with Oya, among whose attributes are thunder and lightning.

###

We left for a home visit in the States on October 27. We went "home," but, because we were mere tourists, we stayed at the Boulevard Hotel. My body weight leveled off, even declined a bit.

Previously when we had lived in Brazil for Whirlpool, John Eser had required that Manny, the children, and I undergo exit-Brazil medical exams at company expense, just as we had undergone pre-Brazil physical examinations. Had we contracted any tropical diseases, his department would have assumed responsibility for treatment.

Because November 1988 was close enough to exit-Brazil time, coming up in March 1989, Manny figured his biennial check-up at the Mayo Clinic would count as an exit-Brazil exam. There-fore, we scheduled my exam as well. The company had paid for my pre-Brazil exam. This one could count as my expatriate exit exam. Such timing offered an advantage, we thought, because in the unlikely event that we had contracted a tropical ailment, we still had time to have it treated in Brazil by doctors familiar with local diseases.

During my exam, I talked to the doctor about my depres-sion, which, having developed and intensified over the two years since we had been to the Mayo Clinic, had become severe. I hoped that she, familiar with corporate examinations and stress symptoms related to corporate life, would have some way of finding relief for the dramatic, dark, intense anger that colored my personality as it turned in on itself to produce depression.

The doctor saw a dishrag of a person. But her only help to me was in listening and sympathizing. She did nothing else be-cause, I suppose, there was nothing else she could do. She did not even mention my emotional condition in the letter she wrote summarizing the examination's findings. Even that omission was for my long-term benefit. It should not be found in the records of a corporate spouse that she was a weak link, that she couldn't take it.

For my first interview and the examination procedures which followed, I wore a plain, zip-front cotton frock to facilitate the frequent disrobing I knew would be part of the package. I had penciled my eyebrows, but otherwise wore no makeup, feeling it was hardly necessary to the circumstances.

This drabness seemed to upset the doctor. My appearance was as depressed as my attitude. For our second and final meet-ing, I made it a point to wear a fine suit, a colorful blouse, rouge, lipstick, and even a little perfume. She looked relieved. I was pleased to be able to brighten her life, even though she could do nothing for mine.

While at the clinic, Manny was acting strangely, penny-pinching in unnecessary and uncharacteristic ways. He called my attention to the size of the hotel dry-cleaning bill, as though I, who had only one item on it, was being extravagant. I planned to buy a dress in one of the fabulous shops in the Khaler Hotel where we stayed. The dress would make its debut at the Newcomer's Club holiday dinner dance held atop the São Paulo Hilton, for which we already had reservations.

Usually I am so frugal that I make many of my own clothes, so Manny never had cause to say what he said to me in Rochester: "I hope you won't spend too much for a dress."

I hadn't planned on spending "too much," whatever amount that was, for a dress, but angry over his unnecessary remark, I upgraded and did, in fact, spend more for a dress than ever before or since. Damn it, I would dress for that event so no one, especially not Manny, would be thinking, as the Rio hotel's doorman did, that he should have a "better woman."

We flew from Rochester, Minnesota, to the Twin Cities and rented a car—which, Manny announced, only he would drive. We stayed with my sister, Nanci, and her husband, Dick Anderson, at their home in Arden Hills.

There we experienced an early snowfall and a slickness under the wheels to which winter drivers must annually adjust. Yet that slipperiness was not the cause of the peculiar accident that occurred as Manny backed the rented Toyota down the incline of the driveway. The accident lay inside himself, in the disheveled snarls of his altering personality. As the rear of the car veered far to the left, leaving the asphalt and knocking over a decorative light pole, he turned to me and blurted, "See? That's what I mean about what can happen. That's why I don't want you to drive."

I took this statement to be an abbreviation for, "See what can happen even with me, the expert, in charge? Imagine how

disastrous this could have been if you had been at the wheel!"
Such had been his rationale during our first stint in Brazil when
I had been denied the opportunity to drive. Nevertheless, I drove
in São Paulo, and I had been driving my own rented car mere
weeks before. Driving, as such, was not the issue. The issue was
control—his need to establish control over me as his own loss of
control over himself and his job became ever more intolerable
to him. Through a minor car collision, the reality of his larger
loss of control forced its way from his subconscious into cognizance, and it underscored our mutual awareness that we were
both on a disastrous collision course. The choice of that course
had been his, not mine. His conscience required that he be the
one at the wheel so that, when the nebulous-but-inevitable
greater accident occurred, he would bear the responsibility.

Sunday, November 6, my sister, my brother, and I held a
family birthday party for our mother, who was turning eighty-
one. Our joint present to her was a bathing suit, which we convinced her she would need, because she was returning with
Manny and me for a visit to Brazil.

She flew with us to South Bend where we rented another
car, drove to St. Joseph, and checked in again at the Boulevard.
With our family, we celebrated her birthday again. Manny and I
also cast our votes in the 1988 presidential election.

The three of us then flew to Miami and on to São Paulo. The
Doans met us at our destination with, literally, armloads of flowers. They had been "alone in Brazil" for sixteen days. Never
before nor since have I been greeted by anyone so happy to see
me. Marcus was there, also, with the second company car, to
handle our luggage and to drive us home.

Mom was going to stay until December 10. On December
13, Manny and I were leaving for Chile and the Antarctic. As
the Doans also had travel plans, we had all decided, back in
October, that the office Christmas lunch would be held on Fri-

day, December 9, to accommodate everyone's travel schedules. It was also known, back in October, that my mother would be with us, and that I planned for her to join us for the party.

The Doans took us out to dinner the night we arrived. They took us out again a few nights later to relay the bad news they had been withholding, not wanting to insinuate it into our home-coming. I feel sorry for them yet for what they had to do, and for what they had to do to us.

Pam and Jim both wanted us to start with a round of *caipirinhas*. I was the only one who abstained from that round and from the next, although even my mother was joining in.

Then Jim, lamenting that I was stone-cold sober—not the best condition for what was coming next—announced he was being transferred out of Brazil. My god—they had just arrived! He was going to work with Phillips in Europe.

Then he told us that Sam Bateman, who was back at the home office, had advised as a personnel strategy that he should not tell Manny about it until the last moment. Devastating as the news was, I admired Jim for breaking it to us as he did, together, and with his family, supporting his decision to violate a com-pany directive.

To Manny the news meant he would not be able to pass on the fullest possible knowledge of the groundwork he had laid to Jim Doan's replacement before he, himself, left to retire in March.

After that news, I ordered a double *caipirinha*, even though it was time for dessert.

All of this and what followed passed over my mother's head, which was just as well.

Groping for something upbeat to say, I offered, "Well, at least there's the December 9 office party to look forward to."

Then Manny, two *caipirinhas* and several beers to the wind, said, "Well, as a matter of fact, there isn't. We had some meetings at the office about establishing policy for Christmas parties and have decided from now on, they will be only for office staff."

All three Doans sat sheepishly while I felt as though my face had been publicly slapped. Clearly, Pam and Angela knew about the decision. It had been discussed with them. Manny probably was supposed to have told me earlier but hadn't, having little realized it would be such an explosive evening.

Pam and Angela couldn't have cared less about the office party. They hadn't been in São Paulo long enough to establish relationships with the office staff. They had not made the investment, as I had, in two previous Brazilian Christmases. In the States I had spent as much of my short home leave shopping for presents for the office staff as I had spent shopping for my own family. In addition to Sandra, Marcus, and the cleaning lady, the staff had come to include an office boy, a junior secretary, and an executive replacement for Manny, George Palmgreen, an American already living in Brazil who was married to a Brazilian.

In reality I had bought two sets of presents: one to give at Christmas and another to give in March when we would be saying a final farewell. At the time I was making the purchases, Manny had seemed grateful for my efforts and found my ideas appropriate. But he lifted not a finger to assist; he was off shopping for something else.

The deliberately careful way Manny phrased his "no Christmas party for you" announcement seemed calculated to give me the false impression that the entire office staff had been involved in discussing the matter, yet I'm sure it had been decided solely by Jim and Manny. They, for sure, had sealed the final decision.

What had the Whirlpool Corporation done to this wonderful, magical youth whom I had followed into post-Nazi Germany and brought back to the U.S., where—to quote Carl

Hennemann in a 1953 *St. Paul Pioneer Press* article—he "really learned about American democracy"?

A further quote from that same article illuminates the tragic transformation Manny had observed: "In a German factory, the foreman is a dictator. He hires a number, fires a number, reprimands a number. There is no human element. You know you've got a boss and what he says goes."

As Manny had remarked in 1953 in an analysis of corporate structure, "It's not much different from the Nazi party." He had thought that knowing of this similarity was enough to immunize him from its effects, even though we both knew he was susceptible when in 1985 he said, "I find working for Whirlpool inconsistent with having a spiritual life."

It was too late. Manny had become one of them. Representing Whirlpool, he who had been duped but couldn't admit it—because corporate men do not make mistakes—was duping me. And issuing fiats. Gone for me was what the journalist Carl Hennemann, in the same article, quoted me as calling "democracy in the family."

The Doans decided they had to cancel the Thanksgiving Day reservation they had made for the American Society dinner. What was the point of trying to make new friends and establish themselves in the community? How would they have responded to the inevitable questions asked new arrivals when they were actually on their way out?

We picked up the Doans' reservations, inviting Joyce and her Argentine painter friend, Raoul, to join us. Raoul was back in South America after spending several years in Italy.

Mom said it was the most beautiful evening she had ever experienced. It made me happy she found joy in my world where, to me, everything had become theater of the absurd.

The next evening, we three disappeared with Joyce into her mists of Embu for the weekend. What a different, healing, milieu.

Monday, Manny reentered Whirlpool's world. Mom and I, with Trude, visited the *favela*. Unlike Lori, Mom was hardened enough not to shed tears at the sight of malnutrition, tattered clothing, and open sewage, but she made a substantial donation.

The night of the ball, at which I wore a dress that cost "too much," Manny escorted Mom and me to the rooftop dining room. That was about all we saw of him until he rejoined us at our assigned table for dinner.

Mom was unable to stand comfortably for the length of time required for cocktail-time circulation. After a bit, I found her a comfortable chair with a view overlooking the brightly lit city and stayed with her, except for periodic replenishment of our punch cups and brief chats with acquaintances along the route to and from the punch bowl.

Manny came by a time or two to hurriedly explain what he had to do that kept him from being with us. His reasons were shades of Flavia, the tour guide whom he "had to" help in Rio, and of the horseback-riding tourists whom he "had to" lead back to the Pousada Caiman guest house.

On another night, Marcus drove Mom and me to a small sanctuary in the suburbs where Joyce had invited us to attend a spiritual meeting of her macumba affiliation. We dressed all in white to be among the people who were basically the same as the ones who made some Christians nervous on New Year's Eve at Copacabana beach in Rio.

I could not understand the Christians' problem. We were greeted at the door and, as guests, given preferred seating, the same way I have been treated when visiting Baptist churches in the U.S. The "problem," if there is a real one, may be that macumbistas honor female manifestations of the deity equally with manifestations of the male.

Two years later when I attended Mom's Lutheran funeral service, I kept my thoughts focused on a photo of her that I brought with me, placed on the altar, and removed for recession, feeling glad for her and for myself that she had experienced the December 1988 evening with the Afro-Brazilian gods and goddesses.

I had urged Manny to go with us that night. He couldn't. Honest and insightful, he knew why he couldn't. It was a recapitulation of feeling that a spiritual life was incompatible with working for Whirlpool. He said, "If I go with you, I won't be able to go to work in the morning."

He could spend weekends at Joyce's, in her company and in her home—and he badly needed that—but he could go no further.

As it turned out, Sam Bateman was in Brazil on business over December 9 and attended the office Christmas lunch, the third annual, which he had missed the first two times. I was treated to Manny's and Jim's accounts of what a great time Sam had at the party I was not allowed to attend. I, who had labored to co-host the two earlier events.

Jim, because he was not in Brazil the two previous Decembers, lacked the personal history that might have made him sensitive to the pain I experienced from their remarks, comments that excluded me from the event completely. Beyond completely. They forgot the event even mattered to me. Jim was crass, because he had not been sensitized; Manny, because—during the years of his will being bent to Sam's—he had become desensitized to the needs of his marriage. These two insensitive men held positions of power that gave them authority over details of my life, the effects of which were truly sobering to contemplate.

Pam Doan is a smart and sensible woman. She worried about

the same threats to her husband's balance and integrity as I did about my husband's. She shared with me an article in Varig's in-flight magazine, *Icaro*. Written by Brazilian journalist Carlos Drummond, the article was entitled, "When you and the company become synonymous." Its thesis confirmed much I suspected—and feared.

Drummond noted that the identification some people have with the company for which they work can become so strong that the border between the individual and the company becomes blurred.

Fusion of personal identity with the company is fed, Drummond says, by the success the company accords an executive as he climbs the ladder. The higher he climbs, the stronger become his needs for self-esteem and personal fulfillment. Balance is called for in how these needs are met. If he works for the company twenty-four hours a day, receiving all his reinforcement there, everything else in his life, including emotional balance, will atrophy. Such a situation is good neither for the executive nor for his company.

Specifically of Brazil, Drummond says it is difficult to strike a happy medium between private life and business life because developing economies tend to demand much more of businesses and employees.

Hear! Hear! To that last sentence, I could add, "especially if they are at the beck and call of superiors in the States who are, through inexperience, insensitive to the pressures under which expatriates work."

As I read the article, the thought hit me that perhaps Sam's anticipated visit was the true reason I was excluded from the office Christmas party. A year and a month had passed since Fran Bateman had ordered me out of her apartment. We had not spoken since, nor had the incident been spoken about between Sam and Manny.

Meanwhile, at the office, Manny was signing both our names to Christmas cards I never saw and sending them out to his "business family," some of whom I never met. At the same time, my exclusion from the office Christmas party sent the clear message I was not a part of that family. Manny did not find this cognitively dissonant. I did.

The papers with which to mortgage our house had at least required my signature, even if after the fact. For the office Christmas cards, both my participation and my signature were forged. I was less than chattel in that my actual existence was not necessary. An abstraction sufficed.

When Mom left, we solved the problem of her frailty, noticeably increased during her month with us, by boarding her as a handicapped person requiring wheelchair service. She had a room reservation at the Miami airport hotel so she could rest between connecting flights. She smiled sweetly and blissfully as a flight attendant wheeled her away from us to the embarkation gate.

Once back home from the airport, Manny and I shifted into the next scenario—packing to leave for three weeks in Chile and Antarctica.

I asked, "In your careful concern about setting policy to provide appropriate Christmas spirit for your 'office family,' which no longer includes me, what consideration have you given to my being able at least to say 'Merry Christmas' to them? Won't you be embarrassed if they're offended by my leaving town without even a gesture?"

From Manny's expression, somewhere between blank and dumbfounded, I gathered that the thought had not crossed his mind. I put together a sack containing boxes of chocolate and personalized mementos for each person at the office. When

Marcus took us to the airport, we gave the sack to him, so he could distribute the gifts at the office the next day.

That year, we could have been home for Christmas, but neither Manny nor I could bear to be in St. Joseph for Christmas merely as tourists. We thought if we went home for Christmas, the pain of withdrawal—to go back to Brazil for the three more months that were contracted—would be greater than we could endure. Better to protect ourselves by doing something else.

Antarctica would be good for us, I thought, because the location would give us a hiatus from the conflicting cultural influences sapping us dry. We planned to sail through pristine seascapes outside the influence of Brazilian social stratification, American linearity and oversimplification and the Protestant work ethic subsumed by the corporation. We were to spend Christmas Eve and Christmas Day at sea, traveling from Elephant Island to the Falklands. Yes! That would put us in the company of an entire shipload of people away from home by choice. In such company, we could pretend that we, too, were, away from home by choice.

We cavorted with penguins of all sorts—chin strap, gentoo, king, magellanic, Adelie, rockhopper—within their other-than-human cultures. We bathed in the hot springs of Pendulum Cove. We basked in the all-but-unbearable brilliance of sun mingled with mountains of ice in the spectacular Lemaire Channel. In inflated rubber rafts called zodiacs, we dramatically, and a bit dangerously, threaded our way through ice to Peterman Island, the southernmost point of our adventure at 65 degrees 12.7 minutes latitude.

Even that paradise of rugged luxury could not undo the damage wrought on us.

What analogy will convey what I felt? What was it most like? After thirty-eight years of marriage to the great love of my life, our relationship was like that of a Siamese twinship in which

the twin to whom I was biologically connected was dying—
slowly, but inexorably. That twin had been drugged and did not
know he was dying. The drug reached me too, but not as fully. I
could still dial 9–1–1. I did that. I dialed repeatedly the number
that rings in the Whirlpool corporate office in Benton Harbor,
Michigan. They refuse to respond. There was no one else to call.

I determined to live as long as I could, as best I could. To do
so, I might have to sever ties to the dying twin.

The stimulating diversion of assimilating into the travel
group in Santiago and journeying on to Punta Arenas served us
both well. In Punta Williams, we boarded the *Society Explorer* as
seemingly well adjusted as any of our companions.

Then the Pousada Caiman experience began all over again,
this time in spades. However, thanks to Pam Doan and that article, this time I understood better what was happening as
Manny, never shedding his Whirlpool personality, set about
courting the ninety-nine other passengers. Those people would
give him all the approval and validation he needed to sustain
the image he had of himself, which was markedly different from
what I perceived. I imagine he avoided conversation with me
because he knew he could count on disapproval from me. The
others were much more reinforcing.

His behavior toward me was calculated to impress the
ninety-nine as being perfectly proper, perhaps even exemplary.
I found no warmth or sincerity in his escorting me to meals, or
in his rising to greet me when I came into the bar–lounge, where
he could generally could be found. Those were postures.

We both experienced the hot springs, but not together. He
was dressed for the zodiac ride before I was, and could not wait
while I bundled into the required boots and parka. It also would
have been hard for anyone to snap our picture together in the
penguin rookeries. Manny always chose to wander in a direction different from mine.

As on our trips to Rio and to the Pantanal, he left our room earlier in the morning than I did and returned to it later, with one remarkable and telling exception. On the white night of solstice, December 21, the sun rose at 2:48 A.M. and set at 11:31 P.M., and I invited Manny to join me for the romantic excitement of photographing a lifeboat in natural light at midnight. He was too tired, he said, accused me of being nonsensical, and went to bed uncharacteristically early. Guilt kills love. Eventually the guilt is so hard to bear that the mind has to fix blame elsewhere.

My heart broke in empathetic anguish and despair as I watched Manny, on some nameless Antarctic island beach, instruct fellow passengers to board the zodiac he had commandeered. He was impressing fewer people than he thought. Most turned away, embarrassed for this man who strolled with a sense of indispensability through misty fantasies of grandeur.

Christmas Eve provided one brief clear view of the deep connectedness we had long known, but which had become so tenuous. He presented me with a gold ring in the form of a serpent with emerald eyes and a diamond crown. The head and neck were like those of a swan. It was a carefully thought-out present, planned well in advance of the event.

I was moved to the core and saw hope. His gift was related to his much earlier comment, "I'm afraid of what you're going to do to me when we get back to the States." Those two actions, separated by months of emotional sterility, came from down deep inside where the family-man personality was dialing his own version of 9–1–1.

The next day was a different story. Our off-course relationship was again in troubled waters; worse, even, than before.

On Christmas Day 1988, the *Society Explorer* crossed the Drake Passage en route to Port Stanley in the Falkland Islands on high seas that sent the ship into a rolling list of thirty-five degrees.

The Expedition Log records: "Breakfast proved to be a disaster! That thirty-five-degree roll put the dishes on the floor, capsized the Christmas trees, and . . . let us know this was no ordinary day on the little red ship, and no ordinary Christmas. It was a Christmas none of us will ever forget."

I do not remember ever being sicker in my life. I was one of many who did not leave my cabin all during that long day. Wearing slick silk long johns as pajamas, my body slid the length of my bunk with each roll of the ship and lay miserably inert until a reverse roll shunted me back to the other end.

The middle finger of my left hand wore the tender gift I had received the evening before, but where was my husband? With a sailor's heart, legs, stomach and love of stormy seas, he went on deck early to revel in the adventure.

As morning progressed to midday, I wretched up all stomach content. By two P.M. when a steward voluntarily brought tea and a sandwich in breakproof containers, I felt my life being saved both by the food and human contact. Where was my husband in this, my direst of hours?

He breezed in late in the afternoon, looking and smelling healthily and wholesomely of cold, moist salt air. He needed more film, or some such thing. He acted surprised to find me there, in bed, ill. Where had he thought I was? He seemed surprised I wondered why he had not wondered, surprised I expected he might have taken some care of me.

I knew where he had really been. He was being young again. He had the glow about him of the youth he was when we first met, when he recalled for me his brief, disastrous career in the German Navy and the several summers following his escape from the Russian prison camp when he skippered a sailboat on Starnberger See for the "Amis," as our occupation troops were called.

Siamese-twinned to him, I felt a bit more of the poison atrophying our union. Alone, without outside help from a support group of any kind, I was not strong enough to endure the disease for both of us.

By dinner time, my body was better. Dressed bravely in my black flared skirt and flowing red silk Cossack shirt, I headed for the bar where I knew I would find Manny. Halfway there, I had to return to the cabin, one more time, to vomit. After that, all was well, as far as appearances were concerned.

The next afternoon as I prepared to go ashore and scout Port Stanley, I was startled by Manny's insistence on accompanying me. I had grown accustomed to his not wanting to do much of anything at the same time I did, which had made me feel melancholy.

We shared a warm, close feeling as we made our way from shops to church to tavern, heads bowed against the gale. What was left of love, we experienced as nostalgia such as one might find at a wake, in requiem for what already had been lost.

We were nearing the end of our journey to the far South and nearing, as well, the end of any magic that once had been between us. That last glimmer of closeness we felt for each other, on a bleak island set in raging waters, was far too little, and it came far too late.

We were at sea three more days. Manny was seldom near. I found myself seeking out the company of second-marriage couples, wanting to hear from them about the mechanics of divorce, about the trauma involved, about the prognosis for one's solitary survival thereafter.

Mechanically, perfunctorily, plane by plane, we threaded our way back to São Paulo. Not to home, to sanctuary, but to the public arena of our domicile, where several more battles had yet to be fought.

###

As humiliating for me—and as depressing—as the *Whirl-pool do Brasil* events surrounding Christmas of 1988 had been, it was worse when the Doans hosted their own farewell lunch for the office staff on January 9, 1989.

Jim Doan might never have realized he erred on the Christmas guest list decision—when "the office" did not consider me "family" enough to go to the company's luncheon—had that guest list not come into juxtaposition with the Doan's list of "office family" guests for the lunch they planned to give as their farewell gesture. *Of course!* I was to be invited to that.

My invitation did not come from Jim nor through Manny. They both convinced Pam it was appropriate for her to call me. She ate the crow that should have been theirs. It was as difficult for her to plead with me that I was "as much family as anyone" as it was for me to swallow the last of my pride and attend. What would the real office family think if I weren't there? It was personally absurd for me to go, but it would have been corporately absurd not to. For the last time, I rose to meet the public relations demands of the Whirlpool Corporation.

A few weeks later, during one of our last "pillow talks," Manny bared the struggle going on in his soul. He debated within himself what to do about the conference call from the Benton Harbor Administration Center he had received from the two former presidents of *Whirlpool do Brasil.* They urged him to alter a report he had submitted so the bottom line for Brazil would appear better than it actually was. I asked if he was going to do it. He replied, "Why not? I don't even care, anymore."

What a turnabout statement from the young man, grown old, who in our first days of marriage had been offended to the core when I did not take his "word of honor" seriously. Manny had said to me during his vulnerable shift from post-Nazi Germany into American democracy, "You have no idea what it feels like to have been taught one way all of your life and then, suddenly, to be told by the U.S. Occupation Forces and most of the rest of the world that everything you believe is wrong." We might both, in 1989, have said to the world, "You have no idea what it feels like to have incorporated into your ethos such elements of American democracy as honesty, fair play, and compassion, only to have the opposites of these virtues practiced against you by the very corporation that for thirty-six years had made you part of its family."

I shed tears for the culture of better values Manny and I had pledged to create. We had created them for a time, at least. Social forces eroded them. I shed tears of personal remorse that those erosions of honor had occurred in my country—that singular gift I was able to bestow on my shining Knight from Paumshausen.

I did everything in my power to maintain my marriage and, with it, the cohesiveness of my family during those last difficult years; everything short of surrendering my own personal integrity, which was something I could not do.

By February 1989, I gave up and set about making arrangements to get myself out of the clutches of the Whirlpool Corporation and beyond the control of my husband.

Every now and then, I listen to men talk about why America's families are breaking up. Most of what they say places the blame, for one reason or another, on women. My experience suggests we might look to corporate behavior as a major cause. The business leaders and captains of industry I have known, by and large, are poor role models for the millions of middle- and lower-class males who esteem and emulate their conduct.

Telltale stories from within corporate walls are rarer than reports from behind royal castle walls. Why? Because fear of the fraternal "power-over" runs even stronger through corporations than it does behind the parapets.

###

Photo by Michael Price, St. Joseph, Michigan, 1986

This final portrait symbolizes Requiem for the
marriage of Emanuel and Rosalyn Von Koenig.

Part Three

File No. 90-659-CZ-T: Complaint and Jury Demand, Second Amended Complaint

The cover reason I gave for returning to the States was that I needed minor, but urgent, surgery. Manny—and Whirlpool—would have to let me go. They, my captors, would not have understood my need to escape them, nor would they have allowed it. During the six weeks between my escape in early February and his scheduled departure from Brazil March 23, Manny and I had little contact. Our few phone conversations were all patched-through business calls he made to the Benton Harbor office.

In one of those calls, he urged me to accept, with him, an invitation for dinner at the Batemans' St. Joseph home early in April "for the sake of appearances." We both understood that the invitation was issued for diplomatic reasons, and Manny said it would be diplomatic of us to accept. How, I wondered, could he even consider asking me to do such a favor for the couple who, in effect, kicked me out and were still shunning me and for the corporation in whose name they had done this? In between the Batemans' seventeen months of silence and their invitation to dinner, my damaged dignity and deteriorated self-confidence needed to hear a statement that started with "I'm sorry."

The only way I could rationalize Manny's inability to understand that an insult to me was an insult to him, as well, was to view his character as having become, by then, protectively Tefloned against feeling the humiliation and other pain I endured.

During those six weeks, Manny wrote to me twice. One cryptic note dealt with disposition of the furniture from our Santo Amaro apartment; a business-like inventory that could have been an accounting of our last years together. Neither the cancer-like depression inside me nor the pains developing in my neck and left arm were relieved by the seven sheets of accounting printout he included to show how financially stable we were. Our marriage, which began in the love and wonder of a great romance, was by that time measured in dollars and cents.

His second note was a perfunctory one-liner: "How are arrangements coming with the medical problem?"

On March 16, 1989, exactly twenty years from that day in 1969 when he first enplaned for Brazil saying, "I don't want to go. I'm scared," Manny celebrated his sixty-second birthday there. I sent a happy birthday streamer to be put up at his office.

During the time Manny stayed alone in Brazil, Joyce looked out for him on my behalf. After a weekend the two of them spent together with her friends, she reported to me, "He knows, Roz. He knows."

Although I had quietly begun divorce proceedings two weeks earlier, I would not tell him until he came home. He knew we were having problems but believed everything to be my fault, and I knew he needed to maintain that belief if he were to get through those last few weeks in Brazil.

Our thirty-eighth wedding anniversary was coming up on March 26, three days after Manny was due to arrive in the States. While I could still pay homage to his birthday, I could not honor the anniversary of a wedding that had lost its meaning. When Manny left Brazil on the twenty-third, he would have to face the actualization of his prophecy "I hate to think what you're going to do to me when we get back to the States."

I truly wish I had been strong enough to brave it out with him those final weeks; that I could have stood by him, followed the script and Teflon-coated the hypocrisy, as he did. Life would have been so much simpler if I had been able to go along with things as they were by pasting a smiley face over the whole mess. But I wasn't able to play life that way. Mind over hives had worked, but migraine blew my mind away altogether, forcing me to do whatever I could to relieve the pain.

On March 23, the curtain would rise to disclose an act-in-progress: Manny's and Roz's Requiem. I no longer could delay telling my sons and daughters-in-law they were about to become part of a broken family. I spoke to each couple separately. They were saddened, but not surprised.

Since divorce was about to become a fact, I needed their concurrence on some of the logistics. Jeff and Nancy were preparing to move into a home they had purchased. I would stay in the Benton Harbor apartment I had taken for the interim, allowing Manny to use the family home, which he did for four months until he bought his own house.

My decision to have Manny stay in what had been our family's home since 1971, the year we came to St. Joseph from our first three-year sojourn in Brazil, was based on wanting him to derive whatever comfort he would accept from it. I would tell him to take whatever household effects he wanted. When he did take some of my favorite things I was pleased, because that meant they held special memories for him, too. Of course, I still loved him, but I understood that he was incapable of making any of the amends that could have allowed us to go on together. He defended Sam. He defended Whirlpool. He, himself, identified with Whirlpool. He could not see "my problem."

I was going to meet him at the airport in South Bend, Indiana, and ask him to be at home the next day because he was going to be served with divorce papers. My sons agreed it might be unsafe for the two of us to make the hour-long drive back in the same car after such an announcement. Doug called the airport and reserved a rental car in Manny's name.

We all speculated about what Manny's reaction would be. Idealistically, I hoped for genuine remorse, protestations of love, and vows to work things out as soon as he effected his retirement from Whirlpool. I did not want a divorce. We were living out a premonition: the one in which I asked, "What am I going to do when I can't reach you any more?" and to which he had replied, "I don't know." I hoped he would recognize my drastic step of filing for divorce as an attempt to reach him. I genuinely hoped he would be responsive and we could reconcile.

However, Doug, himself a corporate man, said, "I hate to say this, Mom, but I think what he might say is, 'How can you bother me with that at a time like this, when you can see how tired I am and know how much work I have to do?'"

When I met him at the airport, Manny did indeed look bent and weary, and I invited him to sit down so we could talk. When I had delivered my message, he looked straight ahead at nothing in particular and said, "How can you bother me with that at a time like this, when you can see how tired I am and know how much work I have to do?"

With that, I had to write off my hoped-for miracle of reconciliation. Responding to the reality of Doug's corporate-wise prediction, I stood and answered, "You've just made this much easier for me. You'll find a car in your name at the counter over there."

At that point, I saw no hope of Manny's realizing what his "corporation first" attitude had done to our marriage unless Whirlpool first admitted its role.

ACLU attorneys I consulted in Detroit and Southfield both agreed that the corporation's actions, as I described them, were immoral, but they were not sure these actions were illegal—a dichotomy I did not understand. At any rate, while they saw the wisdom of my having an out-of-town attorney, they said engaging one who was too far away would give the corporation an advantage; the corporation could maneuver to increase my attorney's travel time and therefore increase my costs. They referred me to an attorney in Grand Rapids, which is two-and-a-half hours closer to the courthouse in St. Joseph, where the case would be filed.

On March 24, while Manny was being served with divorce papers, I was seeking legal counsel in Grand Rapids. The young attorney, dedicated and sympathetic, devoted several intense hours to taking detailed notes of my complicated story. She told me she would present the case to her firm and get back to me.

The following day, I washed my hair and packed. The day after that—my thirty-eighth wedding anniversary—my compassionate friend Ruby drove over from Kalamazoo to deliver me to the Ferguson Clinic in Grand Rapids. There I had my minor surgery the next day.

Flowers arrived from Jim Doan. He even called me from his new assignment in Italy in a show of caring and compassion. He seemed in hopes of repairing what he knew to be my unhappy relationship with Whirlpool, a relationship to which he had, unwittingly, made his own negative contribution. I believe he meant well, but I felt terrorized, as though the sinuous arm of the corporation could reach me anywhere.

The hearing date for the divorce was set for May 30. Never before in my lifetime had April showers threatened to bring forth such an unhappy May flower. I did not want to divorce, to forever separate from the great love of my life, and to break up my family. I had taken a step in that direction to shock Manny into realizing how bad things had become between us. I had hoped for a softening of my husband's hardened heart and some means of our finding a way back to each other. If, however, we could not reconcile, then there had to be a divorce.

Still hoping for reconciliation, and having lost all pride—like Karen Blixen in *Out of Africa*—I tried a desperate measure.

How does one go over the head of Whirlpool's CEO in Whirlpool's own company town? I appealed to the only person I knew whose standing at Whirlpool and in the community could be considered higher. I wrote a letter on April 10 to Elisha Gray, II, retired Whirlpool CEO, who still kept an office at Whirlpool's Elisha Gray II Research and Engineering Center.

In the letter, I acknowledged that my writing to him was unorthodox but not without precedent, because Manny had written to his CEO-successor, John Platts, as the only way to obtain a just evaluation following his 1969–1971 service in Brazil.

I outlined the course of Whirlpool's actions from 1985, covering everything the company did that caused my filing for a divorce—which was still possible to avert because the hearing was fifty days off. My letter concluded with the following paragraphs:

> *Ever since my return from Brazil on February 12, I have been seeking an out-of-area law firm to represent me in a suit against Whirlpool: for having manipulated both Manny and me into the overall situation and then into repetitive sub-situations where family vs. corporation choices were made necessary.*

Until today, when I thought of you and your continued in-volvement with Whirlpool, as well as your support of the Sa-maritan Center (I don't feel that counseling is an answer for me; rather than my adjusting to a situation I did not create, I feel that the victimizer should be called to account), I saw no place within the corporation (our "family!") to turn for re-dress. Manny, in 1971, could turn to CEO John Platts. I can-not turn to CEO David Whitwam; he is the problem.

If you choose to use your influence to have the corporation restore to me the dignity and honor it stripped from me, I would be grateful for a more peaceful settlement than the only alter-native open to me—legal action.

At the bottom of my letter, I typed the names of the four corporate executives to whom I was sending copies: Sam Bateman, Jim Doan, David Whitwam, and Manny Von Koenig.

Even as these letters dropped into the mouth of the large pick-up box at the post office, taking with them some weight from my shoulders, another letter was making its way to me. Weeks had passed during which I had not heard from the attor-ney in Grand Rapids who was going to "present the case to her firm and get back to me." Nor had she returned any of my re-peated phone calls to her office.

At last, a response. I tore open the cream-colored envelope with the embossed return address.

. . . unfortunately are unable to accept your offer of retainership.

So that was how it was going to be. Even a firm with ACLU leanings was not going to touch this feminist case. Did they fear the long arm of the corporation?

Three days later, I met with an attorney who worked alone, Karen Werme. Karen felt too inexperienced to handle such a case herself, but said she would help me find representation. She re-marked she'd be interested in representing Manny against Whirl-pool, because he really had a case. I acknowledged then how difficult my suit would be, because Manny didn't even recognize that he'd been injured; money and status had soothed all for him.

Karen started by calling Irene Piccone in Southfield, the first lawyer I had contacted. Irene recommended basing the case on breach of contract/breach of oral agreement. I felt encouraged by having two supporters in my corner.

If my corporate suit was having trouble getting off the ground, my divorce action made up for it. On May 30, I met with my divorce attorney, and Manny met with his, at the Berrien County Courthouse for our hearing. I felt the power over my own life flowing back into me as I took the stand and responded to all the judge's questions with precisely the lines my attorney and I had rehearsed. In less than ten minutes, the hearing was over and so was thirty-eight years of marriage. My birth name, Reeder, had been restored; I was no longer a "noble" Von Koenig—one to whom, when I married him, honor had meant everything. In divorcing Manny, I felt divorced, also, from the Whirlpool Corporation. They had become one and the same.

On June 12 I received a reply from Elisha Gray:

Dear Mrs. Von Koenig:

This letter is a belated acknowledgment of your letter to me of April 10, 1989, in which you describe the stressful situation you have experienced in the very recent months at Whirlpool.

First let me say I am very sorry you feel so strongly that Whirlpool has not been considerate of your particular needs in its work with Manny. I regret to say that since I have been almost totally removed from the corporation for nineteen years, it would be out of the question for me to interfere or intercede in a personnel problem that might come up at this time.

Since you quite properly included four other active Whirl-

pool executives in this matter by sending them a copy of your letter to me, I am sure that you will have received some reply from the appropriate man in answer to your letter. I hope the matter will not get to the point of seeking a legal solution, because in the many years when I was actively engaged in the company affairs, we never had to resort to that kind of solution to our internal decisions.

I wish you well.

None of the four corporate executives, including my husband, responded. As my idealistic hope for a miracle of intercession died, I knew I had to proceed with my original plan. Having championed the underdog all my life , how could I ever again speak up on behalf of anyone else if I did not have the will to speak up for myself? What kind of example would I be setting for my sons if their mother lacked the will to pursue justice in her own behalf?

Later that summer I wrote to the Esers, who were living in Stuttgart, Germany:

What is the world coming to, you ask, when even Manny and Roz can't stay married? The 1986–89 Brazilian assignment did us in. Corporate mentality got him.

You are going to be hearing all kinds of versions of "what happened." I have always thought enough of both of you to want you to have the facts, as I see them. Edith has been my role model, and I have always admired John's strength of character. I consider, to this day, that he represents the former, honorable Whirlpool that Elisha Gray alludes to in the copy of his letter, enclosed.

It took me quite a while to locate a lawyer who would take the case, but I have one now and am embarking on Reeder vs. Whirlpool. Copies of recent correspondence are enclosed, as well as the complete narrative (actually, I'm working on more).

You don't have to help me, you know that, but let me tell

you, I wouldn't turn down help, if offered. Read what I have sent; absorb it; recover from the shock. Then, if you feel you could write me something like an Elisha Gray letter (although more intimately supportive, because you are, yourself, part of the story and also were deeply wronged in the final days of your career), I'm sure the Court would find it corroborative of my statements.

Whatever. I feel that only after Whirlpool has been hauled before the bar of justice and coerced into some kind of apology will Manny be able to see what he succumbed to and be able to get himself out of it.

You are well off where you are—out of this.

Please wish us well—me in my battle against the dragon; Manny in recovering his senses.

With deepest respect and affection, Roz.

I received no reply from the Esers.

Although Elisha Gray had declined to intercede, his letter nevertheless warmed my heart because it gave me assurance that the kinder, gentler Whirlpool he and others had represented before Jack Sparks became CEO was not an illusion. His letter also affected Karen Werme, enhancing my credibility. Until then, there had to have been moments when she doubted the veracity of my outrageous—but true—tale.

Karen talked with a colleague, the sixth attorney to be consulted about the Whirlpool matter, and followed up that individual's referral to a seventh attorney. However, as she reported to number six, attorney number seven "declined to become involved in this case [because] he fears the client is too emotionally involved, and that anything that goes against her will be blamed on her attorneys."

Karen wrote in reply: "I understand his concern, but I don't think she will do that. . . . I'm hoping you will have time to look over M. Reeder's 'story,' and let me know if you are interested."

Attorney number six declined, claiming that because she knew Elisha Gray she could not possibly become involved. The news was not encouraging.

Karen's next step was to have me undergo psychological evaluation. Because of my own background (B.A. in Human and Animal Behavior, University of Minnesota 1961; M.A. in Educational and Developmental Psychology, Andrews University 1973), I welcomed the move, knowing it would be stuffy but meaningful. Over a period of two days, I spent many hours filling out various personality test forms and being interviewed.

"Aside from a certain amount of situational anxiety related to being evaluated," reported the psychologist, "she appears to be essentially normal. I could not uncover any areas which could be construed as pathological."

I could picture the methodically precise doctor sitting in his perfectly appointed office struggling to capture the essence of my being so he could reduce it to prepackaged citations from the official *Diagnostic and Statistical Manual of Mental Disorders*.

In my official diagnosis, he wrote:

> *She has a certain intensity about her. However, I believe this to be more a character trait or characteristic of her personality make-up and not a symptom, as such. I suspect she may 'front-off' some people because of this quality, but I also believe it serves her well as far as stamina, determination and endurance. As far as the stress-related reactions she reports upon finding out she and her husband were to return to Brazil, while there and immediately after her 'escape,' these would be diagnosed as reactive anxiety and depression. The technical names for these are Adjustment Reactions of adult life with mixed emotional features (309.28) and some physical symptoms (309.82).*

This evaluation reflected what I thought about myself—that I was "essentially normal"—although I felt my stress-related symptoms were considerably more severe than he reported. Still, I thought his diagnosis would lead to a conclusion that the "story" I was telling was true, that it would be clear to everyone that I had been unjustly treated, and that something should be done about it.

The psychologist and I had been close to reaching real rapport at one point. He told me I had checked "yes" to a key statement on one of the tests, and the evaluation guidelines required him to bring it up with me for further exploration. The statement was: "Strange and peculiar things have been happening to me."

"Well, yes," I responded. "I believe all the things I told you about the last three years of my life under Whirlpool management are 'strange and peculiar.' Don't you?"

For a moment, just a fleeting moment, I thought I saw in his eyes a real comprehension of my situation. Then he withdrew, back into the shell of conservative professionalism.

He concluded with a seriousness I could barely comprehend, because it ran counter to my expectation: he suggested I drop my notions of a lawsuit. He didn't think I had sustained sufficient damage on which to base a successful case. He said I should get on with psychological therapy that would help me adjust to what my life had become.

I said to him without hesitation, and probably with the "intensity" that "may front-off some people": "I will not spend one cent for therapy that would help me adjust to an insane situation."

Because the psychologist's report did nothing to strengthen my case, it did nothing to help Karen and me find legal representation for it. The milquetoast conclusions of the report alerted me to the bias of "establishment" thinking, and had the effect of further strengthening my deep-seated need for equitable resolution of my justified complaints. Inside myself, I screamed,

"How bad does it have to get? If I were any further debilitated, I wouldn't even be able to get up off the floor to speak out."

What had I done wrong in my practice of values? The legal profession—everyone but Karen—seemed powerless to help me, even though there was agreement that I had been wronged. I found even my own field, psychology, to be equally impotent.

It became more important than ever to get my case before a jury. Up to that point I had discovered that in the eyes of a corporation, the law, and community mental health—each of them an institution—I had no rights. I did not believe a jury of peers, people like myself, would agree.

A friend and colleague, Vivian Ahlers, an M.A., Limited License Psychologist, had been providing me with psycho-physical therapy, trying to ease the tension and pain from my limbs. She also provided a letter, written "To Whom It May Concern," to document information about me for Karen Werme's use. She began by sharing some background information.

> I have known Roz for a number of years and have greatly appreciated our warm collegial relationship. We met initially at a research conference and were pleased to discover common interests in the field of behavioral science. We have worked together preparing material for professional journals. I have particularly appreciated her lucid, profound, and original thinking. Our dialogues were always a stimulating occasion for new awareness for me. I have also valued her personal integrity, spontaneous good humor, and commitment to enhance her community, particularly working to facilitate good relationships among those of diverse cultural backgrounds. Her self-discipline, vitality, creativity and keen ability to focus on the task at hand have always made working with her a pleasure.

Then Vivian described seeing me again in September 1987 after an absence of several years. We were meeting for lunch during one of my brief visits to the States.

In the lobby of the restaurant, Roz introduced me to Glenn Youngstedt and Bill Gargiulo, whom she identified as being with the Human Resources Department at Whirlpool. Glenn drew her aside to chat for a few minutes while we were waiting for our table.

As we were eating, I remember becoming aware at first and then alarmed at unexpected differences in Roz. I was surprised and saddened at what I experienced as disorientation on her part. Our time together was so brief and I was so taken aback by the changes that I did not at that time question her as to what had brought them about. She seemed too fragile to confront at the time. But I remember turning things over in my mind afterward, trying to make some sense out of what I experienced. It was as though the integrity of her personality had somehow been compromised. I remember asking myself if this could be a manifestation of culture shock, but Roz was a seasoned and experienced traveler, and I had spent time with her following another trip abroad and had not witnessed changes of this nature. I remained puzzled and concerned.

Vivian Ahlers took me with her to Ann Arbor to attend the 1989 conference of the Michigan Society of Forensic Psychology. We thought I might learn how to be an effective witness, should my case get to court, because the subject of seven of the conference's presentations was "Law and the Practice of Psychology: Avoiding the Pitfalls."

For lunch we separated, joining groups at different tables. The three gentlemen with whom I lunched each shared the nature of his practice, whether private or within a corporation. Eventually, all eyes turned to me. I identified myself as "the Plaintiff." Conversation ceased. Fortunately, lunch was about over.

The conference was informative. I believe that had I been allowed a trial by jury, during which I could have taken the stand,

I would have been an effective witness in my own behalf.

At a later time, Vivian stepped in once again to champion my cause and me.

Karen and I settled on Irene Piccone's initial suggestion, breach of contract, for our legal thrust, and Karen made one last valiant attempt to find skilled and courageous legal counsel to prepare and file my suit. Attorney number eight agreed to see us at his office at two P.M. one week later.

Considering how important this appointment was to me, I cannot understand how I came to mark the wrong date on my calendar. Inexplicably, I stood up my legal counsel! The next earliest time for all three of us to meet was November 9.

What happened in the mind of this attorney during the intervening week is a mystery. Supposedly he had been sympathetic and interested on November 2, but not so seven days later. Karen became startled and alarmed before I did. I caught on more slowly, thinking he was merely playing devil's advocate as he threw at me a barrage of cruel and insulting questions.

His thrusts and parries focused on how it had been my own responsibility, as a consenting adult, to have said no in the first place. Moreover, he badgered, "What was keeping you in Brazil once you were there? You could have made your so-called escape at any time." And, "So what if Manny drank heavily in Brazil? He drank before he went to Brazil, and everybody knew it. Why is that Whirlpool's fault?"

Then, gazing across his desk with his weary head resting in his elbow-supported hand, he mildly stated, "These are the kinds of questions you should expect from Whirlpool's attorneys." In hoping to convince me I could not withstand such a barrage, he had convinced himself he could not. He declared such a case could not be won, because Whirlpool couldn't afford for me to win. The world's leading manufacturer of domestic appliances could not afford to be seen as a disrupter of domestic life.

Besides, he added, I did not make the perfect victim. Whirlpool would surely rebut what he saw as the greatest weakness in my case—I wasn't damaged enough. I should, he said, have seen a psychologist immediately upon my return so more damage could have been professionally verified. I wondered if a damaged person would know enough to do that.

In addition, he pointed out, "The defendants will drag up things from your past to make it look like the treatment you were given was justified. The suit will be a major one, expensive and drawn out. The reason for all that is not that your claim is unjustified, but that it probably is justified."

I was given to understand that because Whirlpool and many other corporations probably were similarly abusing spouses, they would fight me tooth and nail to keep me out of court and do everything possible to keep me from winning. If I were to win, not only Whirlpool but also many other corporations would be open to a flood of similar suits.

With frankness the attorney warned me of the covertly arranged misfortunes that might befall me if I persisted. He cautioned that the press, which I would expect to favor me, might choose instead to defame me. His sketch of this worst-case but not unrealistic scenario applied equally to me and to my attorneys.

"This is why I will not take the case and why my professional advice to you is to pursue it no further."

The reasons he gave explained why none of the previous seven attorneys would take my case. I appreciated this attorney's forthrightness. I wish he had represented me, but I would not like to have seen him destroyed.

The seeds of warning he threw at me did not fall on virgin soil. While still in Brazil, I had experienced nightmares over the death of Martha Mitchell, wife of Watergate's John Mitchell, believing she had been murdered for knowing too much and being unwilling to be silent about it.

Also while in Brazil, I had seen and been haunted by the fate of the Empress in the film *The Last Emperor*. She was the only one of the Japanese people who truly understood what the Chinese were doing to her husband in Manchuria, yet she was thought insane because she had taken to eating orchids. I bought potted orchids and planted them in a window box outside my bedroom window. If I started to nibble on the blossoms, I thought, I would take it as a sign that my limit had been reached. But the headaches came first to exile me from my Manchuria.

The attorney was saying that all stops would be pulled out; there would be no mercy. What he wasn't understanding about my relationship with Whirlpool—why I couldn't take his advice—was that I believed they had already pulled out all the stops; there already had been no mercy. They, the world's largest manufacturer of domestic appliances and the producer of beautiful family-oriented commercials, had already broken my family. What had I to lose? My pride was already gone, and I did not have the same personal safety concerns as the lawyers. Uppermost in my mind was that I had a right to demand justice.

Even before Karen and I left his office, for the few minutes when he excused himself to get a legal reference from the library, I was telling Karen of an article I had read about a woman who had represented herself, as plaintiff, in a Florida Court.

"I could do that in Michigan," I whispered, even though the twentieth-century system, under which I was a good citizen, apparently was designed to exclude justice for spouses. Since the beginning of history, men have written laws that had no intention of serving women. Look at the Ten Commandments, I thought.

###

Weather in Michigan during November and December tends to be overcast and dreary, damp and chilly. In Minnesota, my mother was dying. As a parting gesture of appreciation to her for the wonderful life and heritage she had given me, I arranged for all four of my sons and me to be with her December 5 for the annual Lutefisk Supper at the Faith Lutheran Church in Forest Lake where I had been confirmed and married and where my mother was still a member.

We were there on December 5, but she was not with us. Her condition had deteriorated so suddenly and rapidly that earlier the same day I had taken her to the Birchwood Nursing Home. The following three days I helped my brother and sister vacate her apartment at Kilkenny Court, and then I left, knowing I would not see her again. I took her black leather pumps. Our feet were the same size. I would wear the shoes for magic.

One of my Celtic mother's significant gifts to me was bringing my brother and me into a Swedish stepfamily through her remarriage. The Swedes are a stoic people. I must have learned from them the stoicism that has steadied my course.

Michigan seemed even bleaker than before. I kept a December 18 appointment at Karen's office and brought her a cheesecake my son Ed had baked. That day she made a decision. Although she could not represent me any more than could the other seven attorneys, neither could she bring herself to turn me away.

"If you are really up to representing yourself," she said, "I can at least give you piecemeal legal advice. I can be your coach." Her words were a welcome holiday gift.

Christmas, as it had always been, would be at "the house." Doug, Jeff, Ed, their families, and Curt, who was still single, were all counting on the continuity of tradition. They wanted Manny there and he wanted to come, so I could not exclude him. However, under circumstances that had altered drastically since our last normal Christmas in 1985, I could not bear to be there myself. The intervening Christmases of 1986, 1987, and 1988 had been tragic for me, personal disasters of which Manny's behavior had been the immediate cause; and Whirlpool's imposed structure, the source.

I could not pretend to be jolly in my ex-husband's presence in the home that had been ours. Nor could I go to the St. Joseph Holiday Inn, where our family had stayed during the first month of our living in that community, because Whirlpool used it so much that I was known there, and questions would be asked. I booked a reservation at the Holiday Inn in South Bend. I packed nice clothing, took a good book, dined out at good places, and swam. That is how, at age fifty-nine and three-quarters, I survived my first divorced Christmas.

The year concluded with a letter I received from Karen. It documented that I was preparing my own case; she was providing only background research and consultation. The letter was for her protection against Whirlpool's possible retribution. Without that, she felt legally vulnerable. Without her research, consultation, and emotional support, I would not have been able to proceed.

Seeking help wherever available, I asked my friend and minister, Michael Brown, to write some comments from his perspective that would substantiate my distress. Oh, the shame involved in begging friends to say something bad about you! Michael complied, describing my behavior at a meeting of the board of trustees of the Berrien Unitarian-Universalist Fellowship:

> She declared that she would have nothing whatsoever to do with any Christmas activities . . . clearly very agitated by the mere mention of Christmas, which seemed to call up for her some strong negative feelings.

Michael went on to describe how much my behavior shocked those at the meeting:

It also created an organizational problem, since Roz was in the position of organizing Sunday services and ordinarily would have been in charge of the Christmas service. Subsequently, Roz did not, in fact, attend any of the group's Christmas activities. She did mention Christmas on one or two other occasions to me, and each time it was with the same intense quality of upsetness and negativity. As her minister, I was concerned about her emotional state, but I did not put any pressure on her to explain the reason.

Bolstered by Karen's willingness to coach me as I filed my own case, I sought to strengthen the emotional-stress claim by recontacting the psychologist who had evaluated me. I saw him again on January 22, 1990, and asked him to spend time with Vivian Ahlers, whose opinion of the severity of my stress differed from his.

Karen, in the meantime, sent him the following letter:

Rosalyn Reeder asked me to send you a synopsis of my notes of a meeting she and I had on November 3, 1989, with her good friend, Ruby. Ruby visited Rosalyn in Brazil and made the following observations:

Rosalyn appeared stressed. Her speech was very deliberate. Her behavior was very methodical and detailed. The apartment seemed like a prison, because they were safe only inside. The American Consul called and advised Ruby to be careful, and to report any muggings. The Consul had considered putting São Paulo on the restricted list, because of the frequency of crime. She saw armed guards in the grocery store.

I hope this is helpful in your work with Rosalyn. If I can be of any further assistance, please feel free to call.

Two weeks later Karen prodded him further.

Ms. Reeder and I have discussed the meetings the two of you have had. From our discussions, it sounds as if your testimony will be along the following lines:

1. *Ms. Reeder suffers from Post-Traumatic Stress Syndrome.*
2. *She told you about her experiences in Brazil, and based upon your interview and testing, you see no reason to disbelieve what she said.*

Am I correct?

Karen shared with me his reply to her letter of January 20:

Dear Karen:

After anguishing over this case for longer than I even care to admit, I have decided to affirm my original contention. The overall clinical evidence is not consistent with what is needed to undertake a lawsuit. I am afraid Rosalyn may have to take whatever help the mental health system has to offer, even though she sees that (incorrectly) as admitting defeat. I just don't feel I can be of help here. I am truly sorry.

Ten days later Vivian met with him at his office in Kalamazoo and afterwards drove directly to my house, knowing I would be eager to hear her report. She said, "Roz, he's selling you down the river," although his own words, she admitted, were more like "I'm giving myself room to maneuver." In defense of his moderate diagnosis, he noted I could still dress myself, manage money, and keep my weight, cholesterol, and blood pressure down, and I had learned how to relax tension. I was dismayed.

Had I not exerted phenomenal cerebral control over my poor aching body and my broken heart, I would not have been able to function coherently enough to demand justice. Then, of course, there would have been no chance at all for justice, even though clinical evidence might have "been consistent with what is needed." The rules that govern the courts and, apparently, the American Psychological Association, could not have been better written to make justice impossible in a case such as mine.

I do not consider myself a psychologist any more, but at one time, I was. I held memberships in and presented papers before both the American Psychological Association and the Association for Behavioral Analysis, and I taught the subject at the college level for many years.

I did not expect the Court to know about the psychological phenomenon of "learned helplessness," as I knew about it from studying and teaching it; and later, in Brazil, experiencing it. However, among the many expectations I had of my eventual "day in court" was that I would be able to show a jury, as I had my classes, how the phenomenon works. The defendants claimed that once in Brazil I did not have to stay there, that I could have returned to the States at any time, but that was not true. Considerable research shows that when repeated attempts to avoid a punishing situation are unsuccessful, one ceases to have expectations and loses any incentive to try to escape.[1] That was the situation I was in, until the torture of migraine headaches propelled my last-ditch effort to save myself.

Nancy Mason and Joelene Von Koenig were but two of my friends who could not believe the strong-willed person they knew could have become so cowed and helpless.

On February 5, 1990, my mother, Esther Elizabeth Bullis Reeder Nygren, died of pulmonary cancer at the age of eighty-two. According to her wishes, she was cremated. I had her magic black leather shoes in my closet—the "ruby slippers" I would wear, when the time came, to court. I was hard at work producing the Complaint and Jury Demand I hoped to file soon.

A short time before the filing, I was at the office of a St. Joseph attorney who was processing a routine real estate matter for me. I had known without asking that neither he nor any other lawyer in the St. Joseph area would or should be representing me, little David, against Goliath, the community's major employer and dominant economic and political force. Nevertheless, I asked him if he'd like to read over my draft, figuring his curiosity would win out over better judgment. His body language as he read would be informative to me, and my giving him access to "scandalous" information would be payment to him for this service.

He was startled by some of what he read and cautioned me about being allowed to represent myself only "if you don't overtry the patience of the Court." He speculated that on the day I filed the complaint with the Court, "all hell will break loose."

That day came on Friday, February 23, 1990. Early in the morning, shortly after the Berrien County Court House opened for business, I was in an elevator making my way to the office of the Clerk of Court. My real estate attorney and a client were in the same elevator going to the same place. He and I exchanged a surreptitious nod. He knew what I was about to do. At the counter, we were both attended to about the same time. My papers were still being processed when I felt his supportive hands, one on each of my shoulders, and his whisper in my ear, "Good luck," before he turned, and, with his client, walked out the door.

I went from the courthouse directly to the Post Office to send—by certified mail, restricted delivery, return receipt requested—copies of my Complaint and Interrogatories to each of the four defendants named in my Complaint and Jury Demand: the Whirlpool Corporation, David R. Whitwam, Charles D. Putnam, and Samuel M. Bateman.

Then, on that day, as sunless and bleak as a February day can get, I went home to pack for the flight I would take the next morning to Minneapolis. My mother's memorial service was to be held at the Faith Lutheran Church in Forest Lake on Monday, February 26, the same site as my one-and-only wedding on March 26, 1951.

I did not stay in Forest Lake long, feeling a personal urgency to get home and hole up in what had become my own intensely private cave.

All hell did not break loose simply because I dared to file a suit against the Whirlpool Corporation. Nor did it a few days later when the *Herald-Palladium* took the announcement of what could have been a really big story and buried it among fourteen other civil suits.

The media were as cowed by the corporation as were attorneys, psychologists, and even a St. Joseph secretarial service that denied me assistance, fearing culpability by association.

Karen said the next step was to take depositions. I was supposed to prioritize which parties would most likely provide the best evidence in support of my allegations and then issue subpoenas. Manny had to be first. If he would tell the truth—and why wouldn't he, under oath—I might be able to stop right there.

###

My preparations to take his deposition were thwarted by learning that Manny left St. Joseph on the morning of his sixty-third birthday with Judy Clark, a woman I did not know, for a two-week trip out west.

They were married in Las Vegas on the twenty-fourth, one year after—to the day—that Manny had received notice of divorce proceedings and two days before his "other" wedding anniversary. Vivian Ahlers, among the first to hear about it, called to inform me as gently as she could. I felt betrayed, devastated, to realize he had so briefly, if at all, mourned the loss of our thirty-eight years together.

Jeff was elected by his brothers to convey the news to "Mom." The boys had been informed by identical postcards Manny mailed from Las Vegas. I did not envy Jeff his task, but I admired his courage and appreciated his empathy with my distress—which would have been considerably greater in his presence had I not already known, thanks to Vivian's intercession.

###

April 12, 1990, dawned pleasant and sunny, as if to belie the fact that it would become the most difficult day of my life so far. I drove into St. Joseph and parked in the little side street at the door of Murphy Reporting, where deposing would take place. An attendant ushered me into a conference room already provisioned with fresh coffee and water. I sat in silence, focusing on the deep-breathing technique I trusted to steady myself.

Private Counsel Paul Taglia arrived to represent the Whirlpool Corporation, accompanied by Gene Heth of Whirlpool's legal department. Manny came, flanked by his own attorney. The mere five-foot-four of me faced three hulking male attorneys and an obviously hostile remarried ex-husband, who continued to believe everything had been all my fault.

Exchanges between Mr. Taglia and me were testy and contentious from our first moment of contact. I had already heard through the grapevine that he was renowned for his powers to intimidate. Having just come out of a three-year experience of being intimidated by the best, I was not afraid of anything except, possibly, losing my concentration.

I began my questioning by referring to the subject matter in paragraph 7 of the Complaint: my contention that the last few months in Brazil of the first assignment there, 1969 to 1971 (which set the scene for the second assignment), had been extremely traumatic.

I had a hard time getting Manny to admit even the obvious and innocuous truth that John Eser had been his main contact and immediate supervisor at the Whirlpool home office during that first assignment. He showed reluctance in corroborating, although he finally did, that there was terrorist activity in São Paulo and in our neighborhood, that our home had been broken into, and that Whirlpool's Brazilian-affiliate hosts withdrew

social support from us during the last months and caused us to
fear for our safety.

In trying to establish that Whirlpool's attitude of reasonable
dialogue had shifted over the years to an attitude of unilateral
fiat, I delved into Manny's earliest work history with Whirlpool
in 1953.

Mr. Taglia erupted:

> "Well, I'm going to object to that question. That is just
> absolutely wholly irrelevant. It's not reasonably calcu-
> lated to lead to the discovery of admissible evidence. It
> has nothing to do with the issues framed in this lawsuit.
> We will be here for six months if these kinds of questions
> go on. That's my objection. Whatever the witness does is
> up to him. He may answer. I have no control over that."

Manny chose to answer. On this, and on several other points,
something I said managed to pierce the Teflon and lay bare a
nerve still raw from the injustice he had felt at the time. It seemed
to make him feel good to respond, whether Whirlpool's attorneys liked it or not.

Manny agreed, for the record, that John Eser, his Stateside
supervisor while we were in Brazil from 1969 to 1971, had himself later gone to Brazil for a period of about five years, returning in 1982. Manny concurred, also, that John had abruptly
retired six months earlier than he had planned.

When asked, "What was the cause of his earlier-than-
planned retirement?" Manny lied, saying, "He did not personally advise me in detail what the cause was." I knew he was
lying because, contrary to what Manny said, John and his wife
Edith had discussed the matter with me alone as well as with
Manny and me. John, a corporate vice president, told us he left
because CEO Jack Sparks informed him that as of the start of
the next work day, he would be responsible to the very corporate officer who most criticized John's policies and practices.

Whirlpool wanted John "out," and their squeeze-play worked.

For Manny to admit this, even to himself, would be for him to acknowledge that the corporation had achieved his own much-resisted transfer to Brazil through the same squeeze-play method used to terminate John Eser.

Manny corroborated my contention that he had told Jerry Southland he would not go to Brazil the second time because he was planning to retire in 1987. On the other hand, he denied having discussed it with Clara Dansfield, a manager in the department of Human Resources, as she denied it also in her later deposition. Yet I know he obtained through her the printouts of benefit projections he had brought home.

I wanted to establish that Manny was the only person who could do the work Whirlpool required in Brazil. This fact would explain why David Whitwam's goal had been to transfer him there by whatever means necessary. I asked Manny, "Did you ever express anger [to me] with Whirlpool for its shortsighted development of international personnel?"

Mr. Taglia broke in. "Well, I'll object to that question. That is totally irrelevant, immaterial regardless of what he told his wife. It doesn't have any bearing on this case, but you can answer if you like."

I had hit another nerve, and Manny chose to answer, but his response was so abstract that it did not contribute to the discovery process.

Jerry Southland, division vice president of International Sales, had moved off the field after approaching Manny two or three times about going to Brazil. Larry Kremer entered, transforming what had been exploratory inquiry into hard-nosed negotiation. I tried to get an account from Manny of the badgering we both experienced from Larry. The closest I could get was the following exchange:

Me: At the end of a discussion with Mr. Kremer, did he

assume that you had agreed to something you had not,
then leave town and be unavailable for discussion, return, assume that the point had been agreed upon, when
it had not?

Manny: I don't recall that.

I knew Manny was lying. We had frequently discussed this
and anguished about it while it was happening, feeling a trap
was being set. I didn't challenge this, though, because I understood the purpose of taking a deposition was to hope for the
best and get into the record whatever truth you could.

The deposition continued:

Me: During one of his absences, did you go to David
Whitwam . . .

Manny: Yeah.

Me: . . . explaining that Larry had left you hanging and you
needed to know something?

Manny: Well, let me answer the question—the series of
questions—in a different way. Whirlpool handled events
out of phase, the conditions which you and I set out to
Whirlpool which had to be met. And [in] the ultimate
instance, were met, but the way they came about was
inept.

Aha, thought I. At last, recognition from the key man that
he and I had preconditions. Yet he and he alone, not he and I,
was regarded by the corporation and by the Court as being the
only one to judge whether the conditions had been met. In effect, the corporation became the sole judge of its own behavior
because Manny had acquiesced to the conditions of the "Corporate Compensation Policy for U.S. and International Expatriates," which included the statement: ". . . all . . . expatriate
policies . . . will apply to you and members of your family. Such
policies may be changed from time to time by the Company, at
its sole discretion."

Again, to show how my being spirited away to Brazil stemmed from the corporation's conspiratorial squeeze-play on Manny, I tried to elicit from him information about how Dick Litzinger's transfer into the International Division was timed and tuned.

I said, "Whirlpool published an announcement in the *Herald-Palladium* on June 4, 1986, of a new post, that of Division Vice President of International Operations, to be filled by Richard Litzinger. . . . Did his job come to include work you were at that time doing?"

Manny replied, "Of course, because my position was that either we were going to go to Brazil or I'm going to retire. And if I retire or go to Brazil, somebody had to do it."

"What date had you planned to retire?"

"If financially feasible, the intent was in the spring of '87."

"Specifically on your birthday?" I asked.

"Well, thereabouts. . . ."

"If you had not accepted the Brazilian reassignment as you did eventually, what plans did Whirlpool have for you to work at the Ad Center until your projected retirement in spring of 1987?"

"To maintain my current job," he replied, "the job I had at that time, 'til I retired."

I knew that would not have been the case. Manny knew it, too. The same people within the corporation who had forced John Eser into the streets would have done the same to Manny. If he did not go to Brazil where they desperately needed him, they would have no use for him at all. The cover of departmental restructuring was all they legally needed to pull his job out from under him. This was one of the nebulous aspects of the period of our lives from 1986 to 1989. This threatening cloud hung over us, invisible and ineffable, yet modulating our every thought and action.

Then I raised questions about what had led to Whirlpool's publishing in its Administrative Center Bulletin, prematurely and with precognition, that "Bateman and Von Koenig and their families will reside in São Paulo."

His answers were evasive and slippery, with only a trace of the process described as I had experienced it. He restated that yes, "the sequence of events leading up to the assignment in Brazil was handled ineptly."

Because we had left Michigan to attend a reunion of my mother's family in Brookings, South Dakota, on June 26, 1986, I asked Manny: "Had we, when we left on this vacation, agreed to the reassignment?"

"I don't recall the—now, let me clarify that. The agreement to the assignment is better phrased by saying we agreed to the assignment."

"That's not the question I'm asking," I said. "I had not agreed." Manny was making it sound as though I, along with him, had fully agreed to go. I know I had not agreed, and I doubted he had. "I'm asking whether you had agreed."

"It was an understanding that prior to our leaving to [go to] Brazil, whatever questions are open are going to be resolved."

I thought, "Is this not the oral agreement that Whirlpool denies existed?"

So I asked, "By whom? I agree with you, but by whom? Would you elaborate on that?"

"Whirlpool Corporation, whoever is going to be the person who has to handle a particular aspect of that thing."

"But resolved between the Whirlpool Corporation and—"

"And us."

What a victorious moment! My ex-husband had just admitted, under oath, that there was an oral agreement, and it was between Whirlpool and Manny and me. Yet the corporation claimed any agreement was between it and him only; moreover, the determination regarding whether the agreement was honored lay only between him and the corporation. Why would anyone of sound mind make a commitment under such exclusionary terms? I hadn't. The way in which I did end up going to Brazil under the aegis of the corporation parallels the way in which a woman is often led to believe some nice guy is going to give her a ride home, and then, because he manages to hear a "yes" when she is loudly saying "no," she is raped.

I continued my interrogation regarding an oral agreement and who participated in it:

> Me: Since there was no effective formal policy at that time, terms would have had to be based on a broad generalized oral agreement, would they not?

> Manny: No. Whirlpool had a draft, which was probably 95 percent complete, of a foreign policy. It had not been published at that time. It had passed my desk several times as a function as a director in International Division to make suggestions and for modification or comments as I saw fit. So there had been a document which was not officially published, but which was circulated for corrections, and we had access to this document and you and I read this document.

Except for the part about my having read the document, the statement was, so far as I knew, true. I had never seen it. Even if I had seen 95 percent of it, the five percent of the process that was, at the time, incomplete would have been an extremely important part of anyone's decision to accept or reject its terms.

I then said something that I—even allowing for my total lack of experience in the field—felt was unusual in a deposition. But Mr. Taglia allowed it. "Since the purpose of this deposition is to find out what you know and not what I know, this may be inappropriate," I said, "but I would like to state for the record that this is not true. I did not see it. I did not read it."

I stated, in effect, that the deposee was lying. I wanted to get
everything possible into the Court record, under the strong possibility that I would never actually get into court with the case
itself.

The deposition resumed, still focusing on the prematurity
of the Ad Center Bulletin's announcement:

Me: Did you tell David Whitwam I had agreed to go to
Brazil?

Manny: If I told him anything, it would have been to the
effect that there are certain conditions we're working on,
and if they're met, we're prepared to go to Brazil.

Me: I recall answering the phone one evening in either
July or August of '86 when Larry Kremer called to speak
to you. I heard you say to him something like "lay off,
will you? We're still talking about whether I'm going
alone." Do you recall that?

Manny: Not specifically, but this conversation could have
taken place.

Then, hoping to illustrate to the Court generally and to
Manny specifically that his faith in his colleagues as gentlemen
who honored "gentlemen's agreements" was misplaced, I continued:

Me: Did you tell me that if Whirlpool didn't honor its agreements, we could just pull out and come home?

Manny: Uh-huh. Yes.

Me: Did you know about the clause regarding voluntary
termination and payment of your own relocation expenses?

Manny: I know that provision was in the policy, but it
didn't apply. It wouldn't have applied.

Me: Why would it not have applied?

Manny: Because it is my opinion that if we went to Brazil
and found out that the conditions in Brazil were totally

unacceptable to us and we asked to be re-transferred, Whirlpool would have re-transferred us.

What a deluded man he was. I saw him clinging, as I had tried to, to the anachronistic belief that Whirlpool managers dealt honorably with those who worked under their supervision. We had both seen and vicariously experienced how the administration of Jack D. Sparks had polished off the long and effective career of John Eser.

Their having worked as long and as underhandedly as they had to get Manny to Brazil in the first place convinced me there was no way they would have supported his deserting the field of action.

When I asked the final question about the oral agreement, the vehemence of Manny's response as well as its duplicity clearly indicated to me that he had been coached by Whirlpool on this significant issue. "I understood the oral agreement was [to be] between Whirlpool and you and me jointly. What was your understanding?"

"What oral agreement? I'm asking you a question: What oral agreement?"

In spite of this denial of the existence of an oral agreement, he calmed down and was willing to respond affirmatively to my next statement:

> Me: Given that the corporate policy was in draft form, given that anything which came up not covered by the corporate policy—I want to emphasize the incomplete and still-changing corporate policy—was to be resolved to the mutual satisfaction of Whirlpool and the Von Koenigs as they came up.
>
> Manny: True.

This showed, again, that there had been such an agreement and that both he and I were party to it. As a citizen in a democratic society, I had, from the outset, presumed that we were

equally party to it. It never occurred to me at the time that my
voice in matters such as where I should live and in what degree
of dignity would be dubbed-over, first at the corporation's whim,
and then with my husband's complicity. Date rape had turned
into gang bang.

As soon as Manny answered, "True," I introduced the two-
page letter he left behind when he moved out of the house after
our divorce. Addressed to Manny, it had been written three years
earlier, August 26, 1986, by Mike Simeck, staff vice president,
Human Resource Services. It stated that policies may be changed
from time to time by the company "at its sole discretion."

A flurry of activity erupted on the defendants' side of the
table. Mr. Taglia had known nothing about such a letter. He insisted we recess until a clean copy of it could be made and
marked as Deposition Exhibit 1.

The information in Mike Simeck's memo suggested that both
Manny and I had been raped by the corporation. Only the day
before receiving that letter, Manny had already given Sam
Bateman a verbal yes. Machinery had already been set in motion for Sam and Manny to leave almost immediately for the
first round of exploration in Brazil.

The day Manny received that memo, August 27, I had witnessed him cursing over it, but he had not shared its contents
with me—or his thoughts. When I left for Brazil, I had not known
about the unilateral control Whirlpool intended to impose on
our life abroad, nor was I informed of it any time while living
there. "At its sole discretion" meant, effectively, that anything
Whirlpool decreed had to be accepted.

No wonder Manny could do nothing to alleviate the pressures on me! I had kept urging him to defend me, but only he
knew that he couldn't. Manny had adjusted his frame of mind
so he could see as normal that which was insane, since insanity
was intolerable. He had done what Patty Hearst and other

abductees have done; he learned to identify with his captors. I escaped before that happened to me.

Manny's deposition so far had taken us from page one through page thirty. The remaining ninety-four pages tediously documented, blow by blow, the numerous episodes in which my strings were pulled according to decisions made at Whirlpool's "sole discretion."

During a recess, I understood Mr. Taglia's remarks as threatening me if I persisted in going ahead with my "frivolous" action, which, he claimed, amounted to nothing short of harassment:

"Ms. Reeder, I feel it my professional obligation to counsel you that you are treading a very fine line here and trying the patience of the Court. For your own good, you should drop this, and drop it now."

Where the inspiration for my response came from, I don't know. Without hesitation, I replied, "Mr. Taglia, we are here in an adversarial relationship. Anything you tell me is not going to be for my good, but for yours. Give me a break."

Nevertheless, the counsel for the corporation continued his veiled threats, which appear in the deposition transcript:

> Mr. Taglia: I want to caution you in advance that you are perilously close to putting yourself in a position where under the rules of practice and the statutes in this State you can be subjected to financial sanctions for pursuing a frivolous action. I want to put you on notice at this time that the Whirlpool Corporation will, if it follows my advice, vigorously pursue its rights to seek sanctions in the event this case develops in the way I think it will. I want you to understand that—because I know you are not a lawyer—but I also recognize that somewhere along the

line you have talked with a lawyer who has counseled you and who should have better served you, in my judgment, by giving you better advice on this action that you've instituted. . . . [I]f this goes on in this same vein, I am going to get on the phone and call the Chief Judge and ask immediately for a hearing for a protective order that would require you to cease and desist from this sort of harassment, which is subjecting all concerned undue burden or expense, and if you want to persist any further, that you be placed on formal notice by the Court that in the event your action is determined to be frivolous, sanctions will be imposed.

I was not alarmed. Karen had told me expect some such attack.

Karen later read the transcript of the deposition, assessed the situation, and wrote a second letter of self-protection for her file and mine.

On April 23, Clara Dansfield, manager of Benefits and Employee Services of Whirlpool Corporation, responded to a subpoena and appeared for deposition. My intention was to establish that in certain instances there is a legal requirement for the corporation to fully inform a spouse about the retirement benefit choices available—to the point of obtaining a signed form acknowledging explanation, understanding, and agreement with the choice made. Because she and Manny and I had been through this procedure together in 1982, Clara Dansfield readily concurred with my portrayal of these steps.

I pressed further:

Me: You do not expect the Whirlpool employee to be responsible for explaining these options to the spouse?

Clara: No. We sent the information out. Whirlpool wants the spouse and employee both to understand it.

We continued the Q&A, establishing that Whirlpool went

so far as to present a series of seven seminars on this subject to make sure both employees and spouses thoroughly understood all issues.

Clara and I had met a second time in her office following my divorce, and once again it was Whirlpool, not the employee, who was required by law to explain the Qualified Domestic Relations Order so I understood it fully. My signature was required to document that I understood it.

The point I was attempting to make was that when the law requires it, Whirlpool knows how to fully inform spouses on corporate matters that affect them. The machinery to do so is all in place. Hence, the corporation could have—and should have— used that machinery to fully inform me about the "Whirlpool Corporation Corporate Compensation Policy for U.S. and International Expatriates," and they should have done so before I unwittingly came under the corporation's jurisdiction and the stringent provisions of its expatriate policy.

As it was, even though I had been aware that the policy was being drafted, I did not know it had been completed or what its conditions were. Even if I had known its conditions, I would have thought these did not apply to me or to Manny. We both felt we were under some kind of grandfather clause, because that is what our negotiations with Whirlpool had led us to believe. Presumably, that is what Whirlpool wanted us to believe. Even though Manny knew about the policy and I did not, he too considered us to be, in some instances at least, exempt from it, as his testimony shows. He considered us exempt because we were in the position of experimental guinea pigs while the bugs were being worked out of the policy.

Immediately after Clara's deposition, Glenn Youngstedt's followed. Where Clara had been flustered at first, acting as though I shouldn't be putting her through such a process because she hadn't done anything, Glenn was composed. Overly so. He addressed me familiarly by my first name, as though he were my friend. He went to great pains to make it appear as though he had made no preparation for the meeting and had not been coached in any way.

He said he could not remember the date on which he, Bill Gargiulo, Jerry Sorensen, and I had met. But no one was asking him to "remember." Since he knew the subject of our interview, one might expect him to have given the matter some thought and prepared a bit of reconstruction.

"Did you take notes?" I asked.

"I don't believe I did."

Why couldn't he just say no? Or was the real answer, "Yes, but I shredded them one day in late February when Whirlpool was served with your complaint"?

Instead he said, "You and Manny and Sam and Fran were the first two expats that we had worked with." Interestingly, he enumerated four separate names but somehow managed to group us into units of two each, referring to four as two. The two would be Sam and Manny, because—as I was still learning—spouses were not seriously reckoned by the Whirlpool Corporation as being people, except when a federal Qualified Domestic Relations Order required that spouses be recognized and respected.

Glenn seemed embarrassed by the role he had to play that day. He is, I think, a nice person, who, without constraints placed on him by corporate structure, might have been my friend.

I continued my pursuit of justice by deposing Bill Gargiulo, corporate manager for International Human Resources, who, along with Glenn Youngstedt, had interviewed me August 31, 1987. I had earlier subpoenaed Bill's notes from that interview. When the copy was placed in front of him, he found it either impossible or undesirable to read and/or interpret much of his own handwriting in his notes. Across the top of one page he had scrawled, "She is a dramatic/dark character." This was followed by the single word, underlined, all in capital letters:

<u>INTENSE</u>

"Indeed," I thought, "and already in a state of desperation that could, under the prevailing circumstances, only become worse—as, without the help I sought, it had."

Familiar words and sentiments jumped out at me as he read further from the notes he had taken during my plea for help from the corporation: "details of transfer done poorly, liked Brazil but situation—no, office and home become confused—overlap—sometimes Manny is number two and sometimes Fran is, didn't go out at night for two weeks [when left alone in Brazil] because afraid that car would be stolen, structure and dynamics of the tour over there should've been proactively addressed before going. . . ."

As insulting as much of the deposition's content was, I felt I was making progress in establishing the verity of my claims. Three days after the last of these depositions was taken, I unexpectedly received a copy of Defendants' Brief in Support of Motion for Summary Disposition.

Karen had told me many times over what the course of the suit would be, including the likelihood that the defendants would move to have the case thrown out of court. But I was nonetheless surprised that they could do so when the depositions showed my complaints were well founded.

Paul Taglia's defense of his clients' indefensible behaviors introduced me to personal defamation. I read myself described in the Brief as "a divorced woman" and a "disgruntled ex-wife," in contexts that made it sound as though my husband had divorced me, not the other way around.

The Brief stated, "the husband and his employer made an oral agreement (to which she was not a party). . . ." From this phrasing, one would not be able to tell whether I had been left out of all the oral agreements (which I had not, and this was the crux of my lawsuit) or just some of them (which was not contested).

The defendants' premise was that "all details regarding Mr. Von Koenig's reassignment to Brazil were worked out between Whirlpool, through Mr. Bateman, and Mr. Von Koenig to the mutual satisfaction of both, and the conditions of the reassignment were fulfilled by Whirlpool." Also: "If there was an oral agreement, it was between Whirlpool and its employee, Mr. Von Koenig."

My complaint, of course, was not about whether they had satisfied Manny's conditions, but whether they had satisfied Manny's and mine. Yet according to the phrasing in the corporation's Brief, my role in the oral negotiations, limited though it was, was made to appear nonexistent, and the spouse's total exclusion from such negotiations was made to appear as if that's the way it *should* be.

Mr. Taglia cited my statement that my problems in Brazil were "corporate problems organic to the dysfunctional structure of the relationships as set up by Whirlpool," and he diminished these issues in his rephrasing of it as: "Plaintiff was uncomfortable and put upon, and no one did anything about it."

In the Brief, the defendants' version of the divorce was summed up as: "despite [Manny's] efforts to save the marriage," even though, from my viewpoint, he had made no effort at all.

The Brief stated further:

> It is clear . . . that imagined slights, a deep-seated bitterness, and a failed marriage are the stuff of which Plaintiff's pleading is made.

Mr. Taglia summarized the case as follows:

> . . . it is obvious that Plaintiff has failed to state a legally cognizable claim and that she cannot do so, because her several

theories are so flawed and without substance as a matter of law, it follows that there is not and cannot be any genuine issue as to any material fact . . . one need only consider what Mr. Von Koenig has to say concerning the "oral agreement" between Whirlpool and himself. Mr. Von Koenig makes it clear that the conditions he and Whirlpool agreed upon with respect to the assignment to Brazil were met; Whirlpool did what it was supposed to do, Mr. Von Koenig did what he was supposed to do, and in the last analysis Whirlpool acted "fairly and squarely". . . . Defendants are entitled to a full, final and conclusive summary judgment of dismissal. Any suggestion, should it be made, that discovery is not yet complete is irrelevant: "[s]ummary judgment is appropriate, even though discovery is not yet complete, where further discovery does not stand a fair chance of uncovering factual support for the opposing party's position". . . . In the case at bar, there are no cognizable legal claims; and further discovery would therefore be irrelevant, because there can be no "factual support" for that which does not exist.

The conclusion read:

This is a case that ought not to have been filed, but filed it was, and now it ought not be permitted to linger. It is a case grounded on nothing more than hurt feelings and petty grievances, a case based on animosity and personal frustrations, and it should be dismissed with prejudice and with costs.

"With prejudice" meant that the Complaint as originally filed and once amended could not be restated or further amended for submission to the Court. The legal process, at that point, made me feel more like the accused than the accuser. I was having to defend my right to have filed a suit at all.

Clutching for any straw, I made an appointment with a clinical psychologist whose nurturing counsel I had enjoyed when he was the instructor for one of my graduate courses. We met at his office on May Day, 1990. I took with me for him to read the lengthy narrative Karen had insisted I write the previous summer while all was still fresh in my mind.

The psychologist was startled to learn what my life had become. He empathized compassionately and invited me to return two days later, by which time he would have read my story.

Being a sensitive man, his response to my narrative was extremely emotional. In addition to commiserating with me, he showed deep insight, which derived from his placing himself in Manny's situation. He said he had hardly slept during the night after finishing the reading. When he did, his dreams were nightmarish writhings of anguish trying to extricate himself— in the hypothetical role of Manny—from a succession of Catch 22s.

I came to see that Manny's position—in regard to both his job security and his mental condition—had been more precarious than even I realized at the time I filed my suit against Whirlpool. However, the good doctor would not involve himself in the case. He said he could do no more than the evaluating psychologist had done, although his interpretation of the data gathered from my testing might have differed, especially since he had known me for a longer period, and under more normal situations when I was in a much better psychological condition than he found me during the legal proceedings.

He did make a generous offer to be of background assistance if my case made it all the way to trial. Skilled in forensic psychology himself, he offered to teach Karen how to question the psychologist on the witness stand in a way that would leave the jury with the same impression that he, Karen, Vivian Ahlers and I all believed: I suffered Post-Traumatic Stress Disorder, not the milder Adjustment Disorder. Skillful questioning of even a reluctant witness could have elicited testimony that Adjustment Disorder, if of an extreme nature, shades into the area of Post-

Traumatic Stress Disorder and can cross over into it completely. As with all matters psychological, borders are arbitrary.

Again at that point I wondered if only perfect victims—that is, totally destroyed ones—have a crack at justice.

The afternoon of that same day, Elisha Gray came to Murphy Reporting to be deposed. I asked him merely to personally read into the record his letter dated June 12, 1989, in response to mine of April 10, 1989.

He did so, and I thanked him. By way of farewell, he took my hand, looked deeply into my eyes, and said, much to Mr. Taglia's annoyance, "I wish you well."

Karen predicted dismissal of the case, but nonetheless advised me to prepare an affidavit clarifying for the judge those points on which I would testify if and when the case came to court. I went through the Complaint I had filed, correlating supporting statements gleaned from the depositions. To this I added my short list of corroborating witnesses.

The following day I filed the Affidavit along with my opposition to the motion for summary disposition. This latter document concluded:

> I ask the Court to deny Defendants' Motion for Summary Disposition because (1) I have stated a claim upon which relief can be granted, and (2) because there exist genuine issues as to all of the material facts discussed above in Areas of Factual Dispute.

> I request that if the Defendants' Motion for Summary Disposition is not denied, or if any part of it is not denied, the Court allow me to file an Amended Complaint.

By that time, I was finding the constant repetition of basic statements an extremely boring part of self-representation. I had the impatience of one who was not being listened to the first time, nor the second. I was thinking, "What part of 'no, I didn't want to go' do you not understand?" If no one was really listening, did it matter how something was stated? I could never tell the whole story, anyway. I was allowed to talk only about things against which there were already laws or where precedent decisions had been made.

I tried to follow established procedure, much of which I found to be disgustingly irrelevant, rehashing things that had already been said more times than a reasonable person would think necessary. "Proper procedures" took us further and further from reality, ignoring that the case had a heartbeat. The conscience-free behaviors of the corporation that had destroyed our marriage, and as a result our family, had been sanitized beyond recognition, even though I had established that Whirlpool executives lie and that they had lied to me. That was what the case was about—breach of oral agreement. They lied!

The hearing for Summary Disposition was held May 21, 1990.

I expected to be alone when standing—in my mother's "magic" slippers—before the judge. But daughter-in-law Lori Jewell, Ed's wife, would have none of that. In a show of support that overwhelmed me, she arranged for a substitute to take over her duties as director of the Lakeshore High School Band and came to stand with me. Lori's uncle was at that time sheriff of Berrien County, and her father was his chief deputy. Judge Taylor knew who she was. This, of course, didn't matter to him, but it mattered a great deal to me that she put her own reputation on the line to stand with the pariah I had become.

A mere fifteen minutes had been allocated for the hearing, but at Karen's prompting I requested double that time, and the Court granted it. We met in the tiniest hearing room of the courthouse, the media choosing not to attend.

Whirlpool, represented by Paul Taglia, stood on its briefs as filed. I restated my case, as persuasively as possible, in twenty pages.

Following a reference to how Taglia had threatened me with

sanctions for frivolity and harassment, my presentation concluded as follows:

> *It was I who was being harassed, Your Honor, not they. And I, as the plaintiff and as a layperson, could better withstand the harassment than could a member of the Bar who might have been representing me. If the Court rules today to deny the defendants' motion and to allow this case to go to trial, that ruling will provide protection from harassment for both me and whatever attorney may represent me, and I will be able to have the legal representation that I and my case deserve to have.*

Taglia offered several unsolicited explanations for the outburst of his, which I had quoted from Manny's deposition. From the rather startled reaction of both Mr. Taglia and the Court, I concluded that perhaps the Court had not read all my filed materials as thoroughly as it would have me believe.

The Court then spoke, taking the position that the oral agreement, "if any," was that unpredictable problems arising in Brazil were to have been resolved to my husband's satisfaction, not mine. Since this dispute had come to court, the Court would decide whether unpredictable problems arising in Brazil had been resolved to the Court's satisfaction, not mine.

One by one, my Counts fell like dominos, all linked to that first one, the oral agreement. The Court may have been playing dominos, but I felt as if I were Alice engaged in croquet in Wonderland: the wickets—the hoops through which one must jump—arbitrarily moving while the ball is in play.

The session ended with the Court's instructing the defendants' counsel to prepare an "Order of Dismissal With Prejudice"—an order that denied me the opportunity to further amend my complaint and incorporate what I had established in depositions.

That was it for May 21, 1990, but things weren't over yet.

Karen, eagerly awaiting word of how things had gone, was

hopeful. She said it was safe then for her to come forward. I had established in her eyes, if not the Court's, enough substantiating evidence for a trial. The Court, she said, would err by dismissing the case "with prejudice," rather than allowing for restatement and resubmission. She would represent me on June 11 at the final Circuit Court hearing, during which the order would be signed.

If Lori's being with me in court on May 21 had been bolstering, Karen's presence on June 11 was downright inspiring. The form that stated, "NOW COMES KAREN E. WERME who hereby enters her Appearance for the Plaintiff" was one of the most beautiful things I had ever seen.

Judge Taylor greeted her. "Attorney Werme, does your appearance here today mean this case will be appealed?"

Karen's voice rang out loud and clear, "Yes, Your Honor, it does." That day, I needed to do nothing but sit and listen. Was it simply my imagination that both the defendants' counsel and the judge showed a little more respect for me than they had before? How I empathized with all just persons who have been diminished and trivialized by men who are little more than playground bullies in three-piece suits.

The self-protective letter Karen had written me on April 27—which concluded, "I can't give you any encouragement that your case is winnable"—had been written for the record. She believed that the case was not winnable in Berrien County Circuit Court, a conservative and isolated county. But Karen had seen that my case was appealable, even before it was "summarily dismissed" with the added harshness of "with prejudice." She had planned ahead and wasted no time.

Following the initial hearing, Karen and I drove to Kalamazoo to keep the appointment she had made with Ken

Rathert, an experienced attorney who specialized in appeals.

Karen believed and Ken agreed that by dismissing the case "with prejudice," the Court had not served justice. As Karen stated in her April 27 letter, "Manny's deposition . . . supports the theories you hold to support your complaint. Unfortunately, I think it can easily be used to support the corporate theories you expect in response." There were clearly two equally possible interpretations. In such cases, a jury should hear evidence and make the decision. "With prejudice" meant disallowance of further discovery through depositions, disallowance of clarifying and sharpening the case by filing a Second Amended Complaint, and disallowance of bringing the Complaint before a jury.

Ken Rathert saw a winnable appeal and set immediately to work, with the understanding that Karen, as well, would continue to work on the case. I supplied him with copies of everything I had on file to that date. When the Court provided me with a transcript of the May hearing, I forwarded that as well.

On July 12, Ken Rathert entered a Claim of Appeal from the Order of Dismissal. He involved me in every step as he labored through reshaping the narrative of David's experiences with Goliath. The increasing mass of paperwork was so complex that I established a chronologically ordered code system for all documents and used it to help me cite passages to support Ken's work. Under his creative hand, three salient issues evolved.

All through the hot weather of June, July, and August, right through September up until mid-October, we worked hard in kneading the narrative, refining the argument, and bolstering the law citations. Copies of every draft Ken wrote came to Karen and me. Each of us red-penned our corrections and additions, and suggested changes in nuance, until we were all three in total accord that the final product stated, in every way, exactly what needed saying. Only four days ahead of the October 23 deadline, Ken filed the Appeal.

The section of an appeal known as the Statement of Facts is a summary of a case as it has developed to the date of filing; it is "state of the art." The one Ken wrote I will stand on forever:

> *This case involves Whirlpool's inept handling of the transfer of Plaintiff and her then-husband, Emanuel Von Koenig, to Brazil from 1986 to 1989. Whirlpool is a major international corporation. Plaintiff's then-husband, Mr. Von Koenig, was one of its key executives and ultimately became vice president of Whirlpool do Brasil. Although Plaintiff was not an employee of Whirlpool, she was required to perform various tasks and functions for Whirlpool.*
>
> *Plaintiff and Mr. Von Koenig had been previously transferred to Brazil and stayed there from 1969 to 1971.[2] Little was done between 1971 and 1986 to develop personnel in Brazil.[3] So in 1985 when Whirlpool decided to open an office in Brazil, Plaintiff's then-husband, Mr. Von Koenig, appears to have been the only person to whom Whirlpool could turn for help. He was virtually indispensable.[4] Therefore, Whirlpool pressured Mr. Von Koenig, as well as Plaintiff, to accept an assignment in Brazil—despite their firm resolve not to go.[5]*
>
> *In the course of its negotiations and attempts to persuade Mr. Von Koenig to accept the Brazil assignment and in the months following Mr. Von Koenig's actual 'acceptance' of the job, Whirlpool, through its agents, had a devastating impact on the Plaintiff's life and on her marriage.*
>
> *Plaintiff and Mr. Von Koenig had long looked forward to Mr. Von Koenig's retirement on his sixtieth birthday (March 16, 1987) at which time his pension and other financial interests at Whirlpool would be vested.[6] Nevertheless, beginning in November 1985, various Whirlpool officers and employees met with him off and on to persuade him to delay retirement to accept this final project in Brazil where he would be vice president of Whirlpool do Brasil.*

*These negotiations to get Mr. Von Koenig (and the Plaintiff)
to return to Brazil were characterized by Mr. Von Koenig as
'inept.'[7] Although never directly expressed, there was always
the veiled threat in the negotiations that if he did not accept the
Brazil assignment, he would be eased out—even prior to his
pension vesting![8] But Mr. Von Koenig and Plaintiff stood firm
in their resolve to stay in Michigan and not to accept the Brazil assignment.[9]*

*Against this backdrop, Whirlpool (specifically through vice
president David Whitwam) caused a false announcement to be
printed in a publication circulated among all Whirlpool employees and, through them, to many people in the wider community. The statement read: "Bateman and Von Koenig and
their families will reside in São Paulo."[10] Plaintiff had stated
repeatedly and emphatically that she was not going.[11] No terms
of transfer had been agreed on, and, as far as Plaintiff knows,
Mr. Von Koenig had not consented to the announcement.[12]*

*The publication of this false information caused the Plaintiff
a great deal of embarrassment and placed her under a great
deal of pressure. It also was an unwarranted invasion of her
privacy.[13] This unwarranted invasion of privacy caused
Plaintiff emotional stress, and Mr. Whitwam knew or should
have known that it would do so.[14] The Whirlpool community—
as well as the community-at-large, in which Whirlpool is the
major employer—assumed she was going to Brazil, yet she had
not agreed to do so. Plaintiff, faced with the embarrassment
that both the Whirlpool community and the community-at-
large falsely believed that she had already agreed to go to Brazil
and knowing that her husband was under extreme pressure to
do so, began negotiating the terms of her possible 'transfer' to
Brazil.*

*In the summer of 1986, Plaintiff met with Mr. Bateman, who
was the Executive Vice President of International Operations,*

as well as President-Designate of Whirlpool do Brasil.[15] Plaintiff insisted on three conditions being met before she agreed to go. The three conditions were:

1. The use of a car.

2. The use of a computer.

3. An agreement that unforeseen difficulties (certain to come up in a foreign assignment) would be worked out on the spot in Brazil to the satisfaction of Plaintiff and Mr. Von Koenig.[16]

Whirlpool, through Mr. Bateman, agreed to these three conditions before Plaintiff agreed to go to Brazil. In addition to these three conditions, Whirlpool, explicitly and implicitly, had agreed to provide other services and benefits to the Plaintiff (which agreements it later breached). These included language training, interior decorator service, a reliable and efficient system for receiving mail, and a safety system adequate to ensure security in a country commonly known to be dangerous.[17]

Whirlpool's failure to provide adequate security is especially important. Mr. and Mrs. Bateman and Mr. Von Koenig all went to the U.S., leaving Plaintiff alone in São Paulo for two weeks. Because Plaintiff had not been 'abandoned' in this fashion during her 1969–1971 stay in Brazil, she considered the 1987 event an 'unforeseen problem.'[18] She did not 'agree' to stay there alone, so they simply left her; moreover, they left her without making adequate security arrangements. She was left alone in a foreign land, in a land known to be hostile to women.[19]

These agreements to provide services to Plaintiff herself (as opposed to her then-husband, Mr. Von Koenig) were in consideration for Plaintiff agreeing to go to Brazil, which she otherwise had not wanted to do.[20] Mr. Von Koenig would not go to Brazil without her.[21]

At that time, Whirlpool was in the process of rewriting its policies relating to its international expatriates. Plaintiff wanted to be sure that there would be a system of resolving problems *as they came up in Brazil, before she agreed to go. Mr. Bateman agreed to all three of these conditions. He also agreed, explicitly or implicitly, to provide Plaintiff with the above-mentioned services and benefits.*

Despite this agreement, Plaintiff and Mr. Von Koenig remained firm in their resolve not to go to Brazil. So, on Sunday August 24, 1986, Mr. Von Koenig went to the Batemans' home and told Mr. Bateman that he and his wife (Plaintiff) were rejecting the reassignment.[22] The next day, Mr. Bateman informed Mr. Von Koenig that the International Division had promoted him from director to vice president and then acted as if that would resolve all of the issues. On or about August 28, 1986, without further discussion with Plaintiff, Mr. Bateman whisked Mr. Von Koenig off to Brazil to look for office space.[23]

After Plaintiff succumbed to the overwhelming pressure and finally consented to go to Brazil, Whirlpool—specifically through Mr. Bateman—breached its agreement that unforeseen difficulties would be worked out to the Plaintiff's satisfaction in the following ways:

1. Whirlpool (Mr. Bateman) unilaterally attempted to withdraw Plaintiff's previous authorization to attend INLINGUA language school.[24]

2. Whirlpool (Mr. Bateman) interrupted interior decorator service.[25]

3. Whirlpool (Mr. Bateman) abandoned Plaintiff against her expressed wishes in Brazil for two weeks and did so without providing adequate security.[26]

4. Whirlpool (Mr. Bateman) interfered with Plaintiff's receipt of mail and personal belongings.[27]

5. Whirlpool (Mr. Bateman) refused to mediate the unforeseen difficulty which arose with Mrs. Bateman.[28]

6. Whirlpool (Mr. Bateman) continually refused to meet with Plaintiff over grievance matters.[29]

*Even while breaching the agreements with Plaintiff, Whirl-
pool (through Mr. Bateman) required Plaintiff to perform services on behalf of Whirlpool do Brasil: entertaining, helping
secure a qualified maid for Mrs. Bateman, taking care of problems relating to the local populace, and helping with office
Christmas parties, as well as other services.[30]*

*On August 31, 1987, [while on leave in the U.S.] Plaintiff
met with one director and two managers from Human Resource
Services of Whirlpool for over two hours. Despite this lengthy
meeting, the director of Human Resource Services, who was at
the meeting, later admitted that he had no authority to aid the
Plaintiff.[31] On April 10, 1989, the Plaintiff was still trying to
get Whirlpool to live up to its end of the bargain, 'to work
problems out as they arose to the Von Koenigs' satisfaction.' To
that end, Plaintiff wrote a letter about the cumulative problems to former CEO Gray, with copies to Mr. Bateman and
Mr. Whitwam. Mr. Gray responded on June 12, 1989: "I am
sure that you will have received some reply from the appropriate man in answer to your letter."[32] Plaintiff never received
such a reply.[33]*

*Plaintiff initiated proceedings for a divorce, which was
granted, uncontested, on May 30, 1989.[34] After Mr. Von Koenig
had moved out of the house, sometime during August 1989,
Plaintiff discovered, among papers which he left behind, a memo
to Mr. Von Koenig from Whirlpool's Human Resource Services dated August 26, 1986.[35] The memo stated:*

*". . . all . . . expatriate policies as stated in the Company's
International Compensation Policy will apply to you and members of your family. Such policies may be changed from time to
time by the Company, at its sole discretion (emphasis added)."[36]
It was clear to Plaintiff upon reading this memo—first seen by
her three years after its issuance—that Whirlpool did not intend to honor this commitment to her even as Whirlpool*

(through Mr. Bateman) was consenting to point #3 of the oral agreement. It was merely what Mr. Bateman, under Mr. Whitwam's direction, had to say to get her to go to Brazil.[37]

Whirlpool, as a direct result of its failure to live up to its end of the bargain and of its failure to meet its duty to provide an expatriate employee and his family with a reasonable program for coping with their transfer, has recklessly inflicted mental distress on Plaintiff. Plaintiff has suffered the following damages:

1. Loss of professional development and income;

2. Emotional distress (Post-Traumatic Stress Disorder) and the attendant costs of psychological care and treatment; and

3. Emotional distress from the break-up of her family and the attendant costs of setting up a separate residence.[38]

On February 23, 1990, Rosalyn Reeder, representing herself, filed a Complaint and Jury Demand. Then followed the filing of other pleadings and the beginning of discovery. On March 8, 1990, the Plaintiff filed the First Amended Complaint, also in pro per. Then, on April 26, 1990, only two months after the initial complaint was filed, Defendant filed a motion for summary disposition based on MCR 2.116(C)(8) and MCR 2.116(C)(10). The hearing on that motion took place on May 21, 1990, at which hearing, the Court ruled from the bench, summarily dismissing the complaint with prejudice. Plaintiff requested leave to amend her complaint. At the end of the hearing on Defendant's motion, the Court stated:

The Court has also made note of the fact that plaintiff has requested the opportunity to amend. In this Court's opinion, pursuant to 2.116 (I)(5), this Court finds that the evidence before the Court here today shows that that amendment would not be justified. I believe such an amendment would be futile. Accordingly, that motion is denied.[39]

An Order of Dismissal with Prejudice was entered on June

26, 1990. It dismissed all of Plaintiff's claims with prejudice.

The Plaintiff, who now has retained counsel, appeals as of right. For the following reasons, Plaintiff requests this Court to reverse the trial Court's summary dismissal and remand for further proceedings.

The arguments Ken had to make were not the same as the arguments I had made in my Complaint and Jury Demand. His arguments were that the Circuit Court had erred in terminating my case, and that I should be allowed to amend and continue. His arguments covered three issues:

I.   Because Plaintiff, although unrepresented, has stated a viable breach of contract claim against Whirlpool and because there are material facts in dispute regarding that claim, the trial Court erred in summarily dismissing without giving the unrepresented Plaintiff an opportunity to amend her Complaint.

This was followed by ten pages citing legal decisions on relevant cases of record and referring to every single phrase in the *Reeder v. Whirlpool* files which bore on the issue. In particular, Ken homed in on Manny's deposition, highlighting all of the ways in which Manny's statements corroborated mine, even though, by that time, we were divorced, he had remarried, and it would not be an exaggeration to say his attitude toward me was more hostile than friendly.

II.   Because the unrepresented Plaintiff has alleged that Defendant Corporation disclosed embarrassing private "facts" about Plaintiff's intention to transfer to Brazil and the disclosure of this false information placed Plaintiff in a false light in the public eye and caused Plaintiff serious humiliation and embarrassment, the trial Court erred in summarily dismissing Plaintiff's Complaint before Discovery was completed, without granting leave to amend, because genuine issues of material fact remain in dispute.

Four pages of citations followed that argument, with Ken leaning hard on our claimed error of the lower court, by lacing his persuasion with phrases such as, "Summary dismissal when there are disputed issues of fact is disfavored," "Summary judgment is especially suspect," "Summary judgment . . . is particularly inappropriate."

> *III. Defendant Whirlpool breached its duty to Plaintiff, the spouse of a transferred, expatriate employee, to establish and implement a procedure for resolving unidentified problems certain to occur as a result of operating within a foreign environment.*

This was followed by three pages of persuasive citations and these comments by Ken Rathert: "Because the right to trial by jury is so important, summary dispositions of negligence claims are to be granted only in the clearest of cases." "Summary judgment is inappropriate in negligence actions because conformance to a standard of behavior is peculiarly within the province of a jury."

Ken's concluding paragraphs were particularly inspired and represented my sentiments precisely:

> *The unrepresented Plaintiff attempted to present this complex negligence claim against the Goliath, Whirlpool. But the trial Court took the slingshot from Plaintiff's (David's) hands before she could even reach for her pebbles. Appellant admits that the complaint may have to be amended to more clearly articulate Plaintiff's negligence claim against Defendant Corporation. She asks the appellate Court to give her back her slingshot and let her reach for her pebbles. Plaintiff's pebbles might be wide of the mark. But that should be determined by the jury or at least by the trial Court after sufficient time is given Plaintiff to amend her complaint and develop discovery appropriately.*
>
> *The Plaintiff has stated, and the record supports, a viable breach of contract claim against Whirlpool. Plaintiff has also*

two viable invasion of privacy claims. In addition, she has stated a claim, albeit undeveloped, against Whirlpool for its negligent handling of her transfer to Brazil. There are genuine issues of material fact on all of Plaintiff's claims, and Discover, if properly done, could develop additional facts to support her claims.

The trial Court erred in summarily dismissing Plaintiff's claims—especially without giving her an opportunity to amend her pleadings, which opportunity should have been 'freely given.' Not every David slays a Goliath. But every David deserves a fighting chance.

Appellant, therefore, requests that the Order of Dismissal with Prejudice be reversed as to the Plaintiff's breach of contract, invasion of privacy, and negligence claims. The case should be remanded to the trial Court with instructions to grant Plaintiff leave to amend those claims.

With the filing of my appeal, we rested our case—for the time being.

Whirlpool's response was filed November 20. It ran to forty-one pages. Once again, both Karen Werme and I fine–tooth-combed each line. Ken Rathert then studied the comments we'd written so he could further develop his overall sense of the case and be fully prepared for our eventual day in court.

Were I to go over this document again, now, I would perhaps make different comments than I did at the time. Yet I think the comments I made then are more indicative of what this case signifies than the more reasoned observations I might make now, long years after losing the case.

Such intensity of passion cannot be sustained indefinitely; I have since become somewhat more mellowed. At the time, however, I believe I saw it essential to take full advantage of the opportunity to stand firm and talk back. The best case scenario I could see was that standing firm was vital to victory, requiring my fullest and best effort to reverse the disadvantage my side faced. The worst case scenario I could envision at that time was that the case would very likely represent the last chance I might ever have to wax eloquent on the issues. Hindsight now shows that the Court's denying me access to a jury did not still my voice. In 1993, when I sat down to begin again writing the story of Helen of Troy, Divorcing the Corporation is what "happened" instead.

In anticipation of the oral argument Ken Rathert would make before the Court of Appeals, he asked me to comb through the Defendants' reply to the Appellant's Brief, which could be considered Whirlpool's "state of the art" response to our "state of the art." In order to ground and augment his orientation, he needed my reactions, which are as follows:

If what the Defendants say were true, I'd drop the case. But what they say is not true.

The tone of this Brief is consistent with and is an extension of the attitude of the Defendant Corporation toward me throughout the period addressed by the suit, 1986–1989. Every problem which I experienced as a result of being dependent on them in a foreign country on assignment in their behalf was/is either ignored, trivialized, or considered by them to be, after all, my own fault. As they persist in belittling my right even to be heard, the rights of David diminish and the powers of Goliath grow more immense.

Defendant Corporation is correct in its position that this matter should not be taking up the time of the Court, but not because the claim is frivolous. This matter could have been discreetly dealt with within Whirlpool's Human Resource Division if Defendant Corporation had maintained the attitude of Whirlpool's retired CEO Elisha Gray. I had made a last, desperate within-the-family appeal on April 10, 1989, to which he had responded: "I hope that the matter will not get to the

point of seeking a legal solution because in the many years
when I was actively engaged in the company affairs, we never
had to resort to that kind of solution to our internal decisions."

A similar attitude on the part of the Defendants could have
settled this matter without recourse to the Court; could, likely,
even have saved the Von Koenig marriage. Instead of seeking
resolution, they loosed their legal department on me, even go-
ing outside the Corporation to hire an additional mercenary.

We received from the Court of Appeals on November 26,
1990, a postcard informing us that we had "been noticed for the
next available session," but on January 14, 1991, Ken wrote to
me, "Because of a scheduling backlog, it now appears the oral
arguments will not be scheduled until next fall."

By October 3, 1991, a year after my Appeal had been filed,
no court date had been set. A recently passed court rule disal-
lowed oral arguments. Ken responded to the Court, as follows:

We have requested oral argument in the above matter. In
light of the recent changes in the Court rules regarding oral
arguments, I thought it would be helpful to emphasize the im-
portance of oral arguments in this case.

The issues in this case are very complex and there are subtle-
ties which can best be understood through the informal give
and take of oral argument and questioning by the Court. My
client was unrepresented at the trial level and, therefore, it is
important that she be given an opportunity to have 'her day in
Court' with counsel present. Because this case was docketed
and briefed long before the new rule went into effect, it would
be unfair to apply the new rule to my client, who has so pa-
tiently waited for the argument to be scheduled.

Therefore, I request that you allow oral argument.

I expressed my wish to Ken that when such time came, Karen
be there with us to handle, in particular, why the client was unrepresented at the trial level. Karen, in addition, understood the

subtleties and nuances of the case so well that prognosis for the judgment will be better if she were there in consultation, to round out what Ken and I could do.

Ken responded promptly, filling me in on the realities of the Appeals Court situation: "Oral Argument, although important, is not nearly as critical as you may think. A three-judge court usually gives each side only about ten minutes and does not allow any splitting of the argument." In other words, only Ken Rathert could speak, and he only briefly.

Oral argument was granted and the hearing was set, finally, for February 5, 1992, 11:30 A.M. at Grand Rapids.

Ken worked through all the files again, preparing himself for those few minutes he would be allowed to plead. He asked for any further comments I might have on the Defendants' reply Brief, and I added eight more pages to the original eleven.

Not only was it unnecessary, even inadvisable, to have more than one attorney at the hearing, Ken informed me, but even my presence would be considered unusual. There was no arguing with me on that point. I was moderately contemptuous of the judicial system as I had experienced it up to that point. The thought of not being present for the occasion, more momentous to me than to anyone else who might be present, was unthinkable.

I prepared myself to be as relaxed and calm as possible by going to Grand Rapids the day before. My Detroit friend, Millie, spent the night with me there and escorted me to court the next morning. Others who deemed the event auspicious also insisted on being there with me. My son Edward came, on the date only one day short of his thirtieth birthday. My daughters-in-law Joelene Nichols (Doug's wife) and Nancy Beezley (Jeff's wife) came, as did friends Magda Zoschke, Carey Gray, and Joe Bartz.

By 10:45 A.M., Millie and I were in the courtroom waiting area ready for the 11:30 hearing. When everyone else arrived, including Ken and Karen, I issued an invitation to lunch at Millie's favorite Polish restaurant. They agreed that we would lunch together, but Ed led a protest against my paying for it. I dramatized the extravagance by expanding my arms. "This next half hour's 'entertainment' has already cost me $15,000. What's lunch?"

Representing Whirlpool was a solo Paul Taglia. He was visibly nervous. I was not. Whatever the verdict was to be, I was having a good day, because I had done everything I could have done and because my family and friends supported my efforts.

Ken spoke first, then the defendants' counsel, followed by brief rebuttals from each. I had planned to order a transcript of the Court of Appeals hearings, not knowing they would be unavailable. Therefore, I was not taking notes and do not recall specifically what Mr. Taglia said that drew this reaction from Nancy: "I had no idea what they were putting you through! How could you stand being talked about that way?"

The case was heard by Barbara B. MacKenzie, Elizabeth A. Wever, and Robert B. Burns (a former Court of Appeals judge, sitting on the Court of Appeals by assignment). Within half an hour, it was over. Ken and Karen had to get back to Kalamazoo for appointments. The rest of us went to lunch, which my "guests" turned into their treat.

Millie left late in the afternoon. I stayed another night. At dusk, I went alone to the bar atop the Amway Grand Plaza Hotel for an espresso—a delightful habit I had picked up in Brazil—and to think about my mother, who had died on that date two years earlier.

The Court of Appeals originally had received the Brief on my case October 19, 1990. It did not hear the case until February 5, 1992. Somehow I believed the Court would be able to render judgment if not immediately, as in the case of the Circuit Court, within a week or two. I waited, and waited, and waited. As February, March, April, May, June, and July passed and August began, I kept believing optimistically that the delay meant they were giving what Ken had called "complex . . . subtleties" careful scrutiny and deliberation.

Not so. They were merely slow. The opinion they rendered was superficial and uninformed—uninformed because they failed to hear what we clearly said. The opinion began:

> Plaintiff first contends that her amended complaint made out specific allegations regarding the existence of an oral agreement with Whirlpool and that the agreement was breached. However, a reading of the amended complaint reveals that plaintiff did not include a claim for breach of contract among her enumerated claims. . . . We discuss only the three claims plaintiff raises on appeal and affirm as to each.

Ken's argument, which had been stated and restated in every conceivable manner, was (1) that discovery had clearly shown in the very words of Whirlpool's own executive, Mr. Von Koenig, even though he had been divorced by the Plaintiff and was an unfriendly deposee, that there was such an oral agreement, and (2) that the legally naïve, then-unrepresented Plaintiff had, nonetheless, presented sufficient evidence so that she, once she had representation, should be allowed to amend the complaint to include the clearly evident claim.

In ruling serially against each of the three claims, the Court's opinion included a statement I read as an "attitude":

> On appeal, plaintiff fails to cite authority supporting a cause of action for negligent supervision. This Court will not search for authority to sustain a party's position.

To me, this suggested the Court was saying: the Plaintiff, we know, is legally naïve, and her appeals attorney isn't such a hotshot, either.

The opinion continued:

> The Circuit Court correctly held that Plaintiff's tort theory

could not exist independently of the alleged oral contract.

Granted. But why, why did the Court of Appeals not allow me, with representation, to amend the Complaint, continue discovery, and prove to the satisfaction of a jury that there had been, in fact, an oral contract?

Here is Ken's letter to me on that subject:

The Court of Appeals has finally issued its decision, but it is not favorable. The Court has affirmed the Berrien County Circuit Court on all three issues which we appealed.

I am not very surprised about their ruling as it relates to the negligent supervision claim and the invasion of privacy claims. However, I am surprised and deeply disappointed in their cursory treatment of your breach of contract claim. Apparently, the Court did not understand that the contract was between Whirlpool and you, not just between Whirlpool and Mr. Von Koenig. The Court must have misunderstood our Brief and our oral argument or simply chose to construe it as an alleged contract between Whirlpool and Manny only.

Even more disappointing is that the Court's grounds for affirming the dismissal for the breach of contract claim is simply that it was not 'among her enumerated claims.' I thought that we had adequately addressed that issue and shown the Court that although the claim was not 'enumerated' it was spelled out in detail and further that, even if it weren't, you, as an unrepresented Plaintiff suing a large corporation, should be allowed leave to amend your complaint to specifically enumerate the breach of contract claim.

Nevertheless, the Court of Appeals has spoken. I do not think asking for leave to appeal to the Supreme Court would do any good. The Michigan Supreme Court almost never takes cases of this nature. An appeal to the Supreme Court must be filed no later than September 11, 1992.

You may, however, want to consider a motion for rehearing

with the Court of Appeals. This motion would have to rest on the Court's obvious misinterpretation of our argument with regard to the parties involved in the breach of contract claim. Also, we would seek to get the Court to address the issue of whether you should be allowed to amend your complaint.

Filing such a motion, of course, can be expensive and is no guarantee of success. If you want to file it, it must be filed with the Court of Appeals within twenty-one days of August 21, 1992, which is the date of the Court of Appeals' opinion. In other words, it must be filed no later than September 11, 1992.

It is difficult for me to predict your chances of success on a motion for rehearing. The overwhelming majority of such motions are denied. However, I do think the Court of Appeals did seriously misinterpret our Brief and argument in that the Court specifically states you alleged that your then-husband, Emanuel Von Koenig, at that time a Whirlpool executive, entered into an oral agreement with Whirlpool. This simply is not true. Your allegations were that the oral agreement was between Whirlpool and you, as well as your then-husband. You had been very instrumental in Manny's career and Whirlpool knew they needed your agreement to get Manny to go to Brazil and they endeavored to get your agreement. Therefore, you were most emphatically a party to the agreement, which Whirlpool later breached. That, at least, is what you alleged, and the Court, I think, should have acknowledged that.

Please read the opinion carefully and call me to discuss any questions you might have and let me know whether you want to file the motion for rehearing.

I will support you in whatever decision you make on this matter. I know you have gone through a great deal of agony and expense. It may be best to put this litigation behind you. You will have to make that decision.

How I appreciated that outlook! I particularly appreciated

it in contrast to the outlook of the evaluating psychologist, who believed he could make for me the decision that I had no case *and* the decision that I would be psychologically better off dropping the matter.

Whatever I may think of the Berrien County Circuit Court and of the Michigan Court of Appeals, I am enthusiastic about Karen Werme and Ken Rathert, who represented and advised me well throughout the proceeding and through the final moment. I did not hesitate in my decision to go ahead.

The *Herald-Palladium* of Benton Harbor–St. Joseph had chosen not to publicize the case in any way other than the obligatory notice of filing, even though, by any standards, it had to be considered news. One St. Joseph attorney must have learned something more about the powers of the corporation by the fact that the "all hell" he had predicted had not "broken loose." Nor did the Grand Rapids paper pick up on the story. The Michigan Court, in addition to denying the appeal, also deemed it unworthy of publication—meaning it would not even leave tracks in any legal journal.

Because I had not yet been heard, I had to go on. So Ken filed a twelve-page Brief in September 1992 requesting a rehearing. He closed his request with these words:

> Because this Court has made a mistake of fact or has misunderstood or overlooked Appellant's arguments regarding her breach of contract claims, this Court should grant a rehearing and reverse the trial Court's dismissal of the breach of contract claim. The Appellant requests that the case be remanded to the trial Court with instructions to grant Plaintiff-Appellant leave to amend her breach of contract claim.

It had taken fifteen months from the filing date for the Court of Appeals to hear the original appeal. I had no idea how long it would take the Court to respond this time.

My life was pretty much on hold. I couldn't seem to get on

with anything. I had gone back to trying to write the novel I had been working on and reasoned it could benefit by some first-hand research in Sparta, Greece, where my Helen of Troy had lived. This trip could also get my mind off the fact that nothing was happening in my own life. I left September 30 with the feeling that the Court's response, eventually, would be "no," and I would be better able to handle the response if, by then, I had assimilated something of the ambiance of the civilization on which our sense of democracy and justice was based.

I grounded myself in Greece, and returned. Two weeks later the Michigan Court of Appeals made its decision. From its correspondence dated November 3, 1992, I learned: "The Court orders that the motion for rehearing is DENIED."

As Karen predicted, the Court interpreted all the horror stories I told as "just the way corporate America does business."

I sent the following Thanksgiving-time notice to relatives and friends:

It's over. The Michigan Court of Appeals rejected my appeal and rejected my additional appeal for a rehearing of that decision. It finally boiled down to the Court's inability to grasp that I am an individual, that Whirlpool made an agreement with me (which it breached) separate from its agreement with Manny. The Court ruled, in effect, that since my ex-husband thinks they honored their agreement with him, that is all that matters.

I am well and strong and happy, content with my own integrity. I did what needed doing to preserve the values that form my character—as an individual, not as an appendage to somebody else's life.

Financially, this case cost me upwards of $21,000, excluding recompense for the time I devoted to it. This does not in-

clude the cost of the divorce, which debits the ledger of our social structure, as one more broken family is added to the statistical count.

Suing the Whirlpool Corporation and writing this account of the process has not been an easy thing for me to do. I am rewarded, however, both by the cessation of the debilitating headaches with which this narrative begins, and with a sense of the rightness that my voice, long muffled, will be "heard" by a jury of my peers. I continue to believe the values of most people are closer to my values than to those of the corporation, or—even more frightening—to those of the judges into whose hands I placed my hopes for equal justice.

Endnotes to Part Three (pp. 232–263)

1. For example, Depue, R.A., and Monroe, S.M. "Learned help-lessness in the perspective of the depressive disorders." *J Abn Psychol* 87 (1978): 3–20.
2. First Amended Complaint, ¶ 7.
3. Von Koenig Dep., p. 16 § 1; pp. 18–21.
4. Von Koenig Dep., p. 15 § 1.15–p. 16 § 1.19.
5. First Amended Complaint, ¶¶ 9–12.
6. First Amended Complaint, ¶¶ 11–12.
7. Von Koenig Dep., pp. 18–19, 21, 39.
8. Reeder aff., p. 3; Def. First Set of Inter., p. 14; and Von Koenig Dep., pp. 13–14, 19–20.
9. First Amended Complaint, ¶ 14.
10. First Amended Complaint, ¶¶ 13–14, and Answer to First Amended Complaint, ¶ 13.
11. Def. First Set of Inter., insert between pp. 35 and 36: Ivens.
12. First Amended Complaint, ¶ 14; Von Koenig.
13. First Amended Complaint, ¶¶ 35–41.
14. First Amended Complaint, ¶¶ 42–44.
15. Plaintiff's Memo of Law, insert between pp. 5 and 6.
16. First Amended Complaint, ¶ 18.
17. Citations to the record on these points appear on pp. 5–6.
18. Von Koenig Dep., pp 57–60; Reeder Aff., pp. 4–8.
19. Def. First Set of Inter., insert between pp. 35 and 36: Ivens (5), Laundra (4).
20. First Amended Complaint, ¶¶ 7–12.
21. First Amended Complaint, ¶ 12; Plaintiff's Memo of Law, p. 5.
22. Von Koenig Dep., pp. 39–45.
23. Von Koenig Dep., pp. 45–48, especially p. 47 §§ 1.5–19 and p. 48 §§ 1.1–6; Def. First Set of Inter., p. 27.
24. Def. First Set of Inter., p. 15.
25. Von Koenig Dep., pp. 36–37.
26. Reeder Aff., pp. 4–8.
27. First Amended Complaint, ¶¶ 38–39.
28. Von Koenig Dep., p. 55 § 1.13–p. 57 § 1.7.
29. Def. First Set of Inter., p. 28; Von Koenig Dep., pp. 55 § 1.13–p. 57 § 1.7.
30. First Amended Complaint, ¶¶ 23–27; Von Koenig Dep., p. 72 §§ 1.20–25.
31. Youngstedt Dep., pp. 9–10.
32. Gray Dep., p. 5; Plaintiff's Memo of Law, following p. 13; Def. First Set of Inter., p. 28.
33. Plaintiff's Memo of Law, p. 13 ¶ 2; p. 14.
34. First Amended Complaint, ¶ 6; Von Koenig Dep., p. 120.
35. Von Koenig Dep., p. 28.
36. Von Koenig Dep., Exhibit #1, p. 2.
37. Def. First Set of Inter., p. 16.
38. First Amended Complaint, ¶ 21.
39. May 21, 1990, Hearing.

Index